*The author at Megiddo,
site of the biblical Armageddon,
in modern Israel.*

PHIL DONAHUE

THE HUMAN ANIMAL

A Fireside Book
Published by Simon & Schuster, Inc.
New York

A WOODWARD / WHITE BOOK
Gregory White Smith, President / Steven Naifeh, Vice-President

Title page photo by Cameron Beck

Copyright © 1985 by Multimedia Entertainment, Inc. and Woodward/White, Inc.

First Fireside Edition, 1986. Published by Simon & Schuster, Inc.
Simon & Schuster Building • Rockefeller Center
1230 Avenue of the Americas • New York, New York 10020

FIRESIDE and colophon are registered trademarks of Simon & Schuster, Inc.

DESIGNED BY JOEL AVIROM

Production directed by Richard L. Willett

Manufactured in the United States of America

5   7   9   10   8   6   4

1   3   5   7   9   10   8   6   4   2   Pbk.

Library of Congress Cataloging in Publication Data
Donahue, Phil.
The human animal.
Based on a five-part NBC television series
hosted by the author.
Includes index.
1. Psychology.   2. Human behavior.   I. Title.
BF121.D63   1985   150   85-2491
ISBN: 0-671-54696-1
ISBN: 0-671-63035-0 Pbk.

The author gratefully acknowledges permission to reprint excerpts from the following sources:

The Poetry of Robert Frost edited by Edward Connery Latham. Copyright 1923 © 1969 by Holt, Rinehart and Winston. Copyright 1951 by Robert Frost. Reprinted by permission of Holt, Rinehart and Winston, Publishers.

Let's Do It (Let's Fall in Love) by Cole Porter © 1928 (Renewed) Warner Bros., Inc. Used by permission. All rights reserved.

The United Artists release *Annie Hall* © 1977 United Artists Corporation. Reprinted by permission of Woody Allen and Rollins Joffe Morra & Brezner.

The Empire Strikes Back. Reprinted by permission of Lucasfilm Ltd. © Lucasfilm Ltd. (LFL) 1980. All rights reserved.

On the Loose by Terry and Renny Russell. Reprinted by permission of Sierra Club Books.

All You Need Is Love (John Lennon & Paul McCartney) © 1967 Northern Songs Limited. All rights for the United States and Mexico controlled by Maclen Music, Inc., c/o ATV Music Corp. Used by permission. All rights reserved.

I would like to thank the following men and women of science for their generous contributions of time and expertise in the preparation of this book.

Frank Beach, *University of California at Berkeley* / Ursula Beluggi, *Salk Institute* / Vincent Castellucci, *Columbia University* / Noam Chomsky, *Massachusetts Institute of Technology* / Susan Curtiss, *University of California at Los Angeles* / Irven DeVore, *Harvard University* / Marian Diamond, *University of California at Berkeley* / Dorothy Dinnerstein, *Rutgers University* / Irenaus Eibl-Eibesfeldt, *Max Planck Institute* / Halford Fairchild, *University of California at Los Angeles* / Norman Geschwind, *Harvard University* / Langdon Gilkey, *University of Chicago* / Roderic Gorney, *University of California at Los Angeles* / Stephen J. Gould, *Harvard University* / Carroll Izard, *University of Delaware* / Virginia Johnson, *Masters and Johnson Institute* / Jerome Kagan, *Harvard University* / Phyllis Katz, *University of Colorado* / Mark Konishi, *California Institute of Technology* / Melvin Konner, *Emory University* / Christine LaCoste, *University of Texas* / Jerre Levy, *University of Chicago* / Michael Lewis, *Rutgers University* / David Lukoff, *University of California at Los Angeles* / Eleanor Macoby, *Stanford University* / Paul MacLean, *National Institute of Mental Health* / Judd Marmor, *University of California at Los Angeles* / William Masters, *Masters and Johnson Institute* / Carol Meyers, *Duke University* / John Money, *Johns Hopkins University* / Ashley Montagu / Helen J. Neville, *Salk Institute* / David Peretz, *Columbia University* / Michael Phelps, *University of California at Los Angeles* / Robert Reich, *Harvard University* / June Reinisch, *Indiana University* / Leonard Rosenbloom, *Downstate Medical Center* / Peggy Sanday, *University of Pennsylvania* / Arnold Scheibel, *University of California at Los Angeles* / David William Shucard, *National Jewish Hospital and Research Center* / Stephen Suomi, *National Institute of Child Health and Human Development* / Sherman Silber / Nancy Makepeace Tanner, *University of California at Santa Cruz* / Lionel Tiger, *Rutgers University* / Colin M. Turnbull, *George Washington University* / Louis J. West, *University of California at Los Angeles* / John Whiting, *Harvard University* / E. O. Wilson, *Harvard University* / Sandra Witelson, *McMaster University*

CONTENTS

THE HUMAN ANIMAL

Preface

This book began on November 6, 1967, the day my television program premiered on Channel 2 in Dayton, Ohio. During more than four thousand hours of television since, I have played host to almost one million guests who assembled in my studio audience to speak their minds on subjects ranging from world peace to male strippers. Through it all, the underlying questions have always been the same: Who are we, and why are we acting this way?

Those questions were the starting point for this book and for the NBC series that accompanies it. The idea was simply to present some of what science knows about the human animal and what makes it tick. We assumed—probably naively—that there was a large body of research about which the majority of behaviorists agreed, and that their research would provide a "wide road of consensus" down which we could travel comfortably. Once the journey began, however, we discovered that the "wide road" was in fact more like a narrow path—a path that disappeared with alarming frequency. For example, are men's brains different from women's brains? Answers: (a) Yes, (b) We're not sure, (c) Come back next year.

But even if the answers are tentative and incomplete, the questions are still important, and we owe it to ourselves and to our children, who will inherit the world we make, to ask them. Because this inquiry is at the heart of the investigation of who we humans think we are, we shouldn't be surprised that it occasionally provokes controversies more worthy of a barroom argument than a university seminar.

What determines human behavior? Is personality a product of genes and hormones, or of upbringing? Of nature, or nurture? When I asked that question of an anthropologist on my program, he replied promptly, "That's a stupid question." More recently when I asked the same question of other scientists (I am nothing if not thick-skinned), they answered less abrasively but no less tersely: "Both." Nature and nurture are codeterminants of behavior that interact with each other in an astoundingly complex way that produces respectful awe among scientists who are still trying to understand the process, and heated arguments among amateurs who think they already do.

Why is there so much violence in our society? Why do we wage war so relentlessly,

and why are both war and violence such overwhelmingly male activities? Is there a biological explanation for the disquieting fact that the human animal kills its own kind more often, more efficiently, and in greater numbers than any other life form on earth? These questions have assumed an unprecedented urgency, now that the human trigger finger can dispose of the enemy and the whole global neighborhood at the same time.

Why are male–female relationships such a struggle? Sex is a basic human function, yet we often pretend that it doesn't exist, or that when it does exist, it's something to be ashamed of. At least that is the message our children are getting. We should not be surprised that putting love and sex together in a single relationship so often proves to be life's most frustrating challenge. Also, with whom do we fall in love, and why is there so much tension between the sexes? Does "till death do us part" make biological sense for the human animal or are we naturally polygamous?

Where did we come from? Modern elementary and high school biology textbooks continue to ignore or give only passing reference to Charles Darwin. This is startling testimony to the widespread refusal to acknowledge and to *celebrate* the place of *Homo sapiens sapiens* in the drama of evolution. How can we understand ourselves when we continue to flee from an understanding of our beginnings? Does religion make us run away? It shouldn't. Natural selection flatters God. Nevertheless, 125 years after its publication we appear to have more enthusiasm for the classroom use of computer terminals than for *On the Origin of Species*.

Where are we going? From now on, human evolution—our destiny—is in our own hands. Nature was in charge of shaping our bodies, and it may still have a role in determining our behavior, but ultimately, *we* are responsible for shaping our culture. What kind of culture is best for us, and who shall decide, are two of the most important questions on the human agenda—questions that no other species can even ask, much less answer. This book is an effort to provide some of the material that should be considered as the human community struggles with decisions about its future.

How does the human mind work? The human mind is evolution's most magnificent "selection." It is revealing that the great pioneer of the human mind—like the pioneer of the human past—is still a controversial figure. If Darwin holds first place in provoking public outrage, then surely Sigmund Freud is runner-up. In the amateur sport of shoot-em-down-before-they-catch-on, these two giants have become the biggest targets in the whole library. That's because Freud's work, like Darwin's, confronts us with some uncomfortable truths about ourselves—truths we *need* to hear if we are to understand our behavior.

This look at the human animal, its genius and its meanness, has taken me from Switzerland's Mount Santis, where a teenager named Albert Einstein first imagined what it would be like to ride a beam of light, to Dachau, West Germany, where one of Hitler's concentration camps stands in grim testimony to the dark side of the human animal; from the plains of Megiddo in Israel—the Armageddon of biblical prophecy—to Freud's office in Vienna; from the medieval arches of the Chartres cathedral to the launch pad at Cape Canaveral.

Along the way, I have interviewed many of the leading lights of behaviorism at Harvard, Princeton, and U.C.L.A. (to name just three); I have talked with baby-watchers at the University of Delaware, and watched monkeys with the researchers at the Primate Center of the National Institutes of Health in Maryland. From beginning to end, it has been a journey of constant discovery, frequent delight, and occasional frustration.

My partner throughout this two-year enterprise has been Wendy Roth. In addition, I am indebted to Adrian Malone, the series executive producer, and his staff for the ideas and research they gathered in preparing the television production. More recently, I had the assistance of Greg Smith and Steve Naifeh in transforming five hours of prime-time television into a book.

But neither the series nor the book would have been possible without the committed men and women of the behavioral sciences, many of whom generously cooperated with this project. Not only did they express their support for the idea (and not a little surprise that a *commercial* television network was interested in the material); they also demonstrated their brand of courage by entrusting the hard-won conclusions of their life's work to a talk-show host who, if the truth be told, is capable of asking a stupid question.

It is to these scientists, and to the hope they hold for a better understanding of ourselves, that this book is dedicated. Ever since *Sputnik*, the behavioral sciences have been poor stepchildren to the favored technical disciplines. We can peer into the atom and walk on the moon, but we can't stop killing each other. We have failed to interest our children in the pursuit of answers to the most basic questions about human nature. We have committed ourselves to inventions at the expense of understanding the inventor.

By encouraging our children to be curious about these issues, we improve the odds that other Darwins and Freuds will emerge from the next generation to help us understand ourselves better—and that such giants will be received more civilly and their ideas considered more seriously in the future. To do any less would be wasteful. The information we ignore today will affect our decisions tomorrow, and those decisions will, in turn, shape the culture that shapes the future. In the final analysis, encouragement toward better understanding is the most important gift we can give our children, a gift that comes from "the deep heart's core," a gift that only the human animal can give—a gift of love.

P. D.

Los Angeles, 1985

PART ONE

PAST & FUTURE

1. Beauty and the Beast

What a piece of work is a man!
How noble in reason! how
infinite in faculty! in form,
in moving, how express and
admirable! in action how like
an angel! in apprehension
how like a god!

Shakespeare, *Hamlet*

Shakespeare may have been exaggerating a little. We all know politicians who are hardly noble in reason, students who are not always infinite in faculty, children who are sometimes less than angelic, and bureaucrats who respond to our questions with less than godlike apprehension. Yet the words ring true. Every time you see an Olympic record set, or you watch the space shuttle launched, or you read in the paper about some kid who came out of nowhere and rescued a total stranger from a river, you can't help feeling that we *are* noble; that in the whole cosmos, the human animal is something very special.

Compared to the animals around us, there's no doubt we are a remarkable phenomenon. Someone once referred to us as the "superdeluxe model": we walk, we talk, we smell, we taste, we touch, we think. All this in a relatively small and attractive package. We're also very good with our hands. In the comparatively brief time we've been available in the current form—about 50,000 years—we've invented the wheel, the alphabet, the clock, the reciprocating machine, the cyclotron, and everything in between. When we weren't busy making progress, we invented more playful things like music, art, baseball, and bridge. Over the years, we've demonstrated an admirable willingness to cooperate with each other. We assemble in big groups to form towns and cities; we get together in twos to discover love. We've also

---

Every human infant has the potential for both evil and good, despair and joy, fear and love. We are a species of contradictions.

Among animals, humans are relatively slow runners. The invention of the wheel allowed us to increase our speed and extend our range. We've been going faster and faster ever since.

shown a lot of individual spunk. The wheel wasn't invented by a committee, and Albert Einstein, by himself, revolutionized our understanding of the universe.

Of course, most of our uniquely human accomplishments are the result of a combination of cooperation and individual achievement. Even Charles Lindbergh had a ground crew. Beethoven composed the *Ninth Symphony* in the solitude of deafness, but scores of musicians are needed to bring it to life. Neil Armstrong had to have personal courage to step out on the surface of the moon, knowing that he might sink into 15 feet of "moondust," but he had an army of people to help put him there and bring him back.

We can only imagine what it must have felt like to stand on the moon; look back at the earth, suspended like a blue-and-white marble in space; and think how far we humans have come in such a short time. That feeling itself—the tightening in the throat, the tingle up the spine, the tear of pride—is unique to the human animal. Throughout most of our history, that feeling belonged exclusively to religion. When most people's lives were "solitary, poor, nasty, brutish, and short," religion was the only thing that made them feel dignified, special, proud of being human.

The peasants who gazed for the first time at the stained glass in the cathedral at Chartres undoubtedly experienced that same feeling—the most human of emotions

We are creatures of aspiration, always reaching upward, higher and higher, pushing against the biological limits of our bodies and the gravitational limits of our planet. The human animal's home as seen from the moon.

OPPOSITE: In its day, the cathedral at Chartres was no less a miracle of individual achievement and teamwork than the modern effort to reach the moon. The Rose Window, Chartres.

—wonder. Most of them had never been inside anything bigger than a thatched hut and never seen anything more colorful than a piece of dyed cloth. Even today, the sight of this huge, arched space with those luminous windows suspended high in the darkness is almost enough to make a believer of even the most skeptical. In 1260, when the church was consecrated, the peasants who shuffled through those doors must have thought they had died and gone to heaven.

In fact, Chartres cathedral, like dozens of other cathedrals built in the same period, is the medieval equivalent of the modern effort to put a man on the moon. Both represent the perfect combination of individual achievement and group cooperation in the pursuit of something beautiful and lasting. The space program would never have gotten off the ground if Wernher von Braun hadn't made his discoveries in the field of jet propulsion, and the arches of Chartres would never have soared if an anonymous French architect hadn't devised a system of buttresses to support a two-ton block of stone 120 feet in the air and keep it there for a thousand years. But there would have been no stones to support if the wealthier townspeople hadn't dug deep into their pockets and come up with the money needed for construction. The glass in the openings would be clear instead of stained if merchant guilds, members

In 1194, the old cathedral in the middle of Chartres burned down. Within months, the people of Chartres decided to replace it with the most beautiful church in Christendom.

of the nobility, and even the French king hadn't contributed money for the windows. And all the money would have been worthless if legions of craftsmen hadn't been willing to dedicate their skills and often their lives to making this not just another building, but a monument to human achievement.

Bees get together and build hives, termites build mounds, beavers build dams, and spiders spin webs, but what other animal can change stone and glass into poetry? Other animals can alter their environment at the margins, but only we can transform our environment so completely that we reshape our destiny. Alone in the animal kingdom, we can set goals for ourselves and then pursue them. The dream of the medieval craftsmen who built Chartres was to secure a place for themselves in heaven. By lavishing love on this stone and glass, they glorified God and hoped to be rewarded in the next life. But in the process, they changed this life, made it more beautiful and more worth living.

A place like Chartres makes us proud to be human. We can stand tall and hold our heads high. Certainly no other creature could conceive and create something of such sublime beauty. Case closed? Hardly. There is, unfortunately, another side to the human animal that's nothing to be proud of. At places like Chartres, it's easy—

Sometimes we act like saints, sometimes like sinners. The fact that we have such a wide range of responses is both a blessing and a curse. Paul Gauguin's *Self-Portrait* as saint and sinner, 1889.

OPPOSITE: Religion has been a source of inspiration and beauty, but it has also been used as an excuse for senseless bloodshed, from the Crusades to the Salem witch trials.

The human animal's capacity for contradictions extends even into our relationships. Why do we so often hurt the ones we love? Young couple from Gallaudet College for the Deaf making the sign for "I love you."

and tempting—to overlook this other side, the ugly side, of our nature. But we can't begin to understand the human animal without it. Surely there's beauty inside us— but there's also a beast, a part of us that we'd like to deny but can't, a part that gives us a knot in the stomach instead of a lump in the throat.

Even the God-loving people who fashioned the soaring vaults and delicate windows of Chartres had murder on their minds. Some of the workers may well have been veterans of the First Crusade, an expedition to save the Holy Land from the infidel Muslims that was part religious frenzy, part military adventure, and part social fad. On that excursion, begun four years after work on Chartres began, the Crusaders slaughtered thousands of noncombatants, leveled whole communities, and finally "saved" the holy city of Jerusalem by massacring all its inhabitants— men, women, children, Muslims, Jews: everybody. Muslims, after all, were only infidels, not humans, so it wasn't like killing your next-door neighbor.

After the shrines of Christianity were in "safe" hands, many Crusaders returned home and turned their attention to other things, like the cathedral at Chartres.

How could the same hands that carved these stones and stained this glass have wielded swords and butchered women and children? How could so much beauty and so much brutality exist side by side? This is the great contradiction of the human animal. We can be both noble and petty, sublime and savage, beauty and beast. We can pray one minute and kill the next, create one minute and destroy the next, even love and hate simultaneously. We like to think that our erratic behavior is a thing of the past, that we've outgrown the excesses of the Crusades. But nothing could be further from the truth. There are people in Belfast today who will repeat the catechism, then go toss a bomb into a crowded pub; people who grieve for the victims of crime, then pay good money to see it reenacted on a movie screen. The same technological wizardry, individual bravery, and group effort that put us on the moon have also given us weapons that can blow our whole planet into permanent winter.

Far from having disappeared with the last Crusade, the human animal's strange capacity for contradictory behavior still affects our daily lives. As parents, we desperately want our kids to grow up emotionally healthy, able to love and be loved; then our culture teaches them that sex is dirty and they should be ashamed of their sexual desires. Women say they want to marry a nice person who will respect them and communicate with them; then they melt for *machismo* and fall for the strong, silent type. They want a man who will share the housework and feed the baby at three in the morning, but they live in a society in which few bosses grant time off to men who want to share parenting. Cops throw drunken drivers in jail while television sells beer as though it were an American entitlement. The message to teenage males: "You're not a man without a beer can in your hand." But there are millions of teenage drivers and thousands of cloverleaves out there, and the phone rings every day, in homes all across America, and it's the hospital calling—or the morgue.

Why do we do the things we do? Why, after thousands of years of personal tragedies and group catastrophes, do we continue to make the same mistakes? Why do we persist in the same contradictory behavior day after day, century after century, alternating between Chartres and the Crusades, between grief and gore, between moonwalks and megatons?

These questions aren't just for the historians and the sociologists. They're for everyone who wrestles with these contradictory drives in his or her own life. The impulse that sends a society back to war, despite the knowledge that children will die and mothers will grieve, is the same impulse that leads you to light up another cigarette or have "one more for the road," despite the knowledge that it may kill you. We live with contradictions in our own behavior—and the behavior of others—every day. It's about time we tried to understand those contradictions. Are they a permanent part of the human condition, or can we do something about them?

We know that every child has the potential for good and for evil. It's a fact of life that is the hope and the nightmare of every parent. That little bundle of joy scuttering across the living-room floor on all fours and flashing a toothless grin at Mommy and Daddy has every potential locked inside its little head. It can turn out to be a happy adult with a job, a family, and a bungalow with flower boxes, or an angry adult who swears like a sailor and cuts people off on the freeway. As yet, we can only guess about what combination of biology and upbringing determines which path it will take. We do know that both factors are important, and that parents *can* make a difference. We may be a long way from a formula for raising the perfect kid, but we can certainly take the first step down that road by understanding who we are and why we act the way we do.

What do we know about the origins of this bizarre creature, this bundle of contradictions known to the scientific world by the ironic title *Homo sapiens sapiens*, or "man double-wise"? Maybe by looking to our past we can begin to understand more about our contradictory and often self-defeating behavior. For example, what do we have in common with other animals? Are we, as the title of this book implies, like other animals, only smarter, vainer, and more ambitious; or are we a different kind of thing altogether? Some people are uncomfortable with the idea that humans belong to the same family of animals as cats and cows and raccoons. It doesn't sound dignified enough. They're like the people who become successful and then don't want to be reminded of the old neighborhood.

In fact, the proof of our kinship with other animals is everywhere in our culture. From Aesop's Fables to *Bambi*, from Kermit the Frog and Miss Piggy to the Mickey Mouse Club, we've always acknowledged the family resemblance. We treat pets like people and, sometimes, people like unwanted pets. We're intrigued by dogs that can sing, horses that can count, and birds that can talk. Most of our kids grew up glued to the TV set on Saturday mornings watching Yogi Bear, Bugs Bunny, Underdog, and a whole menagerie of other "human animals." In everyday conversation, we often attribute human emotions to animals. We call someone "stubborn as a mule," "smart as a fox," "proud as a peacock," or "wise as an owl."

In these and other ways, our culture reflects the basic notion that animals are like

Some people don't like to acknowledge it, but we humans are not that different from other animals. Popular culture has always enjoyed humanizing the so-called lower life forms. Miss Piggy.

people, just trapped in different bodies. Yet when some know-it-all scientist comes along and says we're just another animal, we bristle. In fact, the similarities between us and other animals, especially mammals, go far deeper than culture. We all have two eyes, one nose, one mouth, and four limbs; our digestive, respiratory, circulatory, and skeletal systems are all cut from the same pattern; we all spend our days raising children, feeding, and nesting, and our nights sleeping.

It was the similarities between animals, not the differences, that attracted the attention of a young Englishman named Charles Darwin. While most of the scientists around him were trying to chop the world into ever-smaller pieces, concentrating on how this plant was different from that plant, or this animal from that animal, he wanted to explain the obvious: Why do they look so much alike? Why is it that plants everywhere in the world have the same structure: roots, branches with stems, leaves made green with chlorophyll, and flowers with modified leaves—sepals, petals, stamens, and pistils? Why do different species of thrushes in South America and Britain both line their nests with mud the same way? Why are the embryos of a lizard and a small bird indistinguishable? Why is human blood chemically closer to the blood of a gorilla than to that of a baboon, and closer to the blood of a baboon than to that of a horse?

Were all these similarities just coincidence? Not likely. The logical answer was that the plant kingdom and the animal kingdom were just like big families in which all the kids look alike—not identical, but alike. After years of researching and

Plants from different parts of the world, no matter how exotic they may look at first glance, have the same basic structure: roots, branches, stems, leaves, and flowers. Aloe.

OPPOSITE: Charles Darwin was only twenty-two when he set out on his historic voyage aboard the Beagle.

On December 27, 1831, Charles Darwin set sail on the H.M.S. Beagle. The ship's five-year journey included the Galápagos Islands and the Straits of Magellan at the southernmost tip of South America.

refining, that simple and very logical notion became the basis for a theory that would revolutionize our understanding of the human animal: the theory of evolution.

Some of Darwin's ideas—like "survival of the fittest"—are so much a part of our consciousness that it's hard to appreciate how risky and earth-shaking they were at the time. No one—with the possible exception of Freud—has contributed more to our understanding of human behavior than Darwin. He opened a door through which all of modern biology and anthropology have passed. Darwin himself was a good example of how traits run in families. Born in 1809, he was the grandson of a distinguished doctor-poet-philosopher-inventor, Erasmus Darwin, on one side, and Josiah Wedgwood on the other. Wedgwood was the man who lent his name to the blue-and-white porcelain that everybody's grandmother has at least one piece of. Like a lot of creative kids, Charles didn't make a very good student. Not surprisingly, given the dry-as-dust subjects taught at Shrewsbury School and Cambridge, he played hooky every chance he got and snuck off to pursue his unusual passion for collecting and studying beetles.

When he was twenty-two, Darwin got a chance to indulge his bizarre obsession. In 1831, the British Navy posted a job for a "naturalist" to accompany a five-year expedition to Brazil, Argentina, Tierra del Fuego, the Galápagos Islands, Tahiti,

New Zealand, Australia, the Pacific islands, and South Africa. Darwin, who didn't exactly have to pry himself away from school, jumped at the chance. During his years on the H.M.S. *Beagle*, Darwin saw earthquakes, cannibals, ancient fossils, and plenty of beetles.

It was the beetles he collected at every stop that began to spark the important questions in his mind: Why were beetles so much alike all over the world? But the same questions applied to every animal he studied: Why did the rhea of South America look and act so much like the ostrich of Africa? Could all of these species really have been created instantly and independently of one another? If God was designing mockingbirds, to use just one example, why would he design three different models for the same environment? Was every species really unique, and did it come into the world fully formed? As any good interviewer knows, asking the right questions makes it a lot easier to get the right answers. Darwin began to think that maybe species that were supposed to be different weren't really so different after all; that they were more like variations on a theme, just as the kids in a family are variations on their parents.

The theory of evolution had its unlikely beginnings in Charles Darwin's childhood fascination with beetles. Among the varieties he could have seen on his voyage aboard the Beagle *were (clockwise from upper left) the weevil of Peru, the itataiai, the tortoise beetle of Brazil, and the longhorn beetle of Peru.*

OPPOSITE: *The infinite variety of life—even within the single family of primates. Darwin was more interested in their similarities than their differences.* Top row, left to right: white uakari, red-bellied tamarin, orangutan, Diana monkey; middle row: white-headed saki, proboscis monkey, pygmy marmoset, mandrill; bottom row: golden monkey, golden baboon, gray-cheeked mangaby, lowland gorilla.

When Darwin published On the Origin of Species *in 1859, "artificial" selection was an established fact. English horticulturists had been breeding flowers like the orchid for centuries. Darwin argued that there was a similar "natural" selection process.* Illustration by Sir Joseph Paxton from *The Magazine of Botany*, London, about 1840.

Charles Darwin didn't *discover* evolution. He was hardly the first person to see the obvious similarities between certain animals. A century before Darwin, some bright people had caught on to the fact that humans and monkeys look and act a lot alike. The German poet Goethe, the French philosopher Diderot, even Darwin's own grandfather Erasmus Darwin had already suggested that these similarities pointed to a common origin. But nobody had figured out *how* they could have evolved. What was the process by which they ended up being similar yet different? Darwin's contribution—and it was great—was to explain the mechanism of evolution.

Any farmer knows that you can get meatier cattle by breeding meaty bulls with meaty cows. Any backyard gardener knows you can get redder roses by crossing reds with reds for several generations. And almost anybody knows that a blond father and a blond mother will produce blond kids. All of that was known in Darwin's time. English farmers had been breeding cattle and English horticulturists had been breeding orchids for more than a century. Darwin's genius was that he saw in that accepted, everyday fact the answer to his questions. Just as the farmer selected his best cattle for breeding and the gardener his best orchids, Darwin figured, nature must have "selected" certain plants and animals to continue reproducing.

Obviously, nature didn't care if cattle were meaty or orchids were beautiful. The only important factor was how well suited a plant or animal was to survive. Given that there are individual variations between plants and animals just as there are

This photograph of Charles Darwin was taken in 1881, when Darwin was seventy-two. He died the following year.

between people—some are stronger than others, some more flexible, some healthier —it was inevitable that some plants and animals were more likely to survive than others. As a species evolved, the features that promoted survival were "selected" for and passed on to the next generation. Those species that "selected" well, like our own, live to this day. Others, like the various dinosaurs, died off because of some unforeseen event against which they had no defense.

Let's take an example close to home. Let's say that a new disease develops that afflicts only blond children. The disease is always fatal—I know it sounds cruel, but nature is cruel. You don't need a grounding in evolutionary theory to know that in succeeding generations there would be fewer and fewer blond people. Blonds wouldn't have grown old enough to have their own blond kids. Before long, the gene for blondness would have been wiped out. Someone looking at us a hundred years later would assume that humans had always been dark-haired, that God had made us that way, when in fact nature had "selected" dark-haired people to survive. When scientists talk about "natural selection," they're referring to this process of weeding out the life forms less suited to the environment and promoting the better-suited ones.

Unlike scientists today, who rush to get their ideas into print before some other scientist scoops them, Darwin kept his ideas about "natural selection" to himself for more than twenty years. He was a gentlemanly English amateur through and through. But in 1858, when he heard that another gentleman-naturalist, Alfred Russel Wallace, was toying with the same basic idea, he decided to go public. The following year his book *On the Origin of Species* was published, and the world hasn't been the same since.

Darwin's theory made it possible to reconstruct for the first time a picture of how life on earth began. It's not a pretty picture, and that's one reason it's not a universally popular picture. As scientists now see it, the beginning began about 4 billion years ago in an unappetizing primeval "soup" of hydrogen, water vapor, ammonia, and methane. When this rich but lifeless atmosphere was zapped with ultraviolet rays and electric discharges from the sun, amino acids—the building blocks of protein—were first synthesized. Not a very glamorous start for the human animal.

One of life's numerous problems for the earliest life forms—one-celled bacteria and blue-green algae—was that they didn't have sex. The result was not just lonely nights, it was complete stagnation. Because they reproduced without sex, there was practically no variation from one generation to the next. Except for the occasional "mutant," each cell "gave birth" to other cells exactly like it. As a result, the blue-green algae you see today on fallen trees, damp rocks, and marine reefs are amazingly similar to the blue-green algae that populated the earth 3.5 billion years ago.

The point is that sex is much more than just a "good time," more than making babies, more than an expression of love. It's also a way for two creatures to mingle their genetic pasts and make new creatures with new genetic combinations. The more variations in genetic makeup, the more chances a species has to survive.

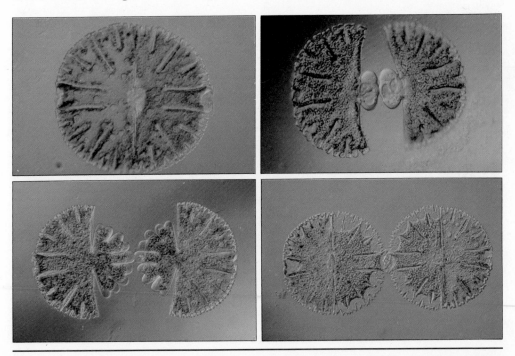

Sex isn't really necessary *for reproduction. Single-cell organisms reproduce just fine without sex, by simply dividing. Cellular division,* Micrasterias denticulata: *interphase cell, three-lobed stage, nine-lobed stage, mature daughter cells.*

The first hint of sex on earth came when two of these one-celled organisms floating around in the soup bumped into each other and "fused" temporarily. Out of this brief but happy fusion came a third cell. They liked it so much that they wanted to make a habit of it; but life wasn't that simple for a one-celled creature, and the result was the world's first identity crisis. In order to fuse with another cell, a cell had to be able to move around. But in order to feed the new cell that came out of their fusion, a "parent" cell had to be able to provide food for it. No one-celled creature, however, could do both jobs—move in order to mate and also provide food for the new offspring—so two different kinds of cells eventually developed: egg cells to provide the baby food, and sperm cells to provide the mobility. Thus, in their most basic form, the sexes appeared.

Roughly half a billion years ago, life took a second major step toward the human animal. After more than 3 billion years of swimming around in water getting bigger, some adventurous organism shuffled onto the beach—probably just looking for more water. The new environment set off an explosion of changes. Our beachcomber needed to move around in order to mate and find food, so she further developed her senses—smell, sight, touch—to locate a delectable bush or an attractive male. She developed bigger bones and stronger muscles to move her toward them and a more elaborate nervous system to control her movements. Her various functions were divided up and assigned to different parts of her body. Because her senses were used mostly to locate food, her sense organs and mouth were grouped at one end and a head began to form. Gradually she developed the ability to gestate a fertilized egg internally instead of in the water as she had done, and to protect it in a shell. All these changes in a couple of hundred million years—a relatively brief period in the long saga of evolution.

The next turning point came when our beachcomber—by now a comparatively sophisticated, reptilelike creature that was no longer confined to the beach—developed the ability to keep her egg inside her body until it was ready for birth. In a forest full of other animals scavenging for food, the ability to protect your young while they developed was a tremendous advantage. It's easy to see why many of the animals that couldn't do it didn't survive. Those that did survive because of this adaptation were the first mammals. Humans are mammals, as are monkeys and cows and cats and almost any other animal you're likely to be friendly with.

The first primates—the branch of the evolutionary tree that we share with the apes—were not so lovable. They were probably something like ugly little tree shrews—an animal that might send you screaming from the house if you saw it in your basement. But the little animal quickly began to change. Think of the process as similar to the transformation of a man into a werewolf in a horror movie, only in reverse. His front paws turn into hands, with opposable thumbs, capable of grasping objects. His claws are transformed into flattened nails. His long snout shortens into

*The first primates were not charming crea-
tures. They probably looked something like
the tree shrew, a small squirrel-like animal
still found in the forests of Southeast Asia.*

a nose as his strong sense of smell fades and his eyes move to the front of his head
to compensate for the diminished sense of smell. You can't see what's happening
inside, but in fact, his visual fields are now overlapping, producing stereoscopic
vision, which allows him for the first time to perceive depth—a key requirement for
making and using tools. Most important, his forehead slowly rises and his head
expands as his brain grows larger and more complicated. On the screen it would
take thirty seconds. In human evolution, it took 70 million years.

During this same period, one of these animals tried balancing herself on her hind
legs so she could use her front paws. It was wobbly at first, but it worked so well
that she kept doing it. Others imitated her, and within a few million years our
ancestors were walking almost exclusively on their back legs. Why did walking on
her back legs make that animal better suited to survive? Why was she "selected"
for upright posture? According to a recent theory, upright posture was a way to
improve on a failing reproductive strategy. She stood up mostly in order to have
more babies.

The problem with walking on four legs is that you can't do anything else when
you're walking. You have to sit down and free your front paws if you want to
accomplish something—like caring for offspring. Our female ancestors discovered
that they could care for more babies, more often, if their front legs—soon to be their
arms—were free. Males discovered they could carry more food, enough for larger
families. Having more babies meant that more survived, and a better survival rate
meant a better chance of surviving as a species. There was a side benefit too.
Standing upright allowed these former tree dwellers to see above the high grass of
their new home on the savanna.

Of course, it's impossible to point to a day, a year, or even a millennium in which
our wobbly, feeble-minded ancestors became human. The emergence of the human
animal was much too gradual a process. But the first primate that is generally
acknowledged as human enough to deserve being called "prehuman" was a lovable,

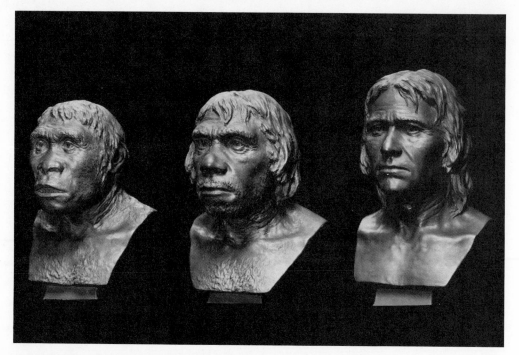

dim-witted creature given the impossible name of *Australopithecus afarensis*. That was too much even for anthropologists to say, so they called her just plain Lucy. She lived about 3.4 million years ago, stood upright and walked on two legs—not bad for an animal with a brain the size of a chimpanzee's.

By evolutionary standards, the transition from Lucy to your next-door neighbor was relatively minor, and it happened almost overnight. During that short period, we went through *Homo habilis*, the first real toolmaker and meat eater, to *Homo erectus*, who discovered fire, and finally, about 400,000 years ago, to *Homo sapiens*. He wasn't quite the next-door neighbor yet, but he was close. He had a big brain—in some cases bigger than ours; he was sophisticated—meaning he had the good sense to come out of the rain and live in a cave; and he was cold—he lived during the Ice Age. From what we can tell, he was also the first human animal to practice religion. Scientists have found his skulls buried at the center of carefully arranged circles of stones, indicating a burial ceremony intended to usher a fallen man or woman into the next world.

That's the history of the human animal according to Darwin and his followers. If it sounded slow and steady, that's because Darwin saw evolution in those terms: slow and steady. Humans, he thought, like all species, changed gradually in response to continuous environmental pressure. Not everybody still sees it that way. Darwin is undoubtedly one of the saints of modern science, and he definitely has his disciples. One of them is Dr. Stephen J. Gould, a professor of biology, geology, and the history of science at Harvard. Gould agrees with most of Darwin's basic theory, but he thinks it needs a little fine-tuning.

In particular, Gould believes Darwin failed to explain "the quirkiness, the unpredictability of evolution." He points to all the fits and starts in the evolutionary story —brief periods of enormous change and long periods where little seems to have happened. For example, animals like Lucy, the first animals that were sort of human, remained more or less the same for at least 1.5 million years. Hard-line Darwinists have always argued that there weren't any periods of inactivity, there are just holes in the record. Changes did take place those years, they argue; we just haven't found any fossil records to prove they did. Gould says there are no fossil records of changes because during those periods there were no changes.

Another knee-jerk Darwinist notion is that *every* feature or behavior in an animal must have evolved as a response to something in the environment. Why does a mammal have four legs? Because four legs make it easier to walk. Why do humans have chins? Because chins make talking and eating easier. Gould responds that a mammal could have four legs simply because it evolved from fishes that had four fins. He compares those who want to believe that every human feature represents a clever adaptation to the comic old philosopher Pangloss in Voltaire's *Candide.* Asked why people have noses, Pangloss answers, "To hold up their spectacles."

Darwin also believed that evolution was a "purposeful" process that moved life "upward and onward" to ever-better adaptations. In this egotistical view, the human

OPPOSITE: Three stages of prehistoric man (from left to right): Pithecanthropus, Neanderthal, and Cro-Magnon. The last of these, who lived about 30,000 years ago, would be virtually indistinguishable from your neighbor.

Skull of Australopithecus africanus.

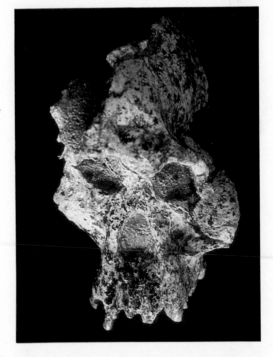

animal is the crowning glory of that process. Gould thinks that notion is arrogant baloney. "Although Darwin encouraged the notion of human evolution as a march toward perfection," he says, a picture with a sense of purpose, there is no reason to think that nature, even given hundreds of millions of years, will draft better eyes, or legs, or brains. Even in matters of sickness and health, the time is long past when our bodies' best hope lay in evolution.

Then what accounts for the difference between a Cro-Magnon man from 30,000 years ago and your next-door neighbor?

According to Gould, there *isn't* much of a difference. If you put the two of them next to each other, gave the old guy a shave, and dressed them up in identical suits, you could hardly tell them apart. Even more important, there would be relatively little "difference in brain capacity and intellectual abilities," says Gould. The difference—the evolution—in the intervening 30,000 years has for the most part taken place in our cultural, as opposed to our physical, development.

But what happened to Genesis? What about Adam and his rib, Eve, and the Garden of Eden? What about the six days of labor and the seventh day of rest? We've traced the development of the human animal all the way back to the primeval "soup" and still no sign of "Him" telling the light to go one way and the dark to go the other. Yet it's all right there in the book. Genesis, Chapter 1, could not be clearer or more eloquent on the issue of creation: "In the beginning God created the heaven and the earth." By the sixth day, God said, "Let us make man in our image." Many theologians—fundamentalists especially—accept these words at face value. In their view, the matter is simple: if man was created in God's own image, as the Bible says, then the idea that man evolved from the ape, as Darwin claims, isn't just sacrilege, it's just plain wrong.

Recent discoveries in Africa now indicate that apes may have some of the rudiments of religious belief. When a family member dies, they not only experience grief, they also enact a ritual-like ceremony. They assemble in a group, stare at the body, then turn to the sunset. Yet we still consider religion a key part of what makes us uniquely human.

It was inevitable that Darwin's ideas would run into trouble from the Church.

According to Dr. Stephen Jay Gould, Darwin failed to explain "the quirkiness, the unpredictability of evolution."

OPPOSITE: According to the Bible, God created man on the sixth day. According to Darwin, the process took billions of years. These two views of Creation may seem far apart, but they're not necessarily contradictory. Europe: A Prophecy by William Blake, 1793.

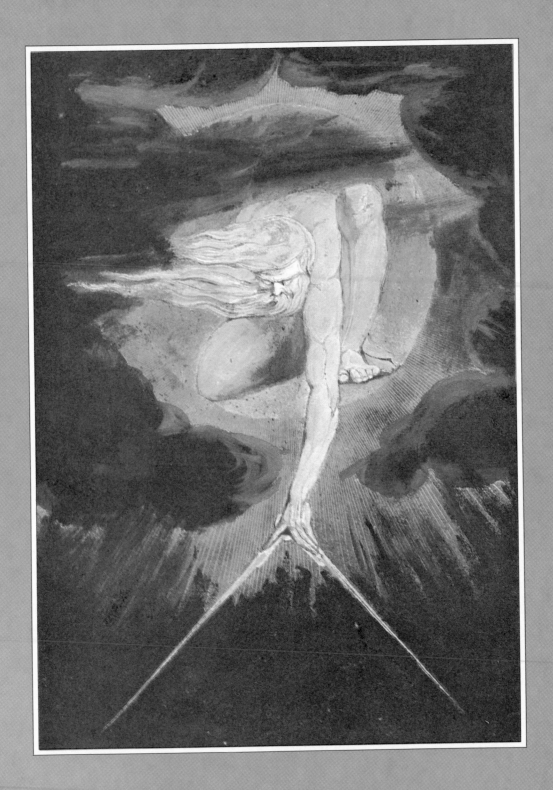

Darwin, who had studied for the ministry himself, was well aware that his theory was at odds with a strict reading of the Bible, and wasn't surprised at all when the theologians rushed to attack *On the Origin of Species*. But even Darwin would have been startled to discover that a hundred and thirty years later, the opposition of religious groups to the theory of evolution is just as loud and bitter as it ever was.

Stephen Gould has campaigned long and hard in defense of the theory of evolution, but he didn't feel the full fury of the opposition to Darwin until he testified at a trial in Arkansas over the validity of a state law requiring that Creationism be taught along with Evolution in the public schools. When he developed cancer, his opponents took it as a sign from heaven, a curse on the nonbeliever: "There was one particularly nasty [letter] from a woman who identified herself as a nurse," Gould recalls, "a preserver of life. She said I was going to die—which I'm not, damn it; I'm going to be a survivor—and that I was sure to burn in hell."

Gould's experience in Arkansas was only the latest skirmish in the battle over Darwin's ideas—a battle that first hit the headlines, and the courtroom, in 1925 when John T. Scopes, a biology teacher in Dayton, Tennessee, was tried and convicted of teaching evolution to his high school class. Scopes' trial brought together two remarkable men, William Jennings Bryan to prosecute Scopes and Clarence Darrow to defend him. Their dramatic confrontation was immortalized in the play and movie *Inherit the Wind*.

Today, the champions may have changed, but the battle goes on. Darwin's latest

"You cannot in academic honesty say that 'I am a Christian' and that 'I am a believer in God' and [at the same time] 'I accept evolution.'" So says the Reverend Jerry Falwell, Darwin's latest nemesis in the continuing battle over the theory of evolution.*

nemesis is the Reverend Jerry Falwell. Falwell's argument is simple, straightforward, aimed right at the gut—like most religious arguments. If you're a good Christian who has faith, says Falwell, then you *must* believe the story of Creation as it's told in the Bible. No room for doubts or reservations, or qualifications, or even just a thoughtful "I'd like to wait until all the evidence is in." A good Christian not only has to believe, now and forever, that God created man in His own image he or she also has to deny that evolution could have been the process by which God chose to create man in his image. "You cannot in academic honesty say that 'I am a Christian' and that 'I am a believer in God' and [at the same time] 'I accept evolution.' "

It's tempting to portray the dispute between Professor Gould and Reverend Falwell as a classic confrontation between the forces of knowledge and the forces of faith. In fact, most of the parties suing Arkansas to prevent Creationism from being taught in the schools were Christian churches. "There may be a conflict between evolution and fundamentalism," says Langdon Gilkey, professor of religion at the University of Chicago, "but all the other major denominations have given up a literalist interpretation of the Bible, and I don't think that means they've given up on the existence of God." In fact, evolution does not, of itself, deny God's existence. It may cause problems with the timing of biblical creation. The "first day" of Genesis may have been hundreds of billions of our days. But the important core of religious sentiment, the conviction that there's a divine presence in the world, is untouched by Darwin. In the end, Darwin's theories, like all great scientific discov-

Our closest relative? Despite the overwhelming scientific evidence, many people —like this demonstrator outside a courtroom in Arkansas—continue to deny Darwin's theory.

eries and all great works of art, make us more deeply aware of the divine.

The human animal has a hunger for knowledge. Just watch a small child some-time. We are irrepressibly curious and playful creatures, and each one of us controls a dazzling array of senses. Of all the animals in the world, we're the only one equipped to go out and search for knowledge, to collect facts, see connections, and then use our conclusions to master our environment. In the end, that's all Charles Darwin did. It's hard to condemn someone for being so eminently human.

But there's another aspect of the human animal that's just as important. The fact is that we crave mystery as much as we crave certainty. We're every bit as fasci-nated by the unknown as by the known. And of all the animals, we're uniquely gifted to be able to imagine mysteries, to manipulate abstract ideas, to believe in the unseen or to take unexplainable joy in the seen. When Shakespeare said that we are "like a god" in apprehension, this may have been what he meant: we can both know things and imagine things. What makes the human animal truly unique is the ability —the *need*—to do both. Does a tree shrew worry about contradictory thoughts? Is a blue-green alga torn between competing ideas? It's not only possible to believe in both God and evolution, it's positively human.

Our capacity for contradiction—the same capacity that fills our lives with absurd-ities and our history books with tragedies—is at the heart of what it means to be human. It allows us to have faith in the unseen, to have hope in the teeth of adversity, to return love for hate, to dream of a better world. Like the builders of Chartres, we continue to dream despite whatever current personal or political cru-sade is giving the human animal a bad name. For ourselves, we may want a house of our own and a happy family. For our world, we may want peace without the threat of nuclear annihilation. Whether medieval workman or modern suburbanite, we have the unique power to imagine beyond the immediate, to envision new ways of living and then work to turn those visions into reality. Whether you march for nuclear disarmament or just go on a diet, you're exercising the uniquely human power to reshape your future by reshaping your present.

Where does this unique human capacity for contradictions come from? Where do all these competing urges and contrary visions originate? In fact, the special equip-ment that makes it possible to satisfy our curiosity, to believe in the unseeable, to hold opposite views from one minute to the next, to ignore the present and dream about the future, it's all in the same place—the human brain. Beauty and beast, saint and sinner, they're all inside. It sits up there controlling our perceptions of the world and our reactions to it, and the only thing that seems to be beyond its power to understand is itself.

Our capacity for contradiction allows us to have faith in the unseen, to return love for hate, to face the future with unbounded enthusiasm.

2. Too Much of a Good Thing?

*A mind not to be chang'd
    by place or time.
The mind is its own place,
    and in itself
Can make a heav'n of hell,
    a hell of heav'n.*

           Milton, *Paradise Lost*

The human brain. For thousands of years it was the most misunderstood and underrated organ in the body. Aristotle thought it was for cooling blood, while the heart was the center of feeling and thought. What is the heart but a few valves and a fist of muscle with some hoses sticking out of it? Yet lovers carve it on trees, Frank Sinatra and Mick Jagger sing songs to it, and Cupid shoots his arrow through it. When was the last time someone said something nice about the brain? Does anyone sing "I Left My Brain in San Francisco" or pound out "Brain and Soul" on the piano? Admittedly, the brain is not a lovable organ. It's the shape of a walnut, the color of a baby's bottom, and the consistency of Jell-O—not exactly a mug you'd want to put on a bumper sticker or a Valentine's Day card.

But what a miracle it is. Packed into this 3-pound package just a little bigger than a grapefruit are something like 100 billion cells. If each of those cells were a grain of sand, they would fill a dump truck. Each of those 100 billion cells is linked to thousands of other cells, creating a dazzling electrochemical circuitry consisting of

Model of the human brain looking through the left eye. The folds of the neocortex loom above. The two heavy filaments leading in from the lower left are the optic nerves carrying visual signals from the eyes to the brain.

trillions of connections that control everything we taste or touch, do or say, see or think. This is evolution's gift to us. More so than the opposable thumb, the vocal cords, the upright stance, or any of the rest of us, this little dynamo is what makes us human.

Ours is not a big brain, by animal standards. If it were a container it would hold about three pints of water, only a third as much as an elephant's brain. If the comparison is based on relative size—the ratio of brain weight to body weight—a human brain looks even worse. A spider monkey, a sparrow, even an ordinary house mouse all have relatively larger brains. Within our own species, brain weight varies. While the average human brain weighs about 3 pounds, the brain of British author Jonathan Swift, who wrote *Gulliver's Travels*, weighed in at a whopping 2,000 grams

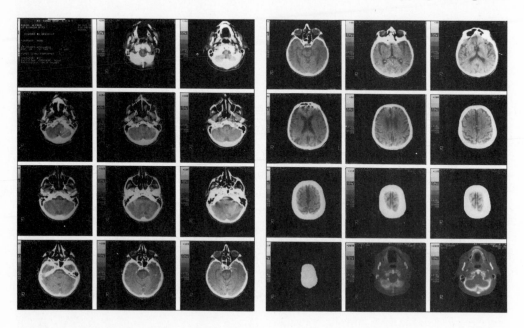

(about 4.4 pounds). Eskimo have bigger brains on the average than any other ethnic group, but that's nothing to brag about. The heaviest brain on record (4.5 pounds) belonged to an idiot. The important feature of our brain appears to be not its size, but its complexity. For example, if you flattened out all those distinctive folds, you'd find that the actual surface area of the brain, where most of our unique intelligence resides, is 324 square inches—about the size of a Monopoly board.

The brain is really three brains: three separate parts, each of which has its own functions and, according to some scientists, its own history. Dr. Paul MacLean, chief of the Laboratory of Brain Evolution and Behavior at the National Institute of Mental Health, argues that the distinctive, three-part structure of the human brain reflects our distinctive evolution. "In fact, we have quite a bit in common with animals,"

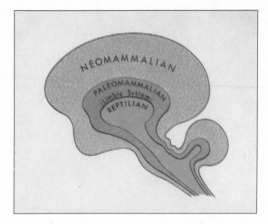

OPPOSITE: The human brain is evolution's gift to us. Portrait of a brain, viewed from above, using computerized axial tomographic (CAT) scan. The horizontal cross-sections begin at the jaw line (upper left) and move up to the crown of the skull (bottom row, third from right).

According to Dr. Paul MacLean, the human brain is three brains in one: the reptilian, the old mammalian ("paleomammalian"), and the neocortex ("neomammalian").

says Dr. MacLean, "right here in our most characteristically human organ, the brain. Our brain is really a 'triune' brain—three brains in one: part 'reptilian,' part 'mammalian' brain and part that's uniquely human. Each of these sub-brains has its own kind of intelligence, memory, sense of time and space, motor skills, and specialized functions. None operates independently of the others, but each has a distinct character. Every one of us carries in his/her head this anatomical legacy of two hundred fifty million years of evolution."

In other words, according to Dr. MacLean, we still have all the brains we ever had. They're not only up there, we're using them. Each of our three brains is like a working souvenir of an important stage in our development. Evolution didn't replace the old brains, it just added new ones—like upgrading a computer instead of buying a new one, or adding rooms to a house to accommodate new kids. The theory makes sense when you realize that all during the evolutionary process we needed the brains we had; we couldn't trade them in or vacate them temporarily. Any improvements had to come in a way that wouldn't interfere with normal functioning.

One clue to the way our brains developed may be the slap-dash way our bodies

Dr. Paul MacLean, chief of the Laboratory of Brain Evolution and Behavior at the National Institute of Mental Health. "Our brain is really a 'triune' brain."

are wired. Do you know why, if you have a heart attack, you may feel it first as a pain under your arm? Because the same nerve pathway that wires the heart to the brain also controls the sensation in that part of your arm. You're not feeling the heart attack because there are no sensory nerves in your heart—if there were, you'd feel every heartbeat as clearly as you feel it when you squeeze your hand into a fist. What you're really feeling is a disturbance in the nerve, but you experience it as a pain under the arm. So our brain is really more like an overwired, rambling old house where three remarkable, but not always compatible animals live. "We might imagine," says MacLean, "that when a psychiatrist bids the patient to lie on the couch, he is asking him to stretch out alongside a horse and a crocodile."

The "crocodile," the most primitive part of our brain, is about the size of a small fist and is located at the very center of the forebrain. It controls simple motor and reflex actions like flinching from pain and bears a striking resemblance—in both form and function—to a reptile's brain. Where in our evolution did we pick this up? About 250 million years ago, even before the dinosaurs roamed or the continents spread, our ancestors were these little doglike reptiles called "therapsids." There's some discussion as to whether they looked more like dogs or more like wolves, but either way they're not the most glamorous page from our past. Although the therapsid itself has been extinct for a long time, we know that it was the branching-off point for mammals and eventually humans.

How do we know our reptilian brain is a souvenir from our therapsid days? According to Dr. MacLean, the therapsid's brain performed many of the same functions our reptilian brain still performs, those unlearned, automatic behaviors like breathing, swallowing, and blinking. Our reptilian brain also makes it possible for us to create new "automatic" routines. When someone says "I could do it blindfolded," he's really bragging on his reptilian brain, which acts as a kind of automatic pilot for certain routine activities. If you do something like brush your teeth or empty the garbage and a few seconds later can't remember doing it, chances are your reptilian brain was directing you.

Lizards are also capable of more complicated activities, and MacLean believes

Reptiles are capable of a few complicated behaviors like fighting and courting. Our crudest emotions—anger, fear, lust—may originate in our reptilian brain. Carolina anolis lizards challenging one another.

OPPOSITE: Like a ramshackle house with many rooms, the human brain developed in stages, from the bottom up, over hundreds of millions of years. Drawing by David Macaulay from *The Amazing Brain.*

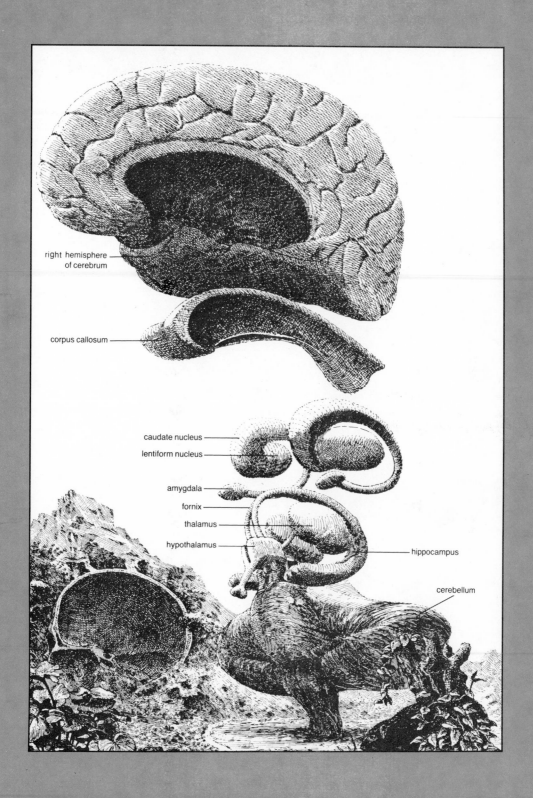

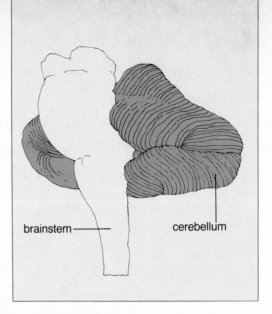

The reptilian brain, located at the base of the brain (see diagram page 47), *dates from the days of the dinosaurs. It controls our unlearned, automatic behaviors like breathing, swallowing, and blinking.*

brainstem

cerebellum

OPPOSITE: Mammalian infants needed care and attention far longer than their reptilian predecessors. That need produced something totally new and different in the world of animal consciousness: emotions. Chimpanzee mother and ten-month-old baby.

that, in humans, these too originate in the reptilian brain. For example, a lizard is capable of identifying itself to other lizards (a behavior called a "signature display"), challenging another lizard to fight ("challenge"), attracting a lizard of the opposite sex ("courtship"), and acknowledging submission or defeat ("submissive display"). So the next time a friend approaches you on the street and says."Hi," or a tough guy in a bar says "You wanna make something of it, buddy?" or you say "I'm sorry," you can bet that your reptilian brain is at work. And no woman who's ever been approached in a bar by a man who says "What's a nice girl like you doing in a place like this?" will be surprised to find out that the reptile in him is at work.

The "horse" in us is the enlargement of the cerebral cortex that surrounds the older reptilian brain and is far more complex. This is the limbic system. MacLean calls it the "old mammalian" brain, because it developed during the early mammalian phase of our evolution. All of our mammal cousins have a similar brain with similar functions, including controlling our senses of smell and taste and our sexual behavior. But the mammalian brain also introduces something totally new and different to the world of animal consciousness: emotions. As far as we know, monkeys and horses don't know joy or sorrow as we do, but they do experience something very close: they play with each other, they care for each other, and they feel lonely without each other. In all mammals, including man, the "old mammalian" brain governs three activities that are never found in reptiles: 1) childish, seemingly purposeless play; 2) nurturing and grooming behavior; 3) and the isolation sounds an animal makes when it is separated from its group. Aside from lust, rage, and fear, all of which are generated in the reptilian brain, most human emotions are derived from these three behaviors common to all mammals and rooted in the mammalian brain: playing, caring, and pining.

Anyone who has lived with two cats or two dogs knows how playful they can be, and has often seen that when one dies, the survivor mourns for weeks and some-

times dies itself soon afterward. But scientists need more verifiable proof. Jane Goodall, for example, has spent more than two decades studying chimpanzees at Gombe Stream National Park in Tanzania, East Africa, because the brain and life cycle of the chimpanzee are so close to our own; it's our closest cousin among all the primates. Goodall's description of the playfulness in one family of chimpanzees sounds like a charming anecdote taken from a book on "How to Be a Mother": "Fifi is a relaxed and affectionate mother. Often she started long play sessions with Fanni, bending over and tickling her with nuzzling movements until the infant was hysterical with laughter. Fifi played often with son Frodo, too—almost always when he got too rough with his small sister."

Looming over its poor relations, the "reptilian" and "old mammalian" brains, is the real star of the show, the last and most human part of the human brain, the neocortex. This is where the real work is done, the work that puts us at the top of the heap in the animal world. The human neocortex is our secret weapon, the advantage that gives us power over the millions of other life forms—some bigger,

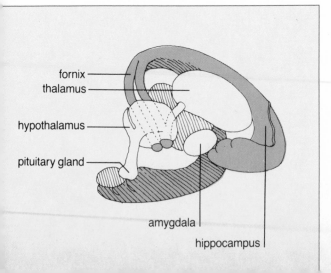

fornix
thalamus

hypothalamus

pituitary gland

amygdala

hippocampus

The "old mammalian" brain, or limbic system, includes the most complex part of the brain, the hypothalamus, a pea-sized structure that regulates eating, drinking, sleeping, waking, body temperature, heart rate, hormones, sex, and emotions. It also directs the brain's master gland, the pituitary. The structures of the limbic system are grouped around the reptilian brain at the top of the brain stem (see diagram page 47).

some faster, some stronger—on the planet. Seventy percent of our entire nervous system is crammed into the neocortex, and then the neocortex itself is crammed into the skull. In and out of and around those folds is a thin layer of gray matter, about a quarter of an inch thick, that contains 8 billion cells, all of them interconnected with fibers so densely packed that there are 10,000 miles of them in 1 cubic inch. If you took all the connecting fibers in your brain and stretched them end to end, they would wrap around the earth forty times. Nothing else produced by evolution is quite like it. Within that maze of wiring reside the unprecedented talents that make us truly human. But it's the combination of all three brains, working with and sometimes against each other, that makes us more than the sum of our past— part animal, part human, and part something more.

When you watch a great artist perform, whether it's Vladimir Horowitz, or Michael Jackson, you're seeing the human brain perform at its peak. The neocortex distills years of learning and practice into effortless virtuosity. It sends a blizzard of messages to the reptilian brain, which coordinates the perfect movements of a hundred muscles every second—sometimes adding a dash of fear or lust or anger. The mammalian brain infuses the movements with love, and passion, and longing, and the result is an instant of such unbearable beauty, of such perfect harmony between the parts of the brain, that another level of consciousness is reached. There are any number of ways to reach that level—religion, science, and art are just the most common—but it's only because we have all three brains working together in the same skull that we can reach it at all. "We have been brought up being told the neocortex does everything," Dr. MacLean says. "We would have an entirely different appreciation of ourselves and the world if we could get a little deeper than the neocortex."

But what about the rest of us? What about those of us who can't perform like Horowitz or Michael Jackson? What has the human brain done for us lately? At the risk of sounding ungrateful, one has to ask the question: Are we too smart for our own good? Most people's days are filled with routine work, shopping for groceries, having friends over for a barbecue, watching television. What happens to all that magnificent machinery up there when it's idling?

"Most of what our brains do," says Stephen Gould, "most of what is essential to our considering ourselves as human is not a product of natural selection, I believe, but arises as a nonadaptive consequence of having a computer as powerful as the human brain. And one of the most unsettling things that the evolution of the large brain has allowed us to do is to look into the future—to feel the tension between today and tomorrow, and to learn the fact of our personal mortality. Think how

---

A great performer represents not just years of practice, but millions of years of evolution. Without our complex brain, we could never do the remarkable things we do. Singer, dancer, performer extraordinary Michael Jackson.

much of human culture has arisen in an attempt to deal with that. You can't argue the brain became large *so that* we would learn the fact of our coming personal mortality."

If it could talk, the Irish elk would probably express misgivings about its ungainly antlers or the peacock about its train. They're great for dominating other males or for attracting mates, but a pain in the neck the rest of the time. Biologists say features like the elk's antlers and the peacock's train are a result of "overspecialization," an evolutionary mechanism that leads to some of the animal world's most distinctive features. "The organism," Gould explains, "is doing what it ought to do as a Darwinian agent: trying to win more copulations to pass on more of its genes to future generations. It does that by developing a highly precise specialized organ which limits the flexibility of the species with respect to evolutionary change, eventually guaranteeing the extinction of the species." In other words, the change may be terrific for the individual peacock, but murder for peafowl as a species.

Is the human brain another example of overspecialization? There's no doubt that its unique powers of intelligence and imagination have served an important adaptive purpose and enabled humans to survive in a world where extinction waits at the end of every wrong turn; but does it now "limit the flexibility of the species with respect to evolutionary change," as Gould says, and constitute a hazard rather than a help to our survival?

Is the human brain a Cadillac engine in a Volkswagen body? Are we all paying a terrible price in terms of frustration and depression by carrying around this overgrown, overwrought, and underworked engine just so a few artists can rev it up to full throttle every now and then? Are we too smart for our own emotional good? It's true that if we didn't have such big brains, we would never have found a preventive for polio or walked on the moon, but we would also have avoided the atomic bomb, ozone depletion, and chronic depression.

Our brain gives us our unique "consciousness" so we can imagine a Sistine Chapel and ask questions about the way the universe functions, but most of the time it's asking all those more mundane questions that keep us awake at night—"Why doesn't she love me?" or "Why am I so unhappy, so depressed?" "Why doesn't anybody like me?" "Why is my sex drive driving me crazy?" "Why do I feel so frustrated?" "What am I going to do with my life?"

Our brains invented radio and television, helping us to exercise our consciousness on the problems of 4 billion people instead of just a few. Every day, a varied crew of people in a variety of straits parade into our living rooms, sharing their anxieties, rekindling our own, causing us to ask questions about ourselves and creating expectations that only make life more miserable, more disappointing, and keep Valium at the top of so many shopping lists. Without radio and television, life would still have problems, but we wouldn't be so aware of them. Without our brains, we might not even be aware of our own eventual death—most animals aren't. Without an aware-

The beautiful feathers of this peacock's train may help it attract a mate, but they also prevent it from flying. When a species evolves in a way that reduces its chances for survival, biologists call it "overspecialization"—too much of a good thing.

ness of death, we probably wouldn't be so much attracted to alcohol or so vulnerable to depression.

If you're overweight, blame it on your brain. The brain has made the human animal uniquely creative, but also uniquely self-indulgent. The number of overweight human beings is unparalleled in any other animal species. Most animals have evolved a biological system linking stomach and brain that makes them automatically stop eating when they're full. It's very difficult to get any other animal to overeat in the wild. But they don't have our mischievous brain. Our bodies were adapted, like all animals', to conditions of natural scarcity. In times of plenty, however, we developed the ability to deny our own regulatory mechánisms. We knew how much food we needed, but we were capable of eating more, and storing it as fat. For most of human history, this ability to overeat had adaptive value: we could overindulge in anticipation of famines to come, much the way a bear overeats during the summer and fall in order to last through a winter of hibernation. Now our brains have devised ways of eliminating scarcity—at least for those of us lucky enough to live in the industrialized world—but our evolutionary override mechanisms haven't changed. We go on blithely stuffing ourselves for a famine that never comes.

If you're overwrought, blame it on your brain. What makes the human animal overindulge in anything—food, alcohol, drugs, work, anything that makes us feel better—is stress. There are two ways to make nonhuman animals overeat. You can destroy part of the animal's brain, or you can subject it to unusually high levels of stress. "What is now popularly known as 'stress,' " says psychiatrist Dr. Michael Weissberg, "is the biological response of the human organism to any demand made upon it."

Some scientists think that a certain low level of stress is built into the human

Our wonderful brain has made us uniquely self-indulgent. The relative number of overweight human beings in Western society is unparalleled in any other species.

animal. "I think that we are set up by our evolution to experience continuously buzzing dissatisfaction, anxiety, maybe mild fear, or mild hunger that goes beyond what we need," says Dr. Melvin Konner, professor of anthropology at Emory University. This "dissatisfaction" is what drives us to work so hard, to achieve so much. Where did we pick up this bee in our bonnet? "We have relieved the stresses, many of the stresses, of the old jungle," says Konner. "We no longer have to fear predation; we no longer have to expect half of our children to die before they grow up. But we *do* have to fear muggers, we have to fear break-ins in our apartments, we have to fear getting run down by cars, and we have to fear that forces beyond our control may turn around and destroy all of life on the planet earth." In other words, what used to be the positive adaptation of alertness that protected us from predators has become a maladaptive vulnerability to stress.

How does the body react to this stress?

"We can measure three stages of that response," says Dr. Weissberg. "The first is an initial alarm reaction, during which the entire body mobilizes to meet the demand. The second stage is resistance, during which the body adapts itself to the continuing demands placed on it and mobilizes its reserves of energy to resist them."

How long can the body put up with stress?

It depends on the individual. According to Dr. Weissberg, we humans possess a deep reserve of what he calls "adaptation energy," an energy that enables us to adapt to changing and perhaps difficult environments. "We don't know much about this energy," says Dr. Weissberg, "except that individuals inherit it in greater or lesser amounts from their parents and that it serves us just exactly like inherited wealth, on which we can draw during our lives but to which we can never add."

And eventually we use it all up?

"Yes," says Dr. Weissberg. "In every response to stress, the third state—exhaustion—arrives when we no longer have the energy to resist. In everyday stress situations—like a hard day's work—we can recoup most of our energy to resist and adapt by getting a good night's sleep or taking a vacation. But we never recover all of it. We use it up over a lifetime, and eventually we have used it all up and we reach the ultimate exhaustion, death. And if we encounter high levels of stress all our lives we will use up our inherited adaptive energy faster, just like a spendthrift heir who squanders his inheritance. And we will die sooner."

It sounds like the best way to live a long and healthy life is not to care; but that would be a boring, undistinguished way to live your life. Is there a healthy way to respond to stress, or do we have to choose between caring and killing ourselves?

"No, not at all," according to Dr. Weissberg. "Remember that I have defined stress in very neutral terms—as a response to a demand. The energy we bring to meeting life's demands is the deepest source of our vitality and joy in life—provided we can actually meet those demands. Work is a basic human need that always

Dr. Melvin Konner, professor of anthropology at Emory University and author of The Tangled Wing. *"We are set up by our evolution to experience continuously buzzing dissatisfaction."*

RIGHT: Depression and alienation seem to be increasingly common side effects of modern life. Some scientists see an "epidemic" of abnormal behaviors designed to help us cope with frustration and unfulfilled expectations. Pablo Picasso's The Tragedy, 1903.

involves stress but should also involve the satisfaction of accomplishing a job we feel a personal pride in doing. In my opinion what our society is suffering from today is not an epidemic of stress but one of *distress*—harmful stress that results from a continuous feeling of failure and frustration."

And why do so many people have that feeling of failure and frustration?

"I think because of the gap we encounter everywhere between our basic needs and our expectations and the realities of our life," says Dr. Weissberg. "For example, we need to work, but many of the jobs we do today are impersonal, boring, and without tangible, satisfying results. Or we are unemployed or don't need to work— idled by poverty or affluence—and suffer the frustration of unfulfillment. We also need a certain balance in life between stressful striving and relaxation, between isolation and companionship, between environments that are stimulating and ones that are tranquil—and in our modern urban existence fewer and fewer people can achieve such a balance. They must adapt themselves to a world that is continually overstimulating, isolating, and stressful without relief—and with less and less of a sense of personal identity and personal self-esteem, another of our basic needs."

In other words, our brain is a delicate hothouse flower that needs rich soil, just the right atmosphere, and the right balance of nutrients to flourish. But in a world of tedious jobs, free time, and personal stress, the brain is alternately overstimulated and understimulated. What happens when the brain, like a sick flower, starts to droop?

"We see today two epidemics: one of distress—related physical ailments like stroke, heart attack, hypertension, perhaps cancer; and another one of depression and abnormal behaviors designed to alleviate our frustrations and narrow the gap between our needs and expectations and our modern realities." According to Dr. Weissberg, "a significant portion of our economy depends on mental attempts to close the expectation–reality gap. And by that I mean drugs of all kinds."

Addiction is the brain's way of coping with a hostile world—a bad day at the office, a dead-end job, no job, family problems, whatever. It's a way of compensating for the stimulation our brain misses, or of calming it down after it's been overstimulated. To pick up the car metaphor again, think of addiction as the stereo in your temperamental Italian sports car. You turn up the volume to avoid hearing how badly out of tune your engine is because it's been idling too long or because you've been racing it too much. Now think of everyday life as heavy downtown traffic and you'll begin to see why some scientists consider the brain a prime example of overspecialization.

America's number-one hard drug, the one that contributes to more than 100,000 deaths every year, the one that costs us $100 billion in damage to our health and the economy every year, is often available right in your supermarket next to the milk. That drug is sold by a billion-dollar industry—entirely legal—that advertises some

---

Alcohol is the number-one hard drug in our society. Even though it contributes to more than 100,000 deaths and $100 billion in economic damage every year, it's often available right in your supermarket.

of its less potent products to an impressionable audience of children as well as adults every night on national television. That drug is, of course, alcohol. And to judge by the most recent statistics on drinking, more and more people in this country are going into their local liquor store to boost the volume on their brain's stereo.

The annual per capita consumption of alcohol in America today is the highest since 1950. Thirty-six percent of the adults who drink are medically classifiable as

alcoholics or problem drinkers. Nineteen percent of young people between the ages of fourteen and seventeen are now also problem drinkers. The percentage of high school students who admit to having been intoxicated at least once has risen from 19 percent in 1966 to 45 percent in 1975. And between 1960 and 1970 the rate of deaths as a result of alcoholism increased 36 percent, to the point where this disease is the second-most-common cause of death in America.

Why is alcohol so appealing to so many people? Because it's legal and relatively inexpensive? Because our society associates drinking with sophistication and maturity? Because it's depicted so alluringly in advertisements? In every case, the answer is yes; but these factors don't add up to a complete explanation of alcohol's enormous appeal. No matter now enthusiastically our culture endorses it, no matter how hard advertisers push it, alcohol wouldn't be so popular if it didn't really *do*

OPPOSITE: Almost all compulsive abuse of substances like alcohol is the result of the same need to alter brain and body chemistry so that we experience reality in a different and less painful way.

The human brain is capable of becoming addicted to almost any substance or activity. Cocaine is only the latest and most fashionable "high."

something for us—or, more accurately, *to* us. "What many people do," says Dr. Konner, "is medicate themselves for their anxiety with alcohol or street drugs, or change their consciousness with these substances, to detach themselves from some of the unpleasant realities, psychological realities, of the environment."

In the brain, alcohol prompts the release of a chemical that slows down the transmission of impulses along and between the neurons of the cerebral cortex.

Remember that thin layer of 8 billion cells connected by 800,000 miles of fiber, packed into 80 cubic inches? It is in this sensitive area that alcohol wreaks the quickest and most complete damage. The first to go are your higher functions—your ability to reason abstractly, make judgments of distance and time, distinguish right from wrong. Then your memory begins to fade in and out. That's the primary reason alcohol is so popular: it releases us from the very consciousness that makes us human; we "forget" ourselves. It's as if the big walnut on top disappears and, for a little while at least, we are mammals again—plain, simple mammals—basically all feeling and fighting. We lose some of that messy neocortical self-consciousness. If you drink long and hard enough, you can even shut down some of your mammalian brain and start to lose your ability to coordinate your tongue to talk or your legs to walk. With the higher brain functions blacked out, there's nothing to check or modify the urges that spring out of your mammalian brain. The direct link between alcohol and child abuse, spouse abuse, murder, vehicular homicide, and suicide has been statistically established and is proved again every day in the news.

Alcohol may be the most popular and the most available form of addiction, but your brain is very inventive when it's looking for ways to escape stress. "An addiction to alcohol," says psychiatrist Dr. Harvey Milkman, "is only one legally and culturally sanctioned way we escape the stress of life by minimizing our awareness of it—'drowning our sorrows.' There are other ways to do this that are just as addictive and achieve the same result. The drug heroin, for example, also minimizes awareness of reality, and so do ordinary drugstore tranquilizers. Or we can make reality seem better by intensifying our awareness of it with amphetamines or cocaine. Or we can escape reality altogether with hallucinogens like LSD. Compulsive abuse of all these substances leads to the same result: the alteration of the chemistry of brain and body so that we experience reality in a different and less painful way. And because we get that result, we use them compulsively."

But the vast majority of adults aren't addicted to any substance. They may have a drink every now and then to relax or socialize, but they're hardly alcoholic. Are some people just better equipped to cope with stress in their lives?

"No doubt many of them are. But there's something most people don't know about compulsive cravings. Human beings can achieve exactly the same minimizing, intensification, or escape from a stressful reality by engaging in compulsive behaviors that have nothing to do with alcohol or other drugs. For example, you can get an amphetaminelike rush to relieve your alienation and feelings of frustration by taking risks—by skydiving, drag-racing, engaging in sexual promiscuity, or committing crimes. Or you can escape reality by compulsively meditating or chanting in a religious cult or just by compulsively daydreaming—your own brain naturally contains several key components of the drug LSD. And you can minimize your awareness of a painful reality by compulsively watching endless amounts of TV, playing video games, becoming a workaholic, or overeating."

Are you saying that people who do these things are the same as alcoholics and other drug abusers?

"We're saying that people who do those things compulsively do so for the same reasons *and* achieve the same results as alcoholics and other drug abusers. They actually alter their brain and body chemistry—and therefore their experience of reality—just as effectively with binge eating or the thrill of crime or meditation as they do with chemical substances. And so they repeat these behaviors compulsively —they become addicted—as a way of narrowing the gap between what they want out of life and what they actually have. In that sense, yes, they are junkies like the substance abusers. Only the addictions are socially acceptable, legal, and enthusiastically marketed to young and old alike."

Apparently, our brains are disappointed with the life they've built for themselves and, like anybody who's underemployed and unchallenged, they're always casting

The human brain is inventive when it comes to escaping stress. Dangerous sports like hang gliding and skydiving produce an amphetaminelike rush that can be as addictive as any drug.

around for something to keep those 8 billion cells either busy or numbed. The logical question at this point is, what can we do about it? Are we stuck with this brain— with all its wonders and weaknesses—or is there some possibility that it will evolve further and, in the process, help us overcome the problems that today drive us to seek escape in alcohol, drugs, and other mind-numbing habits?

"For human beings," says Stephen Gould, "biological evolution is already over. It was completed fifty thousand years ago. There's no reason to think we're going to get bigger brains or smaller toes, or whatever—we are what we are." At this point in our evolution, according to Gould and others, culture, not biology, is the force that shapes our behavior.

But not everyone agrees. In fact, the question of the roles of culture and biology in determining human behavior is at the center of a scientific controversy. Sociobiologists like Harvard's Edward O. Wilson argue that "all domains of human life, including ethics, have a physical basis in the brain and are part of human biology." Biological evolution is not finished, Wilson argues; it has just been joined by another very powerful shaping force, culture. Our behavior is not entirely a matter of cultural evolution; it is the result of "gene-culture" co-evolution.

The very word "sociobiology" implies that social behavior has a biological component, that propensities toward certain human behaviors—aggression and xenophobia, for example—exist naturally in the brain. Critics worry that research into areas like the biological basis of intelligence or competitiveness or prejudice can be used to justify the *status quo* and to forgive racism, sexism, and other evils. Wilson and his colleagues ask not to be criticized for what *might* be done with their research.

Besides, part of the sociobiological argument is that the natural selection process that produced the human brain also equipped it with the ability to overcome biological propensities that have become maladaptive in twentieth-century life. We may have a built-in attraction to addictive behavior, but we can go on the wagon. We may have a violent streak, but through better understanding and more effective cultural control, we can redirect it. In short, we have free will.

Whatever the merits of the controversy, one thing is clear: we have never made much progress by foreclosing inquiry. If we fail to explore the deep reaches of human nature, we are handicapping our children in their efforts to understand themselves and to make a better world.

Our future is in our children's hands, but we have to encourage the inquisitiveness and provide the information they will need to shape that future responsibly. Classroom in Lagos, Nigeria.

3. The Promised Land

Nature never deceives us;
it is always we
who deceive ourselves.

Jean-Jacques Rousseau, *Émile*

Whether culture alone has been directing human behavior in the last fifty thousand years, or culture and biology have been acting together, the results have been truly dazzling—in a period that represents only *one one-hundred-thousandth* of the history of the earth. "When you consider how much has been done in that infinitesimal bit of time," says Stephen Gould, "you realize what a powerful force culture—this project of the human brain—really is. We create culture when we invent things or new strategies for living; and then we pass these inventions on to our offspring, so that what we have created winds up creating us, and alters the course of evolution. For one organism alone, the environment has become a thing to shape, rather than a thing to be shaped by."

And yet the environment we've shaped hasn't made us very happy. Although it's admirable in its advancement and remarkable in its complexity, it doesn't seem, on the whole, to be a satisfying environment. Those of us who are lucky enough to live in the most advanced part of the world have personal computers, supersonic transport, moving sidewalks, CAT scans, and zap mail, but are we really at peace with ourselves—or each other? All that speed and abundance sure is convenient, but as we've seen, it also gives off waves of stress in the same way a nuclear reactor gives off radioactivity.

Why has the human brain created a world that alternately bores it and frazzles it, a world from which more and more people are looking for escape; a world in which extinction is, for the first time, a real possibility? How did we dig ourselves into this hole? Where did we go wrong? At what point did cultural evolution start throwing

Given all the advantages of modern society, you'd think we would enjoy it more. Yet many human animals lead what Thoreau called lives of "quiet desperation." Two shoppers. Sculpture by Duane Hanson.

According to the story of Adam and Eve, life before technology was simpler and less stressful. But we ate from the tree of knowledge, and we've lived to regret it. From the workshop of Albrecht Altdorfer, *The Fall of Man,* c. 1535.

up more problems than it was solving? Maybe if we understand the answers to these questions, we can begin to figure out how to set ourselves back on the right track before—pushed by somebody with his hand on the button—we stumble into a hole so deep and so dark that we'll never come out.

Although the human animal has been around in this form for 50,000 years, our cultural evolution didn't get rolling until about 10,000 years ago when we began to free ourselves from the cycles of nature and the harsh rules of scarcity. It's easy to oversimplify the role of cultural evolution by giving the impression that on January 1, 8000 B.C., nature handed over the mantle of evolution to culture. In fact, the transition began long before then, continued at an extremely gradual rate, and is probably still going on today. To some extent nature is still affecting our evolution: witness, for example, the economic rise of the American "Sun Belt." But by 10,000 years ago, the dominant force in our evolution was no longer nature: it was us. No longer captive to the rhythms of the planet—the moon, the tides, the seasons—we began to evolve in response not to the cycles of nature, but to the pace of our own technological innovations.

It was *then*, according to some, that our troubles began. Technology was the culprit. By insulating us from nature, it introduced new forms of stress into our lives, and we've been going downhill ever since. That's what the story of Adam and Eve in the Garden is all about. We ate the fruit of the tree of knowledge and we've lived to regret it. According to this view, life before technology—life before agriculture, that is—was simpler, less stressful than life today. The world of hunter-gatherer societies is the paradise from which the human race has "fallen." Is that an accurate picture of life before technology? Did our problems begin when that first tribe began to take control of its fate by planting a crop and hanging around to harvest it? One way to answer that question is to look at a society that has only recently taken that fateful step: the !Kung Bushmen of Africa.

Almost none of the !Kung people still wander the bush hunting and gathering their food. They now live in permanent villages and raise their own cattle, which they trade for crumbs of technology like Coca-Cola. Under the careful observation

Primitive tribes are getting harder to find. Most now live in permanent villages and, like the Mbuti tribesmen of central Africa, share the fringe benefits of modern civilization.

of anthropologists like Dr. Richard Lee, the !Kung have recently undergone the same tranformation that our forebears in the Near East went through 10,000 years ago when they switched from hunting and gathering to stock breeding and agriculture and all the other good things that got the cultural ball rolling.

"In some highly significant ways," says Dr. Lee, "it was indeed a fall from paradise. One thing that studying hunter-gatherers has proved to me is that the human species originally evolved and survived not through dog-eat-dog competition for scarce game and the hunting of food, as many earlier theories like Darwinism stated, but rather through cooperation and the sharing of food. It was the food sharing that was the mainstay of traditional !Kung society, and not the aggressive elimination of rivals in some 'survival of the fittest' contest, that enabled us to survive as a species."

What has happened to that cooperative attitude now that the !Kung are beginning to own property and accumulate wealth?

"When the food you're sharing was collected by the group from nature, and will be replenished by nature, food sharing works. But when food becomes a herd animal, owned by one person, which once slaughtered and distributed is not immediately replaceable, sharing becomes an economic detriment. With the beginnings of this kind of economy—our kind—we see the roots of our own 'every man for himself' philosophy, with its various forms of competition and alienation."

So in one sense, at least, our Stone Age ancestors suffered less anxiety than we do?

"Right. They knew who they were, and that they belonged in their society, and that they could more or less rely on their neighbors and relatives. They didn't suffer from the same level of social competition and status inequality that people in more complex, stratified societies do."

So everything was idyllic until technology came along and spoiled it? Not exactly.

"The old !Kung will tell you," Dr. Lee continues, "about how wonderful their life is now with shelter and an assured supply of food, and how anxious they were when they lived as nomadic hunter-gatherers, always wondering if lions would kill them or if they would find enough food to eat. Probably the truest thing we can learn from all this is that human beings have always had stressful situations and anxieties, but that we have traded the original anxieties based on scarcity for different anxieties based on abundance."

In other words, if modern life is a mess, it's not because there's so much more stress now than there was back in the good old days of hunting and gathering. Those who blame technology are wrong. The fault must lie not in the nature of our culture but in the way we *respond* to the culture. "The core of the human problem," says Dr. Ashley Montagu, the anthropologist, "is that human beings are the most adaptable, flexible, and educable creatures on earth. Thanks to this blessing of extreme adaptability, which had enabled us to survive anywhere on the planet and meet any

One of the many "joys" of modern culture: rush-hour traffic. Crosstown traffic in Manhattan moves at the prehistoric average pace of 5.2 miles per hour.

change in our environment with an innovative response, we are also the most confusable creatures on earth, the most prone to success, the most likely to get ourselves into trouble by reason of our adaptability itself."

It isn't technology that has gotten us in a mess; it's what we have done with it, how we have used it—and abused it—that makes our lives so much less happy than they could be. We're often so delighted and self-congratulatory over technological advances that we don't stop to think about the impact they may have on our lives. We swallow things whole and worry about digestion later. Take, for example, the automobile. Marvelous invention, the internal-combustion engine. It set us free, and with the help of Henry Ford, we took to it with frantic enthusiasm and without reservation.

Now look what a jam we've gotten ourselves into. In 1979, crosstown traffic in Manhattan moved at an average speed of 6 miles an hour. By 1982, it had slowed to 5.2 miles an hour. There are 32,000 parking places in downtown Miami. On an average day, 40,000 automobiles compete for those places. If we weren't the most adaptable creature on the earth, could we put up with these conditions? And what about those cities? What a great idea to bring all those people together, to provide so many cultural opportunities, so many choices, and what a miracle that technology can provide the food, water, and other needs of such a densely packed community. Of course, on an average day in Jersey City, there are supermarket lines that start at the cash register and end at the back of the store. Under similar conditions, it used to be thought, our mammal cousins the lemmings would run off to the sea and drown themselves by the thousands. Millions of human animals run to the sea on weekends, too, but not to drown themselves.

And these are only the inconveniences of city life as it is lived by the luckiest of us. In parts of central Detroit, babies die every year at the same rate they do in Honduras, the poorest country in Central America. And in our American cities, you are far more likely to breathe dangerously polluted air—and ten times as likely to be murdered—than in any other industrialized country.

Unemployment among black American teenagers has reached 42 percent; and nearly 30 percent of all black Americans living in cities are under twenty-one. In 1977, the number of American families living below the poverty line—more than 1 family in 5—was higher than in any year since World War II. The gap in income between America's rich and America's poor has *doubled* since 1950.

During the 1970s, 30 of America's 50 largest urban centers actually *lost* population. Philadelphia, Pittsburgh, Chicago, Baltimore, Milwaukee, Minneapolis, Detroit, Seattle, Louisville, Kansas City—they're all shrinking. And not slowly. In Philadelphia, the City of Brotherly Love and the birthplace of American independence, more than 22,000 white families during the 1970s and 50,000 black families abandoned the city.

Is this the Promised Land? Is this the end product of cultural evolution? Is this what scientists call "controlling our environment"? Have we solved life's problems or just created new ones? Have we conquered the stresses of scarcity or just added to them the stresses of abundance? Has our strategy of cultural evolution been to

For many, the "promised land" means a long wait in an unemployment line. As new industries evolve and old ones die out, individuals—and their families—pay the price.

adapt to life merely by solving immediate problems? Have we painted ourselves into a corner that even we can't figure a way out of? These questions may sound abstract and distant, but in fact they're a part of our everyday lives. Every time you go to work in the morning, get caught in a traffic jam, take a breath of polluted air, lock your door at night, or have a nightmare about nuclear war, you're the victim of a cultural evolution that we ourselves have shaped.

Take, for example, the city of Bethlehem, Pennsylvania. The oldest building in Bethlehem is the Community House, built by a band of settlers belonging to the German Moravian Church who huddled together in the snowy woods on Christmas Eve 1741 and founded a settlement which they called Bethlehem in honor of the special day. The Moravians intended Bethlehem to be a community of families leading "blameless" lives, living and working together according to the principles of their faith. They wanted to be governed by their own beliefs, not by others' laws. In other words, they wanted to establish a new culture.

Like many Europeans in the eighteenth century, the Moravians came to Pennsylvania to start over, to free themselves from the Old World with its wars, religious persecutions, social inequalities. William Penn founded Pennsylvania as a "holy experiment" of human communities searching for the perfect relationship between God, society, and the individual. The Moravians of Bethlehem put their hopes in a utopia based on what sounds to us today suspiciously like communism. The goods they produced were shared and held for the common benefit. No one grew richer than his fellows.

That worked fine for a while; but then, around 1857, the first railroads passed through Bethlehem and some enterprising local citizens started a small company to make iron rails. A few years later, after one of the great technological breakthroughs of the nineteenth century, the little company converted from iron to steel and became the Bethlehem Steel Corporation.

If you think Bethlehem Steel is just another steel company, you're wrong. It's an American monument. Bethlehem Steel built Madison Square Garden, the Golden Gate Bridge, the Waldorf-Astoria Hotel, and the first American aircraft carrier. It manufactured and repaired more ships during World War II than any other private shipbuilder in the world. Naturally, in achieving these industrial milestones, it replaced the Moravian Church as the focus of life in Bethlehem. What had started out as a holy experiment became an economic and technological experiment. The religious, communistic culture of the Moravians gradually evolved into the individualistic, entrepreneurial culture of industrial America.

In 1925, on the grounds of its coke works, Bethlehem Steel built a labor camp for newly arrived immigrants from Italy, Poland, Hungary, and Mexico who took the thousands of new jobs for unskilled labor created by the boom. According to accepted business practice, the company paid them as little as it could get away with, gave them twelve-hour, seven-days-a-week shifts, and charged them inflated prices

OPPOSITE: During its heyday in the early twentieth century, Bethlehem, Pennsylvania, was a melting pot for people as well as for iron ore. Workers from Italy, Poland, Hungary, and Mexico came to Bethlehem steelworks to pursue the American Dream.

TOP: Bethlehem Steel's mark is on many of America's landmarks, from the Verrazano-Narrows Bridge outside New York to the Golden Gate in San Francisco.

LEFT: Bethlehem has seen better days. In the 1970s, the city lost almost 10 percent of its population. Is Bethlehem—like hundreds of towns and cities in the industrial heartland of America—a victim of cultural evolution?

at company stores. In addition to work, their lives consisted of bloody strikes, polluted streams, wood barracks and cheap frame houses, outdoor plumbing, and front yards made of slag stones. Occasionally, a company train would stop and dump scrap lumber from the slag banks and the workers would scramble for a few pieces of scarce firewood. The conditions weren't just the result of unique cruelty or greed: they were part of the industrial culture in America before the Depression.

America did offer hope to the unskilled worker—hope that, in his own or in his children's lifetime, his family might get a little piece of the prosperity. The American Dream was in its heyday. And over the hundred years from 1850 to 1950, millions of working Americans in towns like Bethlehem did achieve at least some part of the Dream. Poles, Russians, Portuguese, German, Greeks, Mexicans were all learning English and taking the oath of allegiance. Sons and daughters were rising from unskilled labor to skilled jobs, moving out of the old neighborhoods and into the suburbs. That was also part of our industrial culture.

But what's happened to that culture recently? If you walk around the streets of

Bethlehem today, you feel like you're in one of those Western mining towns just before the last resident packed up and left. If this culture isn't dying, it's very sick. You can see it in the boarded-up shop windows, the idle workers, the deserted streets and stores. If you go over to the steelworks, you'll find half of it closed down. Since 1980, thousands of workers have been laid off, and their prospects for going back to work anytime soon are not good. Out of a population of only 70,000, 5,000 residents left Bethlehem between 1970 and 1980, and more are leaving every year. Is Bethlehem, Pennsylvania—like hundreds of towns and cities across America—a "blooper" of cultural evolution? Are the people in this town suffering from what scientists would call "evolutionary overspecialization"?

Harvard professor Robert B. Reich argues that cultural maladaptation is responsible not only for what's happening in Bethlehem, but also for the larger economic problems that threaten all of us over the long run. According to Reich, people are leaving Bethlehem and towns like it "because the key to the whole local economy—the steel industry—can no longer offer what it once did: first an opportunity, then a steady job. America used to produce fifty percent of the world's steel. Now it produces only sixteen percent and exports only one-tenth of what Japan exports. The old American way of immigrating at the bottom and working up is becoming less and less possible in the traditional industries. And industry and government are moving at a snail's pace toward training and retraining. Our institutions—the invisible 'they' who are supposed to take care of these things—seem to be out of step with the needs of the individuals they serve."

How did Bethlehem—and the rest of us—get into such a fix so quickly after a century of prosperity?

"The way of life that Americans have known since World War Two, when the rest of the industrial world lay in ruins and we were the undisputed economic masters of the world, is dying," says Reich, "the victim of a revitalized foreign industrial competition and a failure to develop an effective strategy for competing

According to Dr. Robert B. Reich, a professor of business and public policy at Harvard University, the future belongs to the most adaptable societies. "The central problem of America's economic future is that the nation is not moving quickly enough out of high-volume, standardized production," says Reich.

OVERLEAF: Kawasaki Oil Refineries in Japan.

with foreign rivals. Put simply, our industrial base is not evolving as fast as it must. As a result, America's standard of living has slipped. But Americans still have in their minds the shining image of the way of life they knew from 1945 to 1975: the end of the industrial era. The move to the Sun Belt is a search for a postindustrial adaptation that will restore to them the fading myth of the American Dream."

Just how bad off are we in comparison to the rest of the world?

According to Reich, "America still has the highest productivity. And on the whole, our people still live better than others on the globe. But in some respects— after-tax income, health care, pollution, longevity, and infant mortality—life in places such as Scandinavia and Japan is better than it is here, and the long-term trend is worrying." Very recently, you were more likely to be unemployed in the United States than in any other highly industrialized country except Canada. Four weeks' paid vacation is the law in most European countries no matter when an employee was hired; in America only 64 percent of all workers get that much vacation even after they've been on the job for twenty years. America ranks eighth in life expectancy for the average male and fifteenth for the average female, while seventeen countries have lower rates of infant mortality. You are about three times as likely to die by someone else's hand in America as in any other industrialized country. We think of America as the land of opportunity, but it's really more a land of opportunity for the rich. In America, 40 percent of the wealth is owned by the top 2 percent of the householders—and that's the most radical concentration of wealth in any industrialized country.

Why are we slipping?

"Because America has failed to adapt to the worldwide reorganization of production," says Reich. Ironically, the very human trait that got us into this mess can, according to Reich, get us out: adaptability. "The central problem of America's economic future is that the nation is not moving quickly enough out of high-volume, standardized production." American factories will *never* regain the lead in production-line manufacturing, because developing countries, with technical assistance, borrowed money, and training, will always have the economic edge of lower labor costs. For that reason, says Reich, trying to compete with them by cutting our wages, devaluing our currency, or imposing import duties to protect less efficient American factories would be maladaptive behavior—we would be solving a short-term problem but making our lives harder in the long run.

More advanced countries like the United States can stay ahead only by shifting into new, more sophisticated industries where our more highly educated population continues to give *us* the economic edge. "As machines and low-wage labor overseas take over those tasks that demand only speed and accuracy," says Reich, "workers' skill, judgment, and initiative become the determinants of the enterprise's competitive success." In other words, we need to be *more* adaptive, not less, if we don't want Bethlehem, Pennsylvania, and maybe even America itself to get left behind on

Technology is advancing quickly, but Japanese children will have the advantages of helpful government policies, responsive management, and a well-educated work force when they grow up.

OPPOSITE: America used to produce half of the world's steel. Today it produces only 16 percent. Japanese businesses and Japanese workers have shown enviable willingness to adapt to rapidly changing market forces. Shipyard worker, Nuraga Heavy Industry.

the scrap heap of cultural evolution.

We've created an environment that will "select" some organizations—firms, industries, whole nations—for their adaptability, the same way that nature selected us for our intelligence. Those that are most adaptable will flourish; those that aren't willing to compromise, readjust, retrain will get left behind. Asked who is most likely to benefit from this movement in cultural evolution, Reich points across the Pacific to Japan.

Everybody's tired of hearing how wonderful the Japanese are, about their great employer-employee relations, their quality control, etcetera, etcetera. But Reich makes a different and more disturbing point about their success. More than robots, or Theory Z, or quality control, it's their *adaptability* that's the real secret of Japan's economic miracle. Unlike us, they've kept pace with changes in production. Both Japanese businesses and Japanese workers have shown their willingness to adapt: when countries like South Korea and Brazil with their low labor costs proved that they could produce simple goods like textiles and clothing more profitably, the Japanese moved away from those goods and into processing industries, like steel and synthetic fibers. When those second-tier countries developed the capability to compete more profitably in steel and fibers, Japan didn't subsidize its steel industry; it moved instead into even more mature industries: from steel, for example, into steel technology, exporting both engineering services and equipment.

Although some critics charge that Japan's economic strength is based on restrictive trade policies, the Japanese continue to demonstrate adapability. Now they are moving into an even more sophisticated stage of production: precision castings, specialty steel, large-scale integrated circuits, and advanced aircraft engines. Because technology is moving so fast, there's never a danger that the Japanese will run out of headroom. They'll always be able to keep one step ahead of the countries with lower labor costs. They may have to move fast, but with helpful government policies, responsive management, and a well-educated, motivated, *adaptable* work force, moving fast isn't a problem.

How does American industry respond to the same challenges? According to

The fabled Silicon Valley was once a sparsely populated corner of California filled with orchards and known as the Valley of the Heart's Delight.

BELOW: Today, the same valley is a late-twentieth-century version of a Western boomtown. Fewer than 100,000 people lived among its orchards a few years ago. Since then, more than a million people have flocked to this new promised land. Will today's boomtown be tomorrow's Bethlehem?

Reich, America has tremendous adaptability—*if* it makes up its mind to change. But, too often, American management would rather use "financial and legal virtuosity" to compete for the artificial profits that come from takeovers and elaborate tax manipulation—what he calls "paper entrepreneurialism." Workers would rather exert union political clout to get import quotas, automatic cost-of-living pay increases, and greater job security in dying industries than retrain for new, more useful jobs in industries of the future. American firms spend billions of dollars in takeover battles, merely transferring the titles of existing industries, while overseas competitors spend the same billions adapting their industries to the real economic competition that lies ahead. Meanwhile, the U.S. government refuses to acknowledge that its welter of subsidies, tax breaks, antitrust rules, quotas, and procurement contracts amount to an industrial policy that is loading the dice in favor of the older, more entrenched industries.

The idle towers of the Bethlehem Steel Corporation, like the antlers of the Irish elk or the peacock's train, are a symbol of the maladaptation of American industry. Does that mean that we're headed for the cultural equivalent of extinction? We wouldn't be the first culture in history to suffer that fate. In the last 10,000 years, many civilizations have come on like gangbusters for a few centuries, then faded into oblivion. Some of them, like the Greeks, the Romans, and the Persians, have essentially disappeared. Others, like the Chinese, the Arabs, and the Indians, live in the shadows of their former prominence. You could argue that we've lived through the decline of European cultural domination, and there are plenty of futurists who believe that America is already being elbowed out of the spotlight by Japan.

But there are hopeful signs. The future is not happening entirely in the land of the rising sun; some of it is happening right here in the U.S.A. in a wonderful, sun-drenched place with the hopeful name of Valley of the Heart's Delight. This is California's fabled Silicon Valley, the ultimate twentieth-century boomtown in the heart of the American Sun Belt. Only a generation ago, fewer than 100,000 people lived in this valley, spread out over 100,000 acres of orchards. Today there are only 13,000 acres of orchard left, and living where all those fruit trees once stood are more than a million people, all of them in search of the new American Dream in the newest and hottest American industry: computers.

From the 1950s to the 1980s the transistor, the integrated circuit, the computer chip, and the personal computer were all invented here, among the vanishing fruit trees. And those inventions spawned a hi-tech industrial revolution that is transforming twentieth-century America just as thoroughly as the revolution in steel and textile manufacturing transformed nineteenth-century America. And just as Polish, Irish, Greek, and Portuguese immigrants came to steel towns like Bethlehem for a chance at the American Dream, twentieth-century Hispanic and Vietnamese immigrants have flooded into Silicon Valley seeking the same things.

Boom and success, unlimited opportunities, enterprise creating jobs for everyone willing to work—this is creative adaptation, with a vengeance, adaptation as America has always practiced it best. Technology appears to be doing for the Silicon Valley today what it did for Bethlehem, Pennsylvania, one hundred years ago. But the question remains whether this community really represents the rebirth of America's industrial survivability or whether it's just another flash in the pan of cultural evolution. Will today's computer-chip boomtown be tomorrow's Bethlehem? The answer to that crucial question appears to depend on whether industry in the Valley can stay on the cutting edge of technology, it should never suffer the fate of the steelworks. If there's one rule of cultural evolution, it seems to be "Keep moving." When we stand still, when we get fat and happy and think we've "made it," that's when we get burned. That's why abundance is such a dangerous thing for the human animal. As long as we had to cope with scarcity, we *had* to keep moving, we had to be light on our feet, adaptable, ready to go where the food was. Abundance allowed us for the first time to think that we had it made, that we could stop trying, stop adapting, that we had arrived. Our arrogance crept into our reading of evolutionary history. We saw ourselves as evolution's final, perfect creation. Why change, why adapt, why try harder if you're perfect?

But magnificent as we are, we're not perfect; cultural evolution goes on relentlessly, and adapt we must. "Three of the fundamental assumptions we humans have always held," says Stephen Gould, "are (one) that we somehow transcend the process of evolution; (two) that everything that has gone before us and coexists with us on earth has been placed here for us; and (three) that a divine hand has given us

The future belongs to those societies, and those individuals, who can adapt to meet the future's challenges. Cultural evolution goes on relentlessly.

dominion over life and the planet. None of these is true, except insofar as the complexity of our brains has enabled us to dominate the earth; and that complexity is a product of evolution, like everything else alive. We are products of the evolutionary process of adaptation. And we must remember what 'adaptation' really means. It doesn't guarantee that we get better, or move higher, or onward and upward, toward some more perfect world. It means we do whatever we have to do to survive. And that's it."

Gould is talking about biological evolution, but the same lessons apply to cultural evolution. With nations as with species, there are no pensions, no leisurely retirements, no Social Security. There's only the law of evolution: you rise and fall according to your adaptability. That's the only promise in this promised land.

4. The Next Step

Some say the world
will end in fire,
Some say in ice.
From what I've tasted
of desire
I hold with those who
favor fire.
But if it had to
perish twice,
I think I know enough
of hate
To say that for
destruction ice
Is also great
And would suffice.

Robert Frost

Some say the world will end in science. They point to the mushroom-shaped shadow that hangs over us and say science and the technology that follows at its heels are the devils in our midst. Others, of course, argue that science and technology are the only forces that can rescue the world. They point to advances in food production, medicine, and energy conservation and say that science isn't our enemy, it's our savior. "On the one hand," says Dr. Melvin Konner, "we have the nuclear bomb, and on the other hand, a vaccine against polio, and tomorrow our technology may lead us to produce wars in space, but it will almost certainly lead us to a malaria vaccine within the next few years, which will save literally millions of lives."

Science is like everything we do: it's a reflection of us. We made it, in all its glory and all its glitches, and like us, it's vulnerable to maladaptation and misuse. But when science or technology is properly created and properly used, it is, like us, a remarkable achievement. Along with art and religion, it represents the human ani-

History is a series of cliff-hangers. One of the most thrilling took place on Switzerland's Mount Santis in northeastern Switzerland, where Albert Einstein hiked as a teenager.

mal's crowning accomplishment—so far. If at some point we were called before God or some alien invader to justify our brief existence on this planet, the argument in our defense would undoubtedly begin with a long list of scientific and technological discoveries. And because all great ideas in science, like all great works of art, start in the individual mind, the list would have to include the men and women who made those discoveries. At the top of that list there would be one special name—and a just God wouldn't have to look any farther. That name would be Albert Einstein.

Our brains have always been tickled by thinking, "What would have happened if . . .?" We like to think that if the slightest detail of our history could somehow be altered, the whole course of civilization would be different. Certainly that's not true of every detail of our lives, but we really can't escape the fact that our history sometimes seems like a series of cliff-hangers. If that bolt of electricity hadn't passed through the primordial soup about 4 billion years ago in just the right way, we wouldn't be here to write about it. If one of our hairy forebears hadn't picked up a stick, or tried balancing on her back legs, or thought of slicing the ends off a round stone to make a wheel, or stuck a seed in the ground and waited around for it to come up rather than move on to another field; if all those discoveries hadn't been made—or if some other animal had made them—we might be living today in a very different world.

One of those "cliff-hangers" in the history of the human animal happened on Mount Santis in the Swiss Alps. It was quite a cliff: 8,000 feet, to be exact—an appropriately dramatic setting for a historic rescue. The year was 1895, and a group of students from the Polytechnic Academy in Zurich were out climbing. Suddenly, on a steep trail leading up the mountain, one of the boys lost his footing and slipped toward the edge of the cliff. Just before he went over, another boy held out his climbing stick. His classmate grabbed it, and a tragedy was avoided. Whoever that rescuer was, he deserves at least a footnote in history and a thank-you from a

Looking out from the summit of Mount Santis, Einstein wondered: Could you run after a beam of light? Could you catch it? And what would it be like if you did?

OPPOSITE: Albert Einstein at age fourteen, only two years before he made his fateful—and near fatal—hike up Mount Santis.

grateful civilization. The sixteen-year-old boy he saved from certain death that day was Albert Einstein.

Whether the close brush with death helped focus Einstein's mind, we don't know, but later that same day, he began to ask himself some questions that would lead eventually to the first of his great contributions to human evolution. After reaching the summit of Mount Santis, above the tree line and overlooking the clouds, he was struck by the quality of light at such a high altitude. Maybe he watched the resident yellow-billed blackbirds slicing through the thin air. We don't know the exact sequence of events and images, but at some point strange questions began to pop into his head: Could you run after a beam of light? Could you catch it? And what would it be like if you did? This was the second cliff-hanger of the day. If he hadn't asked these questions—then or at some point—he might never have revolutionized the way we look at the universe. As it was, Einstein answered his questions a few years later with the special theory of relativity—his famous shorthand, "$E = mc^2$."

Although never better than a B+ student, Einstein had been a naturally inquisitive child. When he was five, his parents gave him a compass, and to their amusement, he spent hours trying to figure out the mysterious movements of its needle. He turned out to be independent, too—more, perhaps, than his parents would have preferred. Just about the time he became a teenager, Einstein's mind turned to religion, and he began to criticize his father, a freethinker, for straying from Jewish Orthodoxy. Finally, at about the time of the hiking trip to Mount Santis, Einstein's head turned for the last time. The subjects he took up at this point—math, physics, and philosophy—would occupy his mind for the rest of his life. They would consume and, eventually, be consumed by his overpowering intellect.

What was so revolutionary about Einstein's theory? To answer that question, we first have to look at what was known about the nature of light at the turn of the century. Although he had been dead for 175 years, Isaac Newton still ruled the world of physics with an iron hand. Like everything else in the physical world, light was understood according to the laws of motion and gravitation that he had formulated. According to Newton, light was no different from the famous apple that fell from a tree. Instead of a single big red fruit, however, light was a stream of tiny particles called "corpuscles." Over the next two hundred years there was some progress in thinking about light, but not much. Scientists reasoned that light was really more like sound than like an apple because it moved in waves, and a few scientists, like Michael Faraday and James Clerk Maxwell, even suggested that electromagnetism as a whole couldn't be explained according to Newton's laws. But no one was prepared to take on the big guy, Newton, openly.

But one idea led inevitably to others. If light traveled in waves like sound, then it shouldn't be able to pass through a vacuum. Sound can't. But light had to be able to pass through a vacuum, because light came from the sun through the vacuum of space. The problem, scientists theorized, must be in their understanding of space.

According to Isaac Newton, light behaved just like the famous apple that fell from a tree: it obeyed the same laws. For 175 years, Newton's ideas ruled the world of physics.

Space wasn't *really* a vacuum, it just looked like a vacuum. There must be something in it that they couldn't see. They promptly named that invisible something "ether." We all know how a wrong idea, once it's accepted, can hang around for a long time, and that's what happened with ether. For years, scientists turned intellectual somersaults trying to prove the existence of this mysterious substance.

Two American scientists, Albert Michelson and Edward Morley, for example, argued that the earth, as it travels through space, generates an ether "wind," just like a cyclist riding on a calm day. To prove this bizarre theory, Michelson and Morley invented a rotating mirror-and-light apparatus. They were puzzled and disappointed to find that the speed of light remained the same whether it was projected against the wind or with it. An Irish physicist, George FitzGerald, demonstrating just how ingenious a scientist can be in trying to salvage a bankrupt theory, postulated that even though resistance by the ether wind slows an object's pace, it also shrinks the object slightly as it approaches its goal, thereby reducing the resistance and increasing the speed. The result, FitzGerald claimed conveniently, was that the object arrived at the goal in precisely the same amount of time it would have taken if it had remained the same size and there had been no ether resistance. Ether became an invisible substance with an invisible effect—a good example of the power of authority over truth.

It was Einstein who dared to claim that the emperor—in this case Newton—had no clothes. The theories scientists had developed to prove the existence of ether, he said, weren't just complicated, they were wrong. And they were wrong for the simple reason that ether didn't exist. As proof, Einstein offered two propositions aimed at the heart of Newtonian physics. First, he said that it was physically impossible to measure absolute speed. At best, a scientist could measure only *relative* speed—meaning the speed of one object relative to another. For example, if a man throws a ball on a moving train, it may look to the man as if the ball were moving slowly. But an observer not on the train would think the ball was moving very fast— at the speed of the ball *plus* the speed of the train. Therefore, any measurements of speed taken by scientists like FitzGerald were invalid because, like the man on the train, he was standing on the earth when he made his measurements, and the earth, like the train, was hurtling through space.

Einstein's second proposition was that light always moves at the same speed, no matter what the motion of its source. In other words, light wasn't like the ball on the train; it didn't travel at its own speed plus the speed of its source. A bullet fired from a warplane travels at a speed equal to that of the bullet plus that of the plane, but the speed of light is the same at all times and under all conditions. Where Newton had assumed that *time* was an absolute—that it moved forward perpetually and at a uniform rate—Einstein said no, the progress of *light* was absolute. Thus, with a single stroke of imagination, he reshaped our understanding of the universe.

To demonstrate the relativity of time, Einstein engaged in another of his "thought experiments." Consider, he proposed, a man standing at a railroad track. Two bolts

In one of his "thought experiments," Einstein argued that a man standing still could see two bolts of lightning as simultaneous, while a man traveling toward one bolt and away from the other would perceive them as sequential. One man's "now" would be another man's "then."

OPPOSITE: By the end of the nineteenth century, time had been enshrined as an absolute. Einstein said no, only the speed of light is absolute; time is relative. Thus, with a single stroke of imagination, he reshaped our understanding of the universe. Chanticleer egg clock by Fabergé, 1903.

In contemplating Einstein's ideas about time and space, it's hard to imagine how anyone could have conceived them, they are so contrary to our everyday experience. Here, Einstein writes out an equation that represents the destiny of our galaxy, the "Milky Way," on a blackboard at the Carnegie Institute in 1931.

of lightning strike the track at the same point and, apparently, at the same time—one bolt of lightning from the west, the other from the east. The logical assumption would be that both flashes of lightning occurred at the same time. But how would the same two flashes of lightning look to someone riding on a train down the track from east to west? To this mobile observer, the flash of lightning from the west would seem to reach him sooner, because he was moving toward it; the flash of lightning from the east would seem to reach him later because he was moving away from it. By contrast, if one flash of lightning followed the other, the mobile observer might view them as simultaneous, the stationary one as sequential.

Two people observing the same sight and seeing two different things. According to one, the lightning flashes are simultaneous; according to the other, they're sequential. How we measure time, Einstein concluded, depends entirely on our frame of reference. Time is relative. One man's *now* is another man's *then*.

Einstein's theory of relativity was soon followed by other explanations of puzzling phenomena. He and his fellow scientists had often observed in the laboratory that when a beam of light strikes a metal surface, electrons are given off—a phenomenon called the photoelectric effect. In 1905, Einstein explained this effect by describing light as tiny particles—later called photons—which actually knock electrons off the metal. This was a key insight into the nature of electricity, without which we would not have a host of devices we consider commonplace today, from the television set to the electric eye.

Also in 1905, Einstein published his second paper on relativity. Arguing from his

Einstein's work belongs in that small circle of achievements for which we have no explanation, only gratitude. Works like Shakespeare's King Lear *make us justly proud of our species.* Lord Olivier plays Lear.

own insights into electromagnetism and the mathematics of relativity, he announced that if an object emits an amount of energy (E) as light, its mass (m) will diminish by the same amount divided by the speed of light (c) squared ($m = E/c^2$). Because the amount of energy given off as light is a very small number and the speed of light is a very large number (300 million meters per second), the formula basically says that when an object gives off light, a tiny, tiny portion of its mass is converted into energy. If a tiny bit of mass is equal to a good amount of energy, then a good amount of mass must be equal to a huge amount of energy. Einstein explored these fateful implications represented by the more famous equation $E = mc^2$, published two years later. The nuclear age had begun.

In contemplating Einstein's ideas, it's hard to imagine how anyone could have conceived them. What connections in that densely packed walnut of his made it possible for him to project his imagination onto a light beam and ride it out to the edge of the universe? Were there, as some scientists have hypothesized, more dendritic connections in his neocortex than in other humans'? Instead of 800,000 miles of connecting fibers, did some fluke of nature give him a million, or was it just one extra connection that happened to be in the right place at the right time on that trip to Mount Santis? Whatever the explanation, Einstein's achievement belongs in that small circle of works—Bach's *Saint Matthew Passion*, Michelangelo's *David*, Shakespeare's *King Lear*—that are inexplicable by any human standard. It's as if he had dropped out of the sky from another planet, stayed just long enough to dazzle and bewilder us, then moved on to more deserving worlds. Richard Feynman, a physicist from Cal Tech who has also won the Nobel Prize and a brilliant man by any measure, said of Einstein's general theory of relativity, "I still can't see how he thought of it."

About the same time that Einstein was hitching a ride on a beam of light, a young woman scientist in Paris was asking herself why, when a photoplate was exposed to a chunk of the mineral pitchblende, an image appeared. According to the known rules of photography, only light striking the surface of the photoplate should produce an image, but she was looking at an image that had been etched in the dark by some unknown, invisible ray.

The woman was Marja Sklodowska. Born in Warsaw, Poland, in 1867, she had overcome poverty and sexism in the academic community to come to Paris and pursue her dream of becoming a scientist. Eventually, she would be honored as the first woman professor at the Sorbonne and the greatest female scientist of the twentieth century. In 1895, Marja—who now called herself Marie—Sklodowska married a French scientist named Pierre Curie.

As early as 1898, the Curies had speculated that the image on the photoplate was created by the rays emitted by a substance called radium. But radium was like ether: no one had been able to isolate it or prove its existence; it was just another convenient explanation for an unexplained phenomenon. To prove their theory, the Curies devoted almost four years to a search for the elusive substance, stirring

heated pots of pitchblende, hour after hour, day after day, for four years. But still no radium. At about nine o'clock one evening in 1902, after Marie had put their four-year-old daughter, Irène, to bed, she and Pierre left their small house and walked through the deserted warehouse district of Paris to the shed which served as their laboratory. The Curies' other daughter, Eve, later described that historic evening when, for the first time, the successfully isolated radium began to glow:

"After the crowded streets of this queer district, with its factory buildings, wastelands and poor tenements, they arrived in the Rue Lhomond and crossed the little courtyard. Pierre put the key in the lock. The door squeaked, as it had squeaked thousands of times, and admitted them to their realm, to their dream.

" 'Don't light the lamps!' Marie said in the darkness. Then she added with a laugh: 'Do you remember the day when you said to me "I should like radium to have a beautiful color"?'

"The reality was more entrancing than the simple wish of long ago. Radium had something better than 'a beautiful color': it was spontaneously luminous. And in the somber shed where, in the absence of cupboards, the precious particles in their tiny glass receivers were placed on tables or on shelves nailed to the wall, their phosphorescent bluish outlines gleamed, suspended in the night."

In 1903, Marie and Pierre Curie shared the Nobel Prize with Henri Becquerel for the discovery of radioactivity. In 1911, Marie received another Nobel for the discov-

OPPOSITE: Marie and Pierre Curie spent four years searching for an elusive substance they called radium. Their work led to the development of X-ray techniques and earned for them a joint Nobel Prize.

RIGHT: Marie Curie suffered at the hands of her own discovery. Over the long years of experimentation and exposure to radiation, she suffered from cataracts, dizziness, and burns. She died in 1934 of radiation exposure. The Curie laboratory, Paris.

OVERLEAF: Wrote one physicist in response to Einstein's formula $E = mc^2$: "It takes one's breath away to think what might happen in a town if the dormant energy of a single brick were to be set free, say in the form of an explosion." That was in 1921. Twenty-four years later atomic devices were dropped on Hiroshima and Nagasaki, Japan. Nagasaki after the blast.

ery of radium and polonium and the isolation of pure radium. Her discoveries led to the development of X-ray techniques that can detect and in some cases cure cancer. Ironically, for all the hope and healing she brought to others, Marie ultimately suffered at the hands of her own discovery. Despite cataracts, dizziness, fever, and radiation burns on her hands, she continued her radium experiments unprotected. In 1934, she died of exposure to the "precious particles" she had discovered. In 1956, her daughter Irène, who received a Nobel Prize in 1935 for synthesizing new radioactive elements, also died of radiation poisoning.

Einstein and Curie have shown us just how much can be done by the human mind: just how far it can strike off into the unknown and return with a brand-new piece of Truth. They're our champions, in the best biblical sense of the word. They represent all of us at the farthest frontiers of human achievement, and when they're successful, we're all successful. Einstein's theories have made possible the exploration of outer space; Marie Curie's discoveries made possible the exploration of the inner body. Just as the human brain is the crowning achievement of biological evolution, Einstein and Curie and thousands of other scientists, artists, thinkers, are the crowning achievement of cultural evolution. They make the long centuries in loincloths and thatched huts seem like time well spent. They also open up the future: they give us somewhere to go, somewhere to direct our energies, a renewed sense of how much there is out there yet to be discovered, yet to be created. Ultimately, that's why we find genius, in any form, so moving. It both validates the past and inspires the future. It makes us feel both our nobility and our potential.

But as in all human achievement, there's a dark side. The brain's accomplishments, like the brain itself, can be magnificent *and* mischievous. Maladaptation is as much a part of human evolution as adaptation. Consider, for example, how we have managed to turn Einstein's wondrous little formula, $E = mc^2$, into a recipe for annihilation. Almost from the moment that Einstein announced his theory, other scientists recognized its destructive potential, but Einstein himself refused to acknowledge it. "It takes one's breath away," said fellow physicist Hans Thirring in 1921, "to think of what might happen in a town if the dormant energy of a single brick were to be set free, say in the form of an explosion. It would suffice to raze a city with a million inhabitants to the ground." In that same year, Einstein was approached on a street in Prague by a young man who told him that he wanted to create a device of mass destruction. Einstein dismissed the idea: "Its foolishness," he said curtly, "is evident at first glance."

The human animal is certainly capable of foolishness, and Einstein lived to see it. When an atomic device was dropped on Hiroshima, Japan, on August 6, 1945, Einstein was at his home in Princeton, New Jersey. Like the rest of the world, he heard the news over the radio, and it must have pierced him like an arrow. Although he had urged President Roosevelt to outrace the Nazis in developing the bomb, Einstein regretted that his discoveries had made such destruction possible. After the war, when a Japanese physicist visited him in Princeton, he apologized in tears for his part in the nuclear devastation at Hiroshima and Nagasaki. It was a noble and human gesture, but it wasn't necessary. His discovery didn't turn cultural evolution toward the nuclear nightmare: *we* did. When evolution is in our hands, we have no one but ourselves to blame for such terrifying maladaptation.

But we do have a choice. Although we're certainly capable of whopping maladaptations, we're still the most adaptable kid on the block, and we continue to show our mastery of the environment in new and even more dazzling ways. Einstein's special theory of relativity opened up many new paths for cultural evolution. Being the eagerly adaptable and impetuous animal we are, we couldn't resist using this new discovery for any purpose that came along. We were like a kid with a new bat: we were going to hit at any pitch that fate threw us. When a war started, without thinking, we adapted our new discovery to war. But there were other paths, other pitches—all of them more worthwhile—and we've pursued all of them. We pursued nuclear energy, although, after Three Mile Island, some people are saying that too was an impetuous, maladaptive move. Still another path has brought us tantalizingly close to a virtually limitless and relatively risk-free energy supply: fusion.

At the immense Tokamak Reactor, located fittingly near Einstein's home in Princeton, New Jersey, scientists are working on a project that sounds suspiciously like science fiction. They hope to re-create the energy of the sun on earth. To do

A cutaway view of the doughnut-shaped Tokamak fusion reactor at Princeton, New Jersey. Here scientists hope to re-create the energy of the sun on earth.

that, they've built what looks like a giant doughnut at a cost of hundreds of millions of dollars. But the shape and size and cost of this device don't begin to suggest its significance. This isn't Three Mile Island. There's no danger of a meltdown here. Unlike other nuclear plants, which are fission reactors, Tokamak is a *fusion* reactor. It produces energy by fusing (joining) light atoms, such as those in hydrogen, rather than by fissioning (splitting) heavy atoms, such as those in uranium. Both processes (fusion and fission) release enormous amounts of energy because whether you join one atom to another or split it into fragments, some of the atomic material is converted into energy. The sustained fusion process being sought at Tokamak is staggeringly difficult to achieve but relatively easy to understand. All it requires is a brief, rudimentary physics lesson. Let's take a quick look at what may be the most important development in cultural evolution since the invention of agriculture.

Each of the 103 elements (from hydrogen, the lightest, to lawrencium, the heaviest) is made up of *atoms:* the smallest part of an element that can exist and still possess the character of that element. An atom, in turn, is made up of a *nucleus* at the center, and around it, a number of *electrons*. The nucleus consists of a number of smaller particles called *protons* and *neutrons*. Like the " + " and " − " poles of a magnet, electrons are negatively charged and protons are positively charged. Neutrons have no charge. Like charges repel and opposite charges attract, so protons are attracted to electrons and vice versa, but protons are repelled by other protons and electrons are repelled by other electrons.

The number of protons and neutrons is what gives an element its character—what distinguishes an atom of gold, say, from an atom of hydrogen. Hydrogen comes in three different forms, or *isotopes*, each of which has a single proton, a single electron, and zero, one, or two neutrons. In all three, the particles are bound together by the attraction between the positively charged proton and the negatively charged electron (the neutron is neutral). If you take another hydrogen atom and try to fuse it with the first, the two atoms resist because they both have nuclei containing positively charged protons, and like charges repel. The only way to overcome this natural resistance to fusion is to shoot one of them at the other with such great speed that they collide *in spite of* their natural tendency to repel. It's the atomic equivalent of a shotgun wedding.

The problem facing the scientists at Tokamak was, how do you get atoms to move that fast? Because atoms move faster at very high temperatures, the only way to fuse them was to heat them. How hot did they have to be heated? What temperature did they set this oven on? In order to produce enough energy to make the fusion possible, hydrogen had to be heated to about 100 million degrees Celsius. To give you an idea how hot that is, the sun, even at dead center, is "only" 15 million degrees Celsius.

Remarkably, the Tokamak scientists haven't had any problem heating the hydrogen to those astronomical levels. The problem has been how to contain it once it

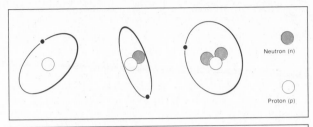

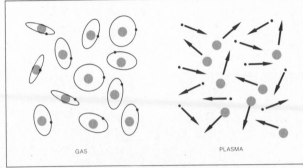

GAS   PLASMA

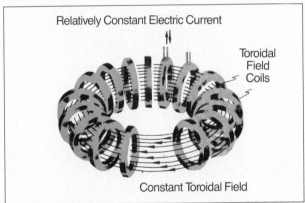

Relatively Constant Electric Current

Toroidal Field Coils

Constant Toroidal Field

TOP: Unlike the nuclear fission process, which breaks up heavy, complex atoms like uranium, the nuclear fusion process at Tokamak fuses together simple, light atoms. Of all the elements, hydrogen is the lightest and has the simplest atomic structure. The three forms of hydrogen differ only in the number of neutrons in the nucleus: (left to right) zero, one, or two.

MIDDLE: One of the many challenges of the Tokamak project has been to control the atomic chaos created when the atoms in a stable gas (left) are stripped of their electrons and transformed into a highly unstable plasma (right).

BOTTOM: By lining the doughnut-shaped reactor with magnets ("Toroidal Field Coils"), scientists have been able to keep plasma from touching the walls of the reactor. The trick is similar to boiling water without letting it touch the sides of the pan.

reached those levels. At 100 million degrees, an electron will separate from its nucleus, leaving a naked nucleus consisting of only a positively charged proton-neutron duo called an *ion*. What's left is a very hot gas, called *plasma*, which contains the positively charged ions separated from the negatively charged electrons. Left to their own devices, these ions and electrons would rush around chaotically, bouncing into the metal walls of the doughnut.

That was a problem because the contact between the plasma and the walls transferred heat from the particles to the metal of the doughnut. The particles would cool and slow down, making fusion impossible. Imagine trying to boil water in a metal pan without letting the pan get hot and you can begin to understand the problem they faced. The solution was to take advantage of the fact that the particles were charged and therefore responsive to magnetic fields. By lining the doughnut with magnets, the scientists were able to suspend the particles between magnetic fields and keep them away from the metal walls.

The only remaining problem at Tokamak is how to heat the plasma so that enough fusion energy is generated to sustain its heat. Currently, more fuel is needed to heat the plasma than is generated by the fusion that results. So the search is for the most efficient heating system. The scientists are experimenting with heat generated by everything from magnetic compression to radio waves. They're even working with old-fashioned "ohmic" heat, the kind that's created in a light bulb or an electric

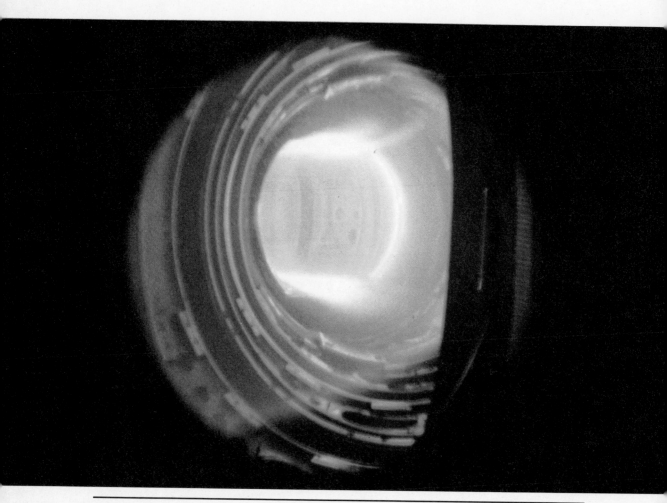

Inside the Tokamak reactor, the temperature reaches 100 million degrees Celsius—seven times hotter than the sun's core.

heater when a current is passed through a poor conductor.

Someday, perhaps someday soon, the scientists at Tokamak will be able to sustain a nuclear-fusion reaction. That will be a day to celebrate for centuries to come. It will be the dawn of the age of fusion, an age in which similar devices will give humanity an almost limitless supply of energy—ten million times the energy we now produce by burning oil or coal. And with fusion, there's no waste—no chemical waste, no nuclear waste. No raping of the environment, either. Tokamak's fuel is an isotope of hydrogen called deuterium that's easily extracted from water. There are more than 10 million million tons of it in the waters of the world—essentially an infinite supply. There's no danger of a meltdown; if a malfunction occurred, the plasma would simply bounce into the metal wall and cool itself off. And, best of all, the material consumed by a fusion reactor cannot readily be used to produce nuclear weapons.

Hiroshima was the nightmare. Tokamak is the dream. We are capable of making a savior as well as a devil, a heaven as well as a hell. And we continue to astound ourselves. Who would have thought we might someday re-create the sun—that distant symbol of light and power and knowledge—right here in New Jersey? Tokamak represents more than progress: it represents salvation. It's proof that we're not headed inevitably into a nuclear winter. This isn't the creation of a pessimistic, doomed species. It could have come only from the hand of that old master of adaptability, the human animal.

Like the Chartres cathedral, Tokamak is a symbol of human achievement, an act of faith in the future, an enterprise that's both ambitious and reverential. Like Chartres, it's a combination of one person's vision and the dedication of hundreds of people to a goal that they may not live to see achieved (a sustained fusion reaction could be fifty to seventy-five years away). But most important, Tokamak is a reaffirmation that we have a choice about the next step in our history. We have the power to destroy the future, and soon we'll have the power to energize it. Which way we choose to go won't be determined by further mastery of our environment. We've already seen that our mastery can be turned to good or to ill. We've shown ourselves capable of both adaptation for survival and maladaptation for extinction.

In the final analysis, the next step will be determined by how well we master ourselves. Ironically, the last, relatively unexplored world is the interior world of human thoughts and feelings. The problems and challenges that remain are here in the labyrinth of the human brain and the tangled web of behavior that it governs. What makes us hate enough to kill? Why does violence thrill us? Why does love so often elude us? We know so much about the broad universe out there and so little about what goes on in this tiny nutshell. It's as if you spent your whole life looking at the world through a lens but never bothered to examine the lens. We need to turn that dazzlingly perceptive brain on itself and get a closer look inside it. Only when we can control ourselves can we truly control our destiny.

PART TWO

LOVE & SEX

5. Vive la Différence

*Men and women
are different.
What needs to be
made equal is the value
placed upon
these differences.*

Virginia Woolf

The human animal, male and female. How similar they are—and yet how deliciously different. No relationship in nature obsesses us more. Certainly no relationship is more widely explored or closely watched. For thousands of years, we've rhapsodized over their differences, celebrated their union, and immortalized their battles: Adam and Eve, David and Bathsheba, Antony and Cleopatra, Romeo and Juliet, Dick and Liz. What would the *National Enquirer, People* magazine, soap operas, romance novels, and Hollywood do if the human animal, like blue-green algae, came in one sex instead of two?

But why only *two* sexes? Why not three or four? If two are fun, think of the possibilities with seven or eight. Are two sexes—and only two—necessary for reproduction? Does the difference in reproductive function explain all the differences between man and woman? To answer these questions and get a better understanding of the differences between the sexes today, we have to go back and see where they came from.

Believe it or not, there *was* life before sex. As far back as 3.5 billion years ago, many simple microscopic species of life, like our old friends the blue-green algae, reproduced themselves quite successfully—and they still do today—without sex. There are no little blue-green alga boys and blue-green alga girls: just one asexual form, which reproduces itself by simply dividing. You might think that this sort of self-reliant, no-nonsense strategy for perpetuating one's species would have solved

Without sex, there would be no variety, just one design, endlessly repeated. Good for the ego, but bad for the species.

the reproduction problem very efficiently, once and for all. No jealousy, no rejection, no bored relationships. So why has most of life switched to sex?

The fact is that when it comes to reproduction, self-reliance is not the best way to go. Suppose that I, Phil Donahue, could reproduce myself the way blue-green algae do—asexually—without the participation of another of my species. The result would be a hundred or a thousand or a million Phil Donahues, all exactly alike. Clones. Perhaps a flattering prospect for me, but rather limited and selfish as far as my species is concerned. Given the ever-changing nature of the environment, a species' chances of surviving if it endlessly reproduces one design without variation —no matter how good the design—are dangerously limited. If something happens that *I* can't survive, my species will die with me, unless by some slim chance I've spawned a mutation of myself that turns out to be more successful than I.

To make sure that it can survive everything that nature might throw in its path, a species needs *variety*. An organism needs to produce offspring that are just different enough from itself, and from each other, in enough different ways, to maximize the odds that no matter what happens, some of them can survive. The only way to get that kind of variety is through sexual reproduction. The division of a species into sexes means that no reproduction can happen unless individuals meet and mate and blend their genes to produce a new generation not exactly like either of its parents, perhaps carrying the genetic key to a better adaptation to life.

As organisms more complex than blue-green algae evolved, they began to develop mechanisms to accomplish this "blending" of genes. Different cells became specialized for different functions: some for digestion, some for transmitting nerve impulses, and some for reproduction. These "sex" cells didn't have the responsibility of passing on all of life's information in one package. Each received only half of its parent's genetic blueprint. To reproduce, this cell had to join up with a sex cell from another organism. There were still no sexes, but these "incomplete" sex cells that needed a "mate" were a beginning.

It may be that we have two sexes today because the reproductive strategy our ancestors adopted involved only two tasks—finding and feeding—and a specialized cell developed for each task. "A sperm is an entity with a mission: search, find, fertilize," says Dr. Martin Daley, a biologist on Prince Edward Island. "In intense competition with other sperms of similar ambitions, it has become stripped down and streamlined. As a participant in a race, it has jettisoned all nonessential baggage. The sperm must, of course, transport chromosomes, but its cellular material is otherwise minimal and is placed in the service of mobility—to find the egg which sluggishly awaits it.

"The ovum's immobility is due to the bulky mass that accompanies her share of the chromosomes. Although each parent contributes almost equally to the genetic resources of the new creature they create, not all contributions are equitable. The female provides the raw materials for the early growth of the offspring. Here, at the very fundament of sexuality, is love's labor divided." If by some fluke our ancestors had devised a more complicated strategy for reproducing—one that involved, say, a three-stage process or three cells uniting, the world would be a very different place: three rest rooms in every restaurant, three figures on a wedding cake, love seats for three, and "eternal rectangles."

But in the system that's come down to us, the process is very simple: the sperm finds the egg and the egg does the rest. The blending of the two sets of genetic materials results in a genetically brand-new organism. The sex of the newcomer will

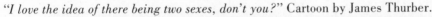

"I love the idea of there being two sexes, don't you?" Cartoon by James Thurber.

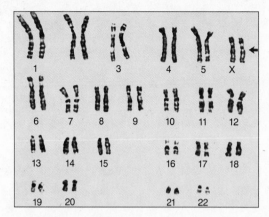

OPPOSITE: The differences between men and women start here, in the basic building block of human life, DNA. Thousands of pieces of information are encoded in the genes that form a DNA molecule. Because such molecules represent the blending of the genes of two parents, the possible combinations are limitless.

be determined by which chromosome the sperm is carrying. "At the time of conception," says June Reinisch, director of the Kinsey Institute at Indiana University, "boys get an X from their mother and a Y from their father. Girls get two X's, one from each parent. It's that Y that is the determining blueprint." (They're called "X" and "Y" for no better reason than because that's what they look like, more or less.) It's this tiny morsel of genetic material that traditionally spelled the difference between an all-star quarterback and a prima ballerina. This is, according to Reinisch, "the biological base upon which society builds its ideas" of what it means to be male or female.

Given how different their biological functions are, it's remarkable that men and women don't look more different than they do. A sperm and an ovum don't look anything alike, yet the differences between male and female humans are small, even in comparison to the sexes in other species. "True—women mature a year or two earlier than males," says Reinisch. "Men have more hair on their faces. And secondary sexual characteristics, such as breast size, do differ. But for mammals, human males and females are much the same." Men do tend to be bigger, have heavier bones, and develop more muscle than women do; women tend to have more

TOP AND LEFT: The genetic difference between males and females is very slight. In place of the two "X" chromosomes in the female (arrow, top), the male has an "X" and a "Y" chromosome (arrows, left). Different genetic compositions—however slight—trigger different patterns of hormonal action and these, in turn, are responsible for most of the sex differences we know and love.

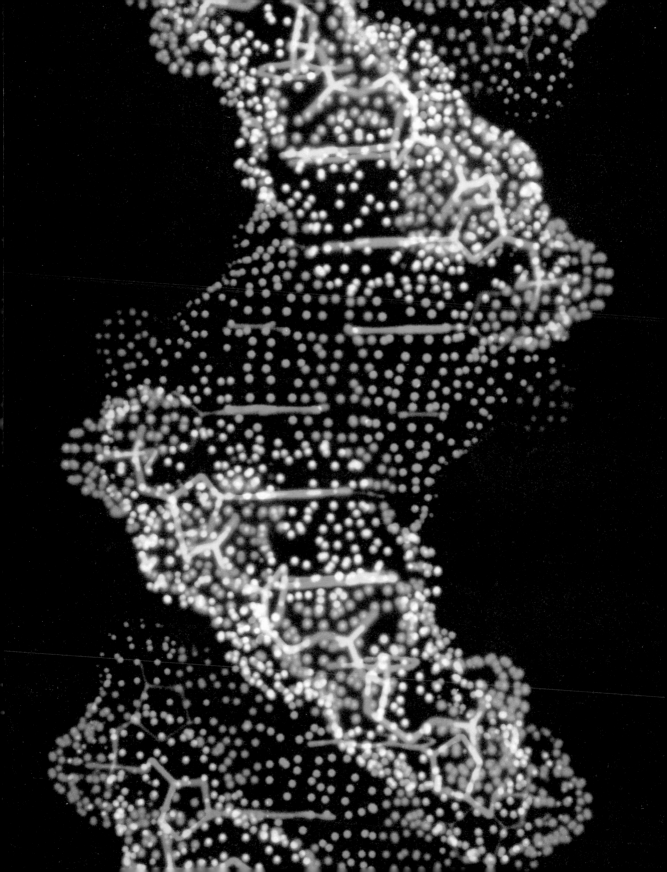

subcutaneous fat. But even these differences are governed by sex hormones and can be minimized by adjusting the balance of hormones. Scientists can't make Scarlett O'Hara into Rhett Butler, but by flooding a woman with male hormones, they can give her a man's muscle structure, his beard, even his voice. Why a woman would want them is another question.

One reason men and women, despite their bickering, are surprisingly alike is that both begin life as the same undifferentiated sex—neither male nor female. That's right: even Indiana Jones started off exactly like Marilyn Monroe—except for the telltale Y chromosome that all men carry from conception. It isn't until the fifth or sixth week *in utero* that the male begins to go his separate way. During that time, every embryo possesses the anatomical beginnings of both male and female sex organs. The changes that make men begin when the male's Y chromosome directs

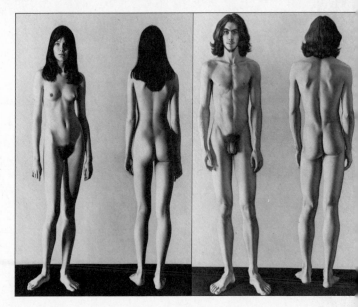

OPPOSITE: *Men and women are both delight-fully different and surprisingly alike. De-spite the so-called battle of the sexes, they are nature's perfect pair.* Merrill Ashley and Peter Martins.

The Bible says God made Eve from Adam's rib. But, according to Dr. June Reinisch, the biology of men and women tells a differ-ent story. Adam and Eve, *drawings by Clau-dio Bravo.*

the production of hormones called androgens. These hormones are directly respon-sible for the production of the male genitalia. If there's no Y chromosome, there is no androgen, no testes, and no male. Instead, about twelve weeks after conception, the female fetus begins to develop ovaries. If a male embryo misses this injection of androgens, which include testosterone, he will grow up looking *externally* just like a female, despite that derelict Y chromosome.

From the moment of that crucial injection throughout a whole lifetime, the only hard-wired difference that develops between the sexes is that men impregnate, while women ovulate, gestate, and lactate. That's it. No other differences are abso-lute or irreversible. Anything else is in the interaction between the culture and the chromosomes—not differences in the brain. Reinisch recalls one scientist's apt comment: "This is only for teaching purposes—because it's biblical and sometimes people are sensitive about it—but he said, now that we know how development works, it's wrong to think that God made Adam and then took a rib from his side and made Eve. A better way to visualize it is that God made two Eves and then he sent down the archangel Gabriel with a large hypodermic needle filled with testos-terone and he shot up one of the Eves and she turned into Adam."

There's an old saw that testosterone is the "male" hormone and estrogen is the "female" hormone. In fact, men and women both have some of each. Women need testosterone for libido, and men need estrogen to produce healthy sperm. There are differences in the way men and women process hormones, and, of course, the levels differ greatly between the sexes, but as Dr. John Money, of Johns Hopkins, points out, there are really no male or female hormones, only "people hormones."

Both the male and the female get their second shot of these hormones at puberty. This is the one that drives them crazy. Ironically, what scientists call our "second-ary" sexual characteristics are the ones we're all obsessed with. Girls get breasts;

Dr. June Reinisch, director of the Alfred Kinsey Institute at Indiana University.

RIGHT: A second shot of hormones at puberty is responsible for most of the "secondary" sexual characteristics that make adolescence an awkward and frustrating time for many young people. Drawing by a student at the Bank Street School, New York City.

boys get muscles, body hair, and baritone voices. There are other changes going on inside, both physical and psychological. In general, it's a difficult time to be a kid, and it's made even more so because you can't do anything about it, you can't talk about it—some parents don't even want their kids to *think* about it. Of course, if you're a kid, it may be all you can think about and all you want to talk about. The primary "secondary" sexual characteristic that develops in puberty is frustration.

Are we slaves to hormones? Do they control our daily actions and reactions? If they have such a decisive effect on the embryo and such dramatic effects in puberty, what kind of mischief do they work the rest of the time? When a man won't open up and talk about his feelings, are his hormones to blame? When a woman always defers to her husband, are her hormones responsible? Dr. Money says that while hormones do dictate behavior in simpler animals, we humans are too smart and sophisticated to be jerked around by our chemistry. Most animals are, in Money's term, sexual "robots." If you flood a female sheep embryo with male hormones, she'll spend her whole life thinking she's a ram. She'll act like a male, even to the point of trying to mount other females. In humans, the effects of hormones are more subtle and ambiguous. If you flood a human female embryo with male hormones, there's only a 50-percent chance that she'll develop bisexual leanings.

There are women who are born with testicles in their abdomens. These women produce as much testosterone as a physiologically normal male—but their bodies refuse to respond to the hormones. If one of them were standing next to you in the checkout line, you wouldn't notice anything unusual. They don't have beards or masculine body hair; they have breasts, feminine features, and feminine manners. They're sexually interested in men, not other women. The only thing that sets them apart from other women is that they don't menstruate. Again, hormones are part but not all of the story.

And as long as we're telling the whole story, we should mention that there are some chemicals other than hormones that may underlie differences in behavior between men and women. For example, in survey responses, women more often report that they're depressed, while men are more likely to say they're moody. These assessments reflect the commonplace that women tend to be more tender than men and men tend to be more emotionally volatile than women. There's certainly no scientific proof to back up either truism, but scientists have recently discovered some intriguing and, *perhaps*, related chemicals. Women, it turns out, tend to have more of a chemical called "serotonin," while men have more of one called "dopamine." "It's interesting to note," says June Reinisch, "that there's more depression among females, and depression has been related to serotonin levels. It's also interesting that there's more schizophrenia among men, and that schizophrenia has been related to dopamine levels." But Reinisch is quick to add that any effort to relate these chemicals to everyday human behavior would be premature. "You've got to keep in mind that there are depressed males and there are schizophrenic females," she says. "It's just that there's more schizophrenia in males, more depression in females."

So it seems that while hormones and other chemicals *influence* our behavior, they don't necessarily direct it. Hack writers may try to convince us that we're slaves of passion; we may even use the excuse ourselves occasionally; but we're only slaves if we choose to be. We're born with a pattern of behavior that's sketched by hormones and other chemicals. But unlike other animals, we don't have to follow the pattern. Our environment can alter it, or we can choose to alter it ourselves.

If hormones don't keep us apart, what about our brains? Maybe they explain why there seems to be such a gulf between men and women. We've all heard men *and* women say, "They just don't think like us." Men are stubborn; women are pliable. Men are logical; women are intuitive. The book of stereotypes is full of this kind of locker-room and powder-room talk. We've always known we had sex *on* the brain; is it possible that we've got sex *in* the brain as well? "The differences in the brain —and what they mean for behavior—are the most important differences for humans to think about," says June Reinisch. "The brains of male and female mammals are not the same. They're not the same chemically, they're not the same anatomically, and they're not the same in terms of connections between neurons. They don't function the same."

Is that why men and women seem to be turned on by different things: women by touching and cuddling and affectionate words, men by X-rated movies and girl watching? Is that why women who want vicarious sexual thrills read steamy romance novels while men feast their eyes on *Playboy* centerfolds? Or do women read romances because they're taught that women are *supposed* to read romances, just as men are supposed to ogle *Playboy?* How important can differences in reading habits be? In fact, these seemingly trivial differences may be a clue to one of the most important biological distinctions between men and women, distinctions that can be traced to that organ that seems to be at the end of every trail when you're exploring human behavior: the brain.

Like any other explorers, brain scientists have spent a great deal of time trying to map the brain, figuring out what function is controlled in what area of the brain. The maps they've produced resemble maps of the moon. Since the surface looks so uniform, it's hard to imagine how they managed to find anything. But in fifty years of surveying, they've been able to locate most of the higher brain functions to the point where they can activate certain functions by stimulating a particular area of the brain. If they poke your brain in one place, you'll smell something that isn't there; if they poke it somewhere else, an old memory will flash into your mind. In one famous experiment, researchers poked a subject in a certain place and an old Bing Crosby song, "White Christmas," popped into his head. The process is still crude, but the possibilities are right out of science fiction.

If you look closely at the cerebral cortex—the "walnut" that's mainly responsible for our thinking and learning—you can see that it's divided into two halves, or hemispheres. In the process of mapping brain functions, scientists have found that each hemisphere is assigned primary responsibility for different functions. They have found, for example, that if you're right-handed and your left hemisphere is damaged, you'll still be able to drive a car and play tennis, but you'll have difficulty talking. If, on the other hand, the damage is to your right hemisphere, you'll be able to talk just fine, but you can probably forget both driving and playing tennis.

In about 90 percent of humans, the left hemisphere governs logic, analytical reasoning, and language. We rely on it heavily when we talk, think, analyze, and argue. The right hemisphere governs the analysis of shapes and spaces. We rely on it to judge distance, the speed of objects, and the spatial relationships between objects. To nobody's great surprise, scientists have discovered that men and women have different cognitive strengths. What's surprising is that they've located those strengths in the hemispheres of the brain. Men, it turns out, *tend* to have stronger right-hemisphere functions. As a result, they tend to excel at math because they can "see" the abstract relationships better. They tend to make better baseball players because they can perceive the spatial relationship between ball and bat better. They tend to be more successful in reading maps because they can relate features on the map to objects in the real world better. And they're usually better at packing the car trunk because they can rearrange objects in space better.

Women, on the other hand, *tend* to have stronger left-hemisphere functions. As a result, they tend to excel in verbal fluency and comprehension. They tend to talk

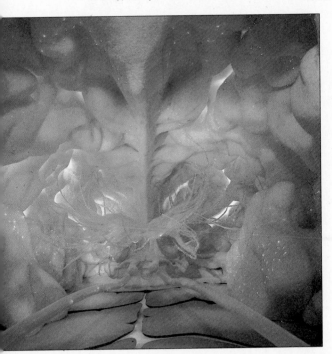

OPPOSITE: Are differences in the male and female brain responsible for the different ways in which men and women seek vicarious sexual thrills? The dominance of the visually oriented right hemisphere in males may account for their interest in centerfolds, while the dominance of the verbally oriented left hemisphere in women may explain their preference for romance novels. Covers of *Playboy* magazine, October 1982, and *The Courts of Illusion* by Rosemary Hawley Jarman.

The two hemispheres of the brain (seen in the model as red and blue) apparently govern different functions. Men seem to be stronger in right-hemisphere functions, while women tend to have an advantage in left-hemisphere functions.

better, argue more persuasively, and learn foreign languages more easily. They're better at expressing their feelings in words—and more likely to do so. They're even better equipped to sing in tune. All these skills appear to be located in the left hemisphere. The relative advantages of each sex do, however, shift over time. For example, girls develop verbal ability much more rapidly than boys in infancy, but boys more or less pull even between the ages of four and eleven. After that, the girls pick up another advantage and take the lead again. On the other hand, boys don't begin to demonstrate their superiority in mathematical skills until adolescence.

How convincing is the evidence for these cognitive differences between men and women? One of the most startling discoveries about these differences is unfolding

Starting at an early age, women tend to talk more often and more fluently than men. They're better at expressing their feelings in words and more likely to do so.

OPPOSITE: Boys tend to be better at activities that involve judging distance, speed, and the spatial relationships between objects. Later in life, they will naturally be attracted to physical activities and be less enthusiastic about expressing their emotions.

even now. It began when doctors treating victims of crippling strokes that had destroyed the speech areas of the left hemisphere noticed that female victims often recovered their power of speech faster and more easily than male victims. Scientists began to speculate that maybe, by some unknown mechanism, women's hemispheres were more closely linked with each other than men's were. It seemed the most likely explanation why the right hemisphere in women was quicker to jump in and take on the tasks, such as speech, that the damaged left hemisphere could no longer handle.

Other researchers soon provided evidence to support the existence of an unknown "link." For example, Sandra Wittelson, a psychologist at McMaster University in Hamilton, Ontario, studied two hundred normal, right-handed boys and girls between the ages of six and fourteen. She gave the children two objects to hold, one in the left hand, one in the right, but didn't let them see the objects. She then asked them to pick the same objects out of a group of similar items. Because sensory information from the right hand travels to the left hemisphere, and information from the left hand travels to the right hemisphere, and because the right hemisphere was known to control spatial skills, Wittelson expected that the kids would be better at identifying the objects they had held in their left hands—the left-hand signals would go directly to the spatially oriented right hemisphere. The boys performed as expected: they were much more accurate in identifying objects they had held in their

left hands. The girls, however, were able to identify objects held in either hand with the same degree of accuracy. Apparently their left brains were feeding information to their right, or vice versa, much more efficiently than the boys' brains.

Finally, in 1983, scientists discovered what they think is the missing link. While studying male and female brains, researchers Ralph Holloway and Christine de Lacoste-Utamsing noticed a peculiar bulge in the corpus callosum of female brains. The corpus callosum is sort of the Grand Central Station for messages between the left and right hemispheres, and the bulge turned out to be an extra bundle of neurons that was missing in male brains. The difference was substantial. The corpus callosum in the female brains was as much as 40 percent larger than in the male brains. Very tentatively, the researchers concluded that female brains are wired with more neural pathways connecting the right and left hemispheres, and therefore they have a greater capacity to integrate the activities of the two sides. Think of the brain as a city divided in half by a river. In the female brain, because there are many more bridges over the river, traffic moves faster and more efficiently between the two halves.

All this plodding scientific work, all this talk of cerebral hemispheres and corpus callosum bridges may lead us back to another old truism. With more connections between the verbal left hemisphere and the spatial right hemisphere, women are better equipped to bring the two kinds of thinking together. The result may be the famous sixth sense of "women's intuition" that results from the blending of logical and creative perception: it's not something they can see, but it's more than just a feeling. Men, on the other hand, have an advantage because communication between their hemispheres is slow. Wittelson points out that men are better at keeping separate tasks separate: talking and running a drill press, for example. If you want to call it an advantage, this biological difference may reinforce the cultural training that makes men better hired killers and combat soldiers—they find it easier to "do their duty" without getting bogged down in second thoughts, moral reservations, or feelings of guilt.

Is this new research into the brain an answer to our question why women read romances and men look at *Playboy?* Are women satisfying their verbally oriented left hemispheres with passionate words, while men pander to their visually oriented right hemispheres with foldouts and porno flicks? While we're on the subject, is this why women want to hear "I love you" so much, or why men seem so unwilling to say it? Are "strong, silent man" and "man of action, not words" just other names for any man dominated by his spatial right hemisphere? Are women who love con-

The left and right hemispheres of the brain are connected by the corpus callosum. The fact that the corpus callosum in the female is as much as 40 percent larger than it is in the male may account for that elusive phenomenon called "woman's intuition."

OPPOSITE: Is the battle between the sexes really just a battle between the hemispheres of the brain? "Human beings are not bumblebees," says Dr. Jerre Levy. "We are not trapped by our biology. [Brain differences] should never be used to limit the way men and women conceive their abilities."

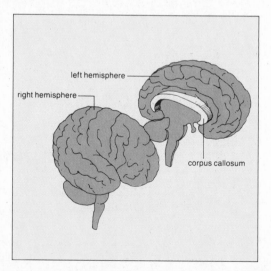

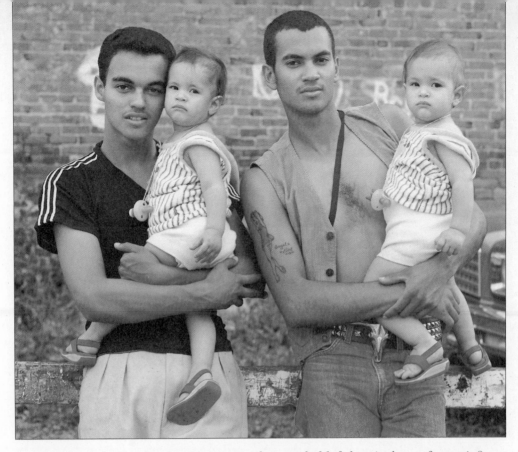

versation and companionship just giving their verbal left hemispheres free rein?

Scientists disagree about the implications of this early research, but the hints are intriguing. Consider, for example, the results of the S.A.T.'s—the Scholastic Aptitude Tests—that high school students take as part of their application to college. Among first-time exam takers who attain top scores (more than 700 points out of a possible 800) on the mathematics part of the test, there are 3 boys for every 1 girl. We still don't know for sure *why* the results are so lopsided. Is it because of the differences in the right and left brain? Or is it because our society teaches kids that boys are *supposed* to be good at math, and girls are *supposed* to be good at English?

Does this mean that the battle between the sexes is really just a battle between the hemispheres? Hardly. "True," says Dr. Jerre Levy of the University of Chicago, a behavioral scientist, "we have observed some biological differences in the male and female brains. And we have observed some behavioral differences between the sexes. But we are just not at a point where we can say one leads to another. You know, human beings are not bumblebees. We are not trapped by our biology. It's probably true that in the beginning men's brains evolved to handle the challenges of the hunt—visual analysis of objects in a landscape, judging distances, making mental maps of terrain, etcetera—whereas women's brains might have evolved a greater verbal fluency to handle the broader responsibilities of family social management. There might be that much link between neurobiology and behavior. But that's a

piece of interesting history that should never be used to limit the way men and women conceive their abilities. Our wonderful cerebral cortex gives each of us the power to choose how we will behave . . . and frees us from biological restrictions."

The biological superiority of women in language—if it exists at all—didn't prevent James Joyce from writing *Ulysses,* and the biological superiority of men in spatial ability didn't keep Amelia Earhart grounded. For the human animal, biology is a cage with very loose bars and no lock on the door. Whether it's men in the translator's booth or women on the balance beam, we do what we damn well please. If differences between the sexes survive in the blood or in the brain or in the body, we don't have to be ruled by them. In our sexual identities as in our destiny, we have the power to choose what we want to be. If we're still hung up on sexual stereotypes, it's our culture, not our chemistry or our cortex, that's at fault. We're the only ones who set the limits, and we're the only ones who can push them.

"We should allow children to do what is comfortable for them," says Reinisch. "We want to expand their horizons, both physically and intellectually. It's the responsibility of both parents and teachers to try hard not to treat boys and girls differently in terms of what we make available to them and what we allow them to experience during their young years." Instead of letting children be confined by their genetic inheritance, we must try to liberate them from it. "Perhaps boys could use some help from the environment—from their teachers and parents—in learning ways to be more cooperative. And, at the same time, perhaps little girls could use help in learning ways to be more assertive."

And what about the differences?

"The differences between the sexes are quantitative, not qualitative," says Reinisch. "Males hear quite well, males taste and smell quite well—well enough to take care of children in a very appropriate way. They have all the skills that are appropriate for doing the tasks that the race needs; and females have all the skills too. It's just a matter of flavoring."

Virginia Woolf had the right idea. As we see more deeply into the biology of the human animal, we may discover more differences between men and women, or we may discover that what appear to be essential differences are, in fact, only superficial ones. Whatever surprises the future holds, we should not fear to explore the possibility of differences simply because we live in a world that exploits them. But we should not view the differences that we do discover as an indication that one sex is superior to the other or that one sex deserves more of life's rewards than the other. Apples are different from oranges, but nobody tries seriously to argue that one is better than the other. They're just different. Each has its own distinctive shape and taste, and the world would be poorer without either one.

Vive la différence!

6. Falling in Love

Birds do it,
Bees do it,
Even educated fleas do it,
Let's do it,
Let's fall in love.

Cole Porter

In fact, birds *don't* do it, bees don't do it, and certainly fleas don't do it, whatever their education. When it comes to falling in love, only *we* do it. The human animal has the distinction of being the only animal that complicates the biological act of reproduction with that elusive something, that distinctive confection of the human brain for which we have many definitions but only one word: love. It's one of our unique additions to the evolutionary process. It turns the somewhat commonplace, necessary animal behavior of sexual reproduction into magic and poetry—so they say. Since Adam and Eve, it has delighted, inspired, and tormented us. Who among us hasn't gone through the bitter ecstasy of infatuation and the sweet agony of "dating." As Elton John says, it "feels so good to hurt so bad."

What the birds, bees, and fleas *do* do is mate and reproduce to perpetuate their species. Although there's some sketchy evidence that female primates get a kick out of sex, most other animals approach their reproductive duties with a hormone-induced sense of purpose. Of course, when we humans fall in love, we too are performing our evolutionary duty to mate and reproduce. Dr. Melvin Konner, chair-

"Falling in love," says Dr. Melvin Konner, "is one of several ways that humans have evolved to ensure that the two sexes get together, mate, and reproduce, thus ensuring the survival of their genes"—and the perpetuation of a dynasty. Charles and Diana, Prince and Princess of Wales.

According to Dr. John Money, the way to the heart may be through the hypothalamus. Brain model.

OPPOSITE: Lovesickness has long been a favorite theme of tragedies and romances, but recent research indicates it may be the result of a malfunctioning hypothalamus. Ophelia drowning herself over her unrequited love for Hamlet: John Everett Millais's Ophelia.

man of the Department of Anthropology at Emory University in Atlanta, says, "Falling in love is one of several ways that humans have evolved to ensure that the two sexes get together, mate, and reproduce, thus ensuring the survival of their genes."

It's an indication of how complicated our brains are that we've developed such an elaborate ritual around such a basic function. No wonder people often express frustration over the delays and pitfalls of romance. Sometimes it's like watching a bad movie in which you know from the first frame that the hero and heroine are going to fall in love but it takes them an hour and a half to do it. You just want to stand up and yell, "Get on with it!" How much of this elaborate ritual is dictated by the past and how much of it is the product of our individual hearts and minds? Is falling in love really "magic and poetry" or is it just evolutionary programming?

What is the mechanism of falling in love? Some people think they can look at you and tell if you're in love. We've all seen movies in which the young boy or young girl comes back from the first encounter six inches off the ground. The mother—using her "woman's intuition," undoubtedly—says to the father, "Can't you see, John?—she's in love." The violins swell while the poor, love-struck youngster stares off into the middle distance. We don't know all the details about how that youngster was "struck," but we do know that the feeling begins deep in her brain in the pea-sized hypothalamus. This dense little cluster of nerves, weighing only a quarter of an ounce, controls hundreds of bodily functions, monitors the entire nervous system, and coordinates the body's response, both physical and emotional, to the outside world: everything from body temperature and blood pressure to appetite, thirst, fear, sleep, sex, and laughter.

According to one theory, within the hypothalamus is an area called the "sex nucleus," the seat of many of the sex differences between men and women. If she finds the guy attractive, the theory goes, the sex nucleus transmits a message, by way of chemicals called releasing factors, to the tiny pituitary gland, which acts as a kind of outlet store for the hypothalamus. The pituitary gland, in turn, releases hormones that fly through the bloodstream like messengers with good news. They tell that news to the sex glands, which respond excitedly by producing three more hormones: estrogen, progesterone, and testosterone. At that point—only a fraction of a second after the hypothalamus got the word—our youngster becomes aware of the process for the first time as she begins to feel a tingling sensation as her muscles tense, a hardening in her nipples, and a lightness in her head as her heart begins to beat faster.

If the people who wrote love songs were true to human anatomy, they'd be writing songs not about the heart or even the eyes, but about the hypothalamus. If you want someone to love you, this is the hard little nut you've got to crack. This is where you'll find the *true* chemistry of love, the exact formula of which is still a mystery. "My theory," says John Money, "is that the nerve pathways produce substances that induce what people refer to as falling in love." According to Money, the way to a man's heart—and to a woman's—is through the hypothalamus.

How do we know about the critical role played by the hypothalamus, and especially the sex nucleus within it? The way we so often do: by observing the behavior of people whose bodies, through some misfortune, have been damaged. We know that if the sex nucleus is harmed—it lies so close to the pituitary gland that it can be accidentally damaged during pituitary surgery—the entire process of falling in love is affected. When the hypothalamus goes haywire—when messages aren't properly transmitted either from the hypothalamus to the pituitary gland or from the pituitary gland to the rest of the brain—the resulting neurohormonal imbalance can wreak havoc with a person's romantic life. It can lead to romantic obsessions, anxieties over separation, lovesickness, and love-blindness. We're not talking about

Precious.

Chocolate contains the same chemical, phenylethylamine, that the brain produces when it falls in love. Not surprisingly, people often have a craving for chocolate after the breakup of a relationship.

the problems of head-over-heels infatuation that are—relatively speaking—normal for humans. We're talking about the kind of lovesickness that can turn into a destructive obsession, or the kind of love-blindness that prevents a person from falling in love at all. People who suffer from these neurochemically induced problems may marry and try to have sex, but the results are almost uniformly unsuccessful or unsatisfying.

Among the first sure "signs" of falling in love that our youngster will feel is "a giddy high similar to an amphetamine boost," says Dr. Michael R. Liebowitz of the New York State Psychiatric Institute. That "high" is a sign that her brain has entered a distinct neurochemical state by releasing a chemical substance related to amphetamines (probably phenylethylamine) which, like any "upper," makes her heart beat faster, gives her energy, and generally improves her emotional outlook. But like any "high," it has to end. "The crash that follows a breakup is much like withdrawal," according to Liebowitz, who notes that people who break up often have a craving for chocolate, which, like love, is high in phenylethylamine.

It sounds more and more as though falling in love is like using marijuana or cocaine, only legal and safe because your brain does all the work and supplies all the candy. Apparently that description may not be so far off the mark. Jaak Panksepp, a scientist at Bowling Green State University in Ohio, says that the brain produces substances called opioids that are similar to opiates. "At a neurochemical level," he argues, romantic "attachment is essentially an addictive phenomenon involving opioids." Early in life, pleasurable stimuli such as contact with our parents "trigger the release of opioids," which in turn sedate the anxiety of separation when Mommy or Daddy walks out of the room. We become addicted to these infusions of sedative and, in later life, search for relationships that provide them. Dr. Panksepp's theory may account for the glazed look in our youngster's eyes when she returns—"withdraws"—from her first encounter with her new crush. It's probably the same look that her mother noticed and pointed out to right-hemisphere Dad.

When people say "You always hurt the one you love," or talk about a soap-opera star you "love to hate," they're pointing up a contradiction in human behavior that has always befuddled us. Why does there seem to be such a thin line between hate and love? If a houseguest leaves the cap off the toothpaste, you're unperturbed; if your husband or wife does the same thing, you're furious. One minute it's hugs and kisses; the next it's World War III. Why do we get so angry at people we love? Scientists may have found a partial explanation in the chemistry of love. That chemistry, it turns out, is very similar to the chemistry of other emotions such as anger or fear. Only the circumstances distinguish one emotion from the other. Your pulse may beat faster and your palms may begin to sweat whether you're furious at someone, terrified of someone, or infatuated with someone. The physiological signs are identical.

To prove this, some imaginative scientists in British Columbia selected two bridges—one a rickety footbridge 230 feet above a rocky gorge, the other a sturdy concrete bridge only a few feet above a sandy riverbed—and placed the same attractive woman at the end of each bridge. She asked men who came off the bridge to help her fill out a questionnaire and during each brief encounter gave the man her phone number. Result: a significantly higher percentage of the men who had crossed the rickety bridge made follow-up phone calls. Conclusion: those men were in a high emotional state after crossing the dangerous bridge, but when they met the attractive woman at the other end, they thought their trembling hands and pounding hearts were the result of sexual excitement, not the result of fear. The chemistry was the same; the circumstances made the difference.

What happens after chemistry starts the romantic ball rolling? Just as most animals have developed a routine for attracting mates of the opposite sex, the human animal surrounds the complicated chemical process of falling in love with an even more complicated ritual of approach. As any teenager knows, it's easy—too easy—to fall in love. The hard part is setting the other person's chemistry in motion. To do that, our species has developed an elaborate behavior pattern we call "flirting." You may think that everyone has his or her own unique approach to flirting, or that you can learn "new techniques" from books like *How to Pick Up Girls* or *Sex and the Single Girl*, but according to Dr. Irenaus Eibl-Eibesfeldt, a professor at the Max Planck Institute in Munich, West Germany, who spent years traveling to different countries recording on film the flirting behavior of different cultures, the human animal flirts pretty much the same way the world over. According to Dr. Eibl-Eibesfeldt, when you're attracted to someone and you want him or her to be attracted to you, you're very likely to exhibit some or all of the following behaviors:

☐ You give the person a slight smile and a bashful look, lower your eyes, then turn them away. You may repeat the pattern several times.

☐ You hold your gaze for just a fraction of a second longer when you look into his or her eyes.

☐ You make small touching movements.

☐ You let your hand rest briefly on some part of his or her body.

☐ You move closer than you normally would.

☐ You keep your mouth slightly open, looking unconsciously at various parts of his or her body.

☐ You nod your head in agreement—no matter what the other person says.

☐ You face the other person head on.

☐ You use your hands more than you usually do to emphasize your points.

☐ You check frequently for his or her reactions to what you're saying, commonly by raising your eyebrows and opening your eyes wide.

☐ You moisten your lips often.

☐ You make an effort to find subjects of conversation about which you're likely to agree.

Dr. Eibl-Eibesfeldt's work indicates that flirting behavior, like falling in love, may have a biological and/or chemical component we don't yet understand. After all, if the flirting pattern is indeed universal—if flirting in Tokyo looks about the same as flirting in Chicago—then it probably has more to do with our species' evolution than

Dr. Irenaus Eibl-Eibesfeldt, professor at the Max Planck Institute, Munich, West Germany. The fact that flirting patterns are the same the world over may indicate that flirting behavior, like falling in love, has a chemical or biological component.

OPPOSITE: *Universal flirting patterns as demonstrated by a Glui Kalahari boy (top) and a Himba girl (bottom). From left to right: averting eyes, slight smile and bashful look, checking for reaction by raising eyebrows and opening eyes wide, moistening lips.*

with our personal identities.

Even that old troublemaker jealousy may say more about the evolution of the species than about the response of individuals. Shakespeare called it "the green-eyed monster," and today it's still responsible for a high percentage of the murders committed in this country. Most of the inmates of our crowded prisons are male, and most of them got there through violent crimes that were sex-based. Who among us hasn't felt that burning sensation that can turn any Dr. Jekyll into a raving Ms. Hyde. Dr. Melvin Konner says that jealousy, like all romantic passion, is part of our biological legacy. "We have been selected to be wary whenever we get a feeling of sexual arousal," says Dr. Konner. "I think that, for a female, the reasons for wariness are obvious. You have to be afraid of pregnancy, and you have to be afraid of being harmed by a male who's likely to be more powerful physically than you are. For a male, the same feelings put you in a situation of potential competition with other males.

"We can't read the emotions of other animals. But we can see behaviors in many species that make it absolutely clear that they resent intrusions by other males into their sexual relationships with 'their' females. And females have similar reactions to desertion by males whom they are paired with or attached to. Some cultures have a

"Everybody noticed it. You gawked at her all evening." Jealousy appears to be a built-in feature of the human animal in all ages, in all cultures. Cartoon by James Thurber.

OPPOSITE: What determines whom we fall in love with? Some experts believe that the "choice" of lovers is made according to unconscious patterns that are set very early in life as the result of childhood experiences. Nineteenth-century engraving.

little more jealousy, some less. We write poems and songs about it. And we complain about it in the courtroom. But fundamentally we are having the same emotion that's been handed down to us by our evolutionary legacy."

Why do we get jealous? Why do we care?

"Males that didn't care were cheated on by their mates," says Konner. "They brought up the offspring of other males and didn't pass on their own genes to subsequent generations. Females didn't want to be deserted, to be left with offspring they would have to raise alone, without a male."

Is jealousy still necessary—or have we outgrown it?

"As long as we need deep attachments between men and women," says Konner, "we need jealousy to ensure that they continue."

With all this new research into human behavior, one has to wonder, what ever happened to "doin' what comes naturally"? Scientists have explained the mechanism, the chemistry, and the role of evolution in the "behavioral pattern" of falling in love. Does science leave any room for the magic of "love at first sight"? Is some researcher going to publish a paper on the neurochemical basis of Kismet or the evolutionary origin of puppy love? Sometimes it seems as if we no longer have any autonomy in our love lives; we're just the helpless puppets of chemical, biological, or evolutionary directives. At least we can still show some individuality in the person we fall in love with. Right?

Well, not exactly. In fact, the person you fall in love with—or the *kind* of person you're likely to fall in love with—may be yet another aspect of your love life that's beyond your conscious control. If you think about it for a minute, that's not such a shocker. A lot of people have found themselves walking into a bad relationship just like the bad relationship they just left, all because they couldn't help falling in love

with "the wrong person." Our soap operas and movies are filled with "impossible love"—stories of people who fall in love when they know they shouldn't, when there's no possibility the relationship will work out, when it's doomed from the first furtive glance; yet they do it. They say, "Love is blind." Their friends say, "They're just fools for love." Elvis Presley sang, "Wise men say only fools rush in, but I can't help falling in love with you."

If *you* don't control choosing the person you fall in love with, who or what does? If you were any other mammal, that question would be easier to answer. It would all happen in the nose. In four-legged animals, like dogs, the male is turned on by the smell of chemicals called pheromones that the female produces when she's in heat. The seductive allure of pheromones is so strong that, with the right wind, a dog can pick up a female's scent from a quarter-mile away. According to Dr. John Money, after one whiff he'll set off in pursuit of the bitch with "his snout in the air, his tail curled up, and one thought on his mind." When he arrives on the scene, of course, he has to cope with the problem created by the female's public advertisement of her availability for sex: other dogs. It's usually the female—*not* the male—who then decides which of the males she's attracted will be her mate.

As we evolved away from the lower mammals, the nose gradually lost out to the eyes. In primates, says Dr. Money, "the sense of smell is augmented by the sense

of sight, and partnerships are not random but are established partly on the basis of some as yet unknown principle of individualized preference." Until recently, scientists thought that humans were attracted to each other on the basis of sight alone, that smell no longer played any role in the mating dance. But a recent discovery made scientists rethink the role of smell. At the base of human hair follicles, researchers discovered a tiny gland called an apocrine gland that secretes a chemical with a distinctive scent. Although the exact role of apocrine glands in the dating game is unknown, it's clear that they play a role in sexual behavior because they don't begin to develop until puberty. Whatever their role, we probably won't like it. We've become so accustomed to the masking scents marketed by the multibillion-dollar perfume-and-cologne industry that the subtle human pheromones scarcely stand a chance.

Okay. Assume the scientists are right and that sight, not smell, is the first thing that turns us on. Hardly a revolutionary notion, but it leaves the main question unanswered: why is it that one person is more physically appealing—more attractive—than another? One person goes gaga for blondes, another for redheads. One person likes hairy chests, another "sensitive" eyes. Are these preferences simply a matter of taste? If so, when did we develop those tastes? Or are they part of our genetic inheritance? Will you inevitably choose the same kind of mate your mother

Why is it that we find one person more physically appealing—more attractive—than another? Why are some people attracted to hairy chests, others to blond hair, others to legs or bosoms or buttocks? Men's and women's rear ends, Manhattan Beach, California.

Dr. John Money, professor and director of the Psychohormonal Research Unit at Johns Hopkins University. "We all fall in love not with a partner, but with a fantasy superimposed or projected onto a partner."

OPPOSITE: Soon after birth, most infants, like the goslings of Egyptian geese, are genetically prepared to attach themselves emotionally to, or "imprint" on, a mother figure. In humans, the time for attachment is more flexible.

or father did? Are we doomed to fall in love with the same type of person over and over again, no matter how bad a match, or can we change our preferences in midstream?

The news from the scientific community isn't encouraging. According to Dr. Money, our preferences aren't as much a matter of free choice as we'd like to believe. Money says each of us has in his or her head a "lovemap" that's drawn sometime between the ages of five and eight and is based on early experiences with parents, siblings, relatives, and the environment. This lovemap determines who attracts us erotically. It's "a pattern in your brain that's going to tell you what is the perfect love affair and who is the perfect person to fall in love with," says Money. It's as if you've got this sketch of a person in your head and you're running around looking for the person who matches the sketch. The old concept of "Mr. Right" or "Ms. Right" wasn't so far off.

How are these lovemaps drawn? Although we don't know much about the process, it's likely that the broad outlines are sketched in our genes. We come into the world wanting certain relationships—the outline may be as broad as that. The details—blond hair or redhead, hairy or "sensitive"—remain to be filled in. Money suggests that the process can be compared to the "imprinting" of newborn animals on their mothers. Soon after birth, a young animal is genetically prepared to attach itself emotionally to—"imprint" on—a mother figure. Usually, because she's there and taking care of it, the newborn attaches to its real mother. But not necessarily. If another animal, even a human being, is around at the right time—the time when the newborn's genetic clock tells it to imprint—the newborn will attach itself to the other animal.

In humans, the time for attachment is more flexible than it is for most animals. But we do go through periods when we set the pattern for our later attachments—

when we draw the individual lovemaps. Usually, we choose one person, grow obsessed with that person, and eventually he or she becomes the model for all future loves. Although this imprinting on a love object commonly takes place during adolescence, it can happen earlier or later, and it can happen more than once in a lifetime. But once drawn, the map remains with us throughout our lives.

Just as a young animal is likely to imprint on its mother, aren't human kids likely to imprint on members of their family? Is this just a scientific version of the Oedipal phenomenon?

"We know from studies of population genetics that people tend to love and marry people like themselves," says Dr. Melvin Konner. "That's even true in the people who come together and produce an illegitimate offspring. They tend to be more alike in height, weight, intelligence, skin color, and so on, than two people drawn at random from the general population. And that's certainly true in marriage. We tend to pick people like ourselves. Maybe this is because of our feelings about ourselves. Maybe it's because we tend to pick people who are in some ways like the siblings or the parents we grew up with."

In fact, Dr. Konner attributes much of our notion of love to the long attachment between the human child and its parents—one of the longest childhoods in the animal world. "We have an exceptionally long childhood," says Dr. Konner. "Very

few animals take as long to grow to maturity as we do. This gives us an impressive dependency, and an impressive opportunity to develop a profound and lasting attachment to our parents. That probably helps give us the capability to form lasting attachments later in life. But you also have to recognize that there are animals like geese that form lasting attachments in adulthood without having had a long childhood. So there might be something in the brain that makes this happen, *in addition to* our long childhood experience."

Too often, this interminable childhood encourages us to become obsessed with one of our parents. Many people spend their entire lives after leaving home looking for a way to get back in by looking for a husband or wife who matches the parental model in order to replicate their parents' relationship. According to Dr. Roderick Gorney, professor of psychiatry at the University of California at Los Angeles, " 'Mother' is the first person to fulfill our needs and she is the first with whom we 'fall in love.' She protects us, cares for us, provides all the satisfactions we crave. So as adults men tend to look around for the perfect Mommy forever and find someone who resembles her—or sometimes, if their experiences with her were bad, someone who is reassuringly unlike her." In the same way, women often search for men who are like (or unlike) Daddy.

Of course, no matches are perfect. Most of the time, most of us have to settle for husbands, wives, or lovers who don't look *exactly* like the lovemaps we have in our heads. They're somewhat alike, and it's the similarities that bring us together. But it's the differences that inevitably get us into trouble. The discrepancy between the person we're prepared to fall in love with and the person we *actually* fall in love with is the root of many of our romantic difficulties. Even among most "normal

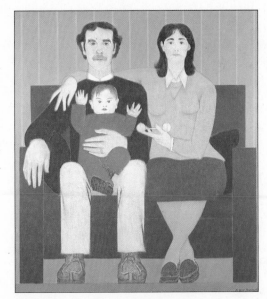

OPPOSITE: Parents are the first people to fulfill our needs, and they are the first with whom we "fall in love." So as adults, we look around for the perfect mommy or daddy. Mother and Children by Adolphe William Bouguereau, 1879.

Two years is about the natural life of the high flame of a love affair. But by then nature has usually created a baby, so the bond becomes three-way. New England Family by Will Barnet, 1983–1984.

couples," says Dr. John Money, "each partner projects onto the other his/her ideal image of erotic arousal. Otherwise stated, this means that we all fall in love not with a partner, but with a fantasy superimposed or projected onto a partner."

Have you ever come to the end of a jigsaw puzzle and there's one piece left and one hole in the puzzle but they don't match? You just *know* that piece fits into that hole, and you try like crazy to force it in. You mangle the piece, you work yourself into a frenzy; you want so badly for it to be right—but it just *isn't* right. That's what happens in a relationship when you try to make your partner fit some ideal lovemap you've got in your head that he or she doesn't know about and maybe even you don't know about. The harder you try to make it fit, the more trouble it causes. "Should the partner not embody that projected fantasy," concludes Money, "sooner or later the pair bond begins to become unbonded."

How could something as vague and often subconscious as a lovemap cause so much disappointment and disillusionment? Are people really that picky?

"Falling in love," says Dr. Money, "is a very self-centered kind of experience, because it's based on your own emotion, and your own intensity of feeling about how absolutely flawless and wonderful and perfect the love is. It's often love at first sight, so that when you get beyond the vision of what the other person is to the reality of how you fight at the breakfast table, you can have some terrible disillusionments. I think that explains why some people, after the disillusionment arrives, hate each other with the most unmitigated hatred that human beings are capable of."

But I thought falling in love was one of evolution's strategies for mating. What kind of strategy is it that gets us together only to have us fight and break up?

"Even if it's a relatively poor match, it can last for as long as two years. That's about the natural life of the high flame of a love affair—and then it begins to burn lower. But Nature is very clever. She gives you long enough to create a pregnancy and have the baby delivered, and then the pair bond of the two lovers has to enlarge to include the baby, and it becomes a three-way bond."

Is falling in love another form of maladaptive behavior? Has our hypercomplicated brain, with its highfalutin notions of love and romance, gotten us in trouble again? Because of it, do we expect more when we fall in love than a real relationship can possibly deliver? Because of it, do we expect perfection from our mates and set ourselves up for inevitable disappointment? Have we evolved a system for attracting mates that's terrific in the short run—sure, falling in love is a wonderful feeling— but destructive over the long haul? Is the high rate of divorce in this country, like our industrial decline, another symptom of overspecialization?

To answer those questions, let's look at one particular form of falling in love: homosexuality. Sex researchers continue to insist that homosexuality is a relatively rare phenomenon *if* you define a homosexual as a man or woman who has sex *only* with people of the same sex. Alfred Kinsey put the number at 4 percent of men and 2 percent of women. But the latest evidence indicates that while exclusive homosex-

Some scientists explain differences in sexual preference by pointing to the fundamental bisexuality of the human fetus. But why does this seed of bisexuality develop into homosexuality in some people and heterosexuality in others? Gay Pride street fair, Christopher Street, New York City, June 1984.

uality is still rare, homosexual *interest* is widespread. "Every one of us has a homosexual side," says Dr. John Money, in the sense that "we can be attracted by both sexes." Dr. Money attributes this element of bisexuality in all of us to the fundamental bisexuality of the human fetus. For the first few weeks after conception, the fetus is both male and female, and it continues to carry the legacy of that bisexuality even after it begins to differentiate according to its chromosomal sex. "No matter what we become," says Dr. Money, "male or female, we always carry with us some hint of our early bisexual (both-sexed) nature. Female genital organs contain vestiges of male structures, and the male breast has its nipples, which do not have the same function as those of a female but are there nevertheless."

But why does this seed of bisexuality develop into homosexuality in some people and heterosexuality in others? Or, as mothers and fathers of homosexuals inevitably ask: "Why is my child gay?" The familiar response is to rip a page from Freud and hand it to the distressed parents. "Typically," says Dr. Charles W. Socarides, professor at the Albert Einstein College of Medicine, summarizing the accepted Freudian view, "we find a pathological family constellation in which there is a domineering, crushing mother who will not allow the developing child to achieve autonomy from her, and an absent, weak, or rejecting father." In other words,

controlling Mother plus weakling Father makes Junior gay. Simple as that?

Hardly. Although one study does show a slight connection between the family situation described by Dr. Socarides and a homosexual son, the reality of human behavior is far more complicated. For example, Dr. Ray B. Evans, a psychologist, cautions against looking only at the parents' effect on the child. What about the child's effect on his parents? "It is just as tenable," says Dr. Evans, "to assume that the father of a prehomosexual son becomes detached or hostile because he does not understand his son, is disappointed in him, or threatened by him, as it is to assume that the son becomes homosexual because of the father's rejection. Similarly, it is as reasonable to assume that a mother becomes intimate and close-binding with her potentially homosexual son because of the kind of person he is as to assume he becomes homosexual because she is too binding and intimate with him." To further confuse matters, a study of homosexual men conducted by doctors in Boston and St. Louis found that most of them were well adjusted, and most reported that their fathers, not their mothers, were their dominant parents.

In trying to understand the formation of our sexuality, both hetero- and homo-, researchers have recently turned their attention to possible biological factors, especially hormones. If falling in love with someone of the opposite sex is in part a chemical process, then perhaps falling in love with someone of the same sex indicates an alteration in that chemical process. For example, the study in Boston and St. Louis showed significantly lower levels of testosterone in a group of homosexuals than in a control group of nonhomosexuals. Although the results of these tests are hotly disputed in the scientific community, they do at least raise the issue of whether homosexuals who want to can be reoriented to a heterosexual lifestyle. Body chemistry is much more susceptible to change than fifteen or twenty years of upbringing. But at the same time, a combination of chemical predisposition *and* upbringing is far more formidable and resistant to change than simple learned behavior.

Dr. Money, like most scientists today, believes that homosexuality is a function of both nature and nurture. In only a small percentage of individuals, who receive an unusually large rush of masculine hormones *in utero*, does there seem to be no propensity whatever toward bisexuality. But the nurture part of the equation, Dr. Money says, is more than a matter of controlling mothers and weak fathers. According to Money, there are three leading causes of homosexuality: the effects of hormones before birth and soon after birth; gender learning that occurs between the ages of eighteen months and four years; and lastly, the lack of sexual and erotic rehearsal play among juveniles. But Dr. Money's theories, like most theories of sex-role formation, are largely unproved and widely disputed.

Scientists are only just beginning to understand the biological and environmental dimensions of sexual attachments. Why, for example, do our teenagers come together so often for backseat encounters that result in millions of unwanted pregnancies? Why do we so often fall in love with the "wrong" person and end up just another name on the divorce-court docket? Why does transsexualism seem to be on the rise? These and other forms of sexual behavior are unlikely to encourage long-lasting relationships or successful reproduction.

We have to ask ourselves, what have *we* done to encourage these maladaptive solutions to the problems of sexual attachment and reproduction? Of course it will help to know how these behaviors are influenced by biology and chemistry. Scientists have discovered, for example, that a hormonal chemical called LHRH, a substance long used to trigger the pituitary gland to send its "releasing factors" to the sex glands, can stimulate sexual interest even in animals that would normally be impotent because their pituitary glands have been removed. Although a lot of testing remains to be done, the end result may be a cure for impotence. "I know of no other brain chemical," says Dr. Robert L. Moss, professor of physiology and neurology at the University of Texas, "that can produce such a narrowly specific response." In LHRH, we may have finally discovered a true aphrodisiac.

But we can't look to chemistry for all the answers. Most of those will come from looking at ourselves more closely. What role does sex play in our society? What do we teach our children about sex? What do we fail to teach them? The answers to these questions—more than history, more than chemistry, more than legislation, more than sermons—will determine our sexual future.

Given how magical love can be, it's a tragedy that so many people have trouble finding and sustaining it.

7. The Dirty Joke

"Sex without love is an empty experience."
"Yes, but as empty experiences go, it's one of the best."

Woody Allen, *Annie Hall*

The dry, rocky terrain around Mount Carmel in northwest Israel doesn't look anything like the Garden of Eden, but it was here, in the caves that dot these barren hills, that the real-life counterparts of Adam and Eve may have lived. Like other human "couples," they hunted and gathered in this area just as their not-quite-human ancestors had done for almost 150,000 years. We don't know for certain, but they may have had conversations that sounded roughly like Woody Allen and Diane Keaton. We know that they had the capacity to feel love as well as the urge to have sex. Whether they felt any conflict between these two needs, we don't know. But by the time the story of Adam and Eve was written down in the Bible, original sex had become original sin.

Ever since, our society has been split on the subject of sex. We haven't been able to make up our minds whether sex is the perfect union of two people or a disgusting remnant of our animal origins. On the first night of a honeymoon, it's a beautiful experience; in a dirty theater in the red-light district, it's degrading. One minute we rhapsodize about it; the next minute we don't want to talk about it. We love to watch it, but we prohibit it from being shown. Every major city has a citizens' movement

OPPOSITE: Woody Allen and Diane Keaton in Annie Hall.

In caves like this one near Mount Carmel in Israel, our early ancestors tried for the first of many times to put love and sex together in a single relationship.

to close down "dirty-movie" theaters, yet half the theaters in the country show pornographic movies only. The English language has one phrase—"making love"—for the beautiful act, and half a dozen widely used words for the brutal act. We long for it, fear it, revile it, and delight in it.

Supposedly, the key ingredient that distinguishes "making love" from just "doing it" is love. But is that *really* the test? Or is the real distinction just a piece of paper from City Hall saying it's okay for these two people to "do it"? When a husband and wife get together in their suburban bedroom it's okay, even though she's cheating on the side and he's fantasizing about his secretary. *But* when Junior and the girl next door get together one night when her parents are out, it's dirty, even though they're madly in love with each other.

Part of the confusion results from not trusting our own motives. Why do we want sex? Do we want it for the animal gratification of copulation leading, if all goes well, to orgasm? Of course. Nature has ensured that we reproduce by endowing us with a strong sex drive and a remarkable capacity for orgasmic pleasure. Do we want it so that we can consummate our feelings of intimacy with another person? Sure. That too. And that's where we differ from other animals. In addition to a powerful sex drive, we come to the mating act loaded down with expectations, anxieties, social taboos, and cultural responsibilities. For other animals, reproduction is little more than a chemical response, at best a few seconds of excitement in an otherwise unremarkable day. But for us, the decision to unite with a member of the opposite

sex is made amid a swirl of romantic imagery, intoxicating fantasy, and fear—the fear of loss, the fear of broken promises, the fear of failure, and the fear of success (which means facing the challenges of a lifetime of living together).

No wonder we're confused. We humans need to mate, we love to mate, but human mating is by far the most complicated, problematic coupling on planet Earth. On the one hand, we're animals and we crave sexual gratification; on the other hand, we're humans and we crave the higher fulfillment we call love. We're the victims of our own advanced status. It would no doubt provoke something like amazement in our animal relatives if they could comprehend the agonies and the ecstasies we endure in the effort to accomplish something that comes so naturally to them.

Apparently, we've always been ambivalent about sex. Dr. John Money says that, during most of the history of Western civilization, we have separated sex from love. "Love is above the belt, and sex is below the belt," says Dr. Money. "Love is beautiful and lyrical and romantic, and sex is filthy and bawdy and carnal because it involves the sex organs." At the height of the Inquisition in the fifteenth century, people were so obsessed with the "sin" of sex that hundreds of thousands of men and women were burned to death after being tortured into confessing that they had engaged in sex with the devil. "Entire villages in southern Germany and Switzerland were exterminated."

The Victorian period "tabooed sexual frankness but produced Freud and other

OPPOSITE: Human pairing may be the most complicated, problem-filled coupling on planet Earth, but when it's successful, there's nothing more beautiful or more fulfilling.

We can't decide what to think about sex. Is it a dirty and degrading act of animal gratification or an act of love? We treat it both ways.

We refer to prudish attitudes about sex as "Victorian," but in fact the Victorian period was just as confused on the subject as we are today. French burlesque dancer Mademoiselle Aimée, about 1880.

OPPOSITE: The human female is the sexiest animal on the planet. But only recently has society given her the opportunity it has always given men to indulge her sexual appetites openly at "ladies only" clubs and other forms of "beefcake" entertainment. Chippendales, Los Angeles.

great founders of sexology," says Money. "It preached the sanctity of the family while making a big business of prostitution. It imposed a church-appeasing censorship on erotica and ran burlesque shows in its big cities. It warned against the moral and psychic degeneracy of masturbation and encouraged it by supplying no other outlet. It abhorred homosexuality, while segregating boys from girls in the adolescent years. Sex was identified as sacred, spiritual, and beautiful, but vetoed until marriage. Simultaneously it was carnal, lustful, and dirty, but to be shared with the loved one."

Dr. Money believes the continuing separation of sex from love is responsible for most of our difficulties in making relationships work. "I'm not going to guess the figure, but it's not even fifty percent of the people in our civilization who are lucky enough to grow up to have a real union between love and sex, as a pair in a partnership." The challenge is complicated by medical discoveries that add years to our lives almost as fast as we take them away. During most of existence, the average human being died between the ages of twenty and forty. Because the idea of single, lifelong partners is central to our culture—unlike the rest of the mammalian world—now we not only have to combine love and sex in a stable relationship, we have to keep it up for fifty or sixty years instead of just ten or twenty. That's a trick that taxes even our adaptable brain.

It's bad enough that sex is so complicated, but it's also so *available*. Ever since the first rubber condom was displayed to the public at the Philadelphia Centennial

Exposition in 1876, birth control has increasingly separated sex from procreation and created in the process a whole new phenomenon: "casual sex." Sex with many partners—consecutively or concurrently—has become relatively common. The rising tide of casual sex may have crested in the seventies, when people typically slept together after the third date, if not the third drink. It was an era of sex at first sight. Looking for justification, people responded enthusiastically to therapists Abraham Maslow and Carl Rogers, claiming for themselves the right to sexual adventurism under the banner of self-actualization. For many people, the prevailing morality of the period could be summarized: "If it feels good, do it."

Of course, it almost always feels good. Sex is not only culturally more available now than it used to be, it's also more *biologically* available to us than to any other animal. The human animal is among the most sexually active creatures on earth. If two people are willing, sex is biologically possible any time of the day or night. We humans don't realize how lucky we are. For some lower life forms, sex is a once-in-a-lifetime event. Even for our cousins the primates, sex isn't always available. According to biologist Sarah Blaffer Hrdy, gibbons, although monogamous like humans, can mate during only a few months every two or three years. Imagine how different our lives and our society would be if we could only have sex for a brief period every two or three years.

Why are we the sexiest animal? What makes it possible for us to have sex any time we want it? In fact, we owe our enviable capacity to the female of our species, who, unlike all other females, is not burdened by *estrus*. Estrus—sometimes known as "heat"—is the period during which a female is biologically ready to receive a male's sperm. Someone referred to it as a female's "business hours." Among other animals, those hours can range from only a few days every year to several months two or three times a year, depending on the female's flow of hormones. Whatever her cycle, when a female is open for business, she puts out a sign. A female baboon, for instance, develops a swelling in her genital area to indicate her readiness for sex. A langur monkey shakes her head and her rump violently from side to side— when this lady says "no" she means "yes." The female horse is available only twice a year, and the males know it because the rest of the time, a membrane closes and covers her vagina. Perhaps in an effort to reduce frustration, male horses produce sperm only when the female is available.

For women, the freedom from estrus has meant the deregulation of sex. Unlike any other female animal, women choose when they want to have sex. "The human female," says Dr. Hrdy, "is the only mammal that is *continuously* sexually receptive, although as you go higher on the primate scale there is more tendency for females to be sexually receptive at nonreproductive times. It is in humans that sex is truly 'deregulated' and female sexuality flourishes." Of course, the human female does have a cycle that determines when conception is possible. According to recent studies, it may also determine when she is particularly eager to be aroused. But she can have sex anytime during that cycle. In other species, biology controls the decision to have sex. In the human species, the female gets to choose with whom, when, how, and if she will have sex. By far the most important sex organ in the human body is the brain.

According to Dr. Hrdy, a side benefit of being liberated from estrus may have been female orgasm. "The female's ability to climax orgasmically, although a potential not always realized, appears universally throughout human societies. There are other primates who seem to experience this positively reinforced genital stimulation we call orgasm. But only in our species are the woman's readiness and potential pleasure in sexual activity so great that the male has made efforts to control it."

For a long time, those efforts to "control" the female orgasm consisted of denying that such a thing existed. Some people still do, by pretending that women are really asexual. Denial has taken more brutal forms over the years. In some societies, women are deprived of orgasm by amputating the clitoris or by infibulation—sewing the vagina shut until marriage.

But facts are facts. Women do have orgasms, and they're very similar to male orgasms. "Physiologically," says Dr. William Masters of Masters and Johnson, "what happens is that there's a great increase in the blood supply to the target organs and a great increase in the muscle tone in the body. With orgasmic release, these two physiological changes are neutralized. It doesn't matter whether it's male or female, the same things happen in terms of release." It's also widely known by now that the female is capable of multiple orgasms; the male isn't. After a man ejaculates, he has to wait at least a few minutes, no matter how young or potent he is, before he can ejaculate again. But a woman can move immediately from one orgasm to another. "The human female," says Dr. Masters, "has an infinitely greater capacity to respond to effective sexual stimulation than the male ever dreamed of having. It's apples and oranges."

Obviously the loss of estrus was a good thing for women, but what did it do for men? There's a great deal of disagreement among researchers about the relationship between the loss of estrus and male behavior, but one thing is clear: just as women developed sexual behavior patterns unique among animals, so did men. In all species besides ours, males have developed a specific "strategy" for mating. The two-ton elephant seal, for example, is what scientists call a "tournament strategist." In a tournament species, the male either is larger than the female, like the elephant seal; has a more flamboyant display, like the peacock; or is more dangerous, like the antlered male deer. The sexes come together only to have sex and the males compete with each other for access to the female—the right to impregnate her—in a "tournament" that coincides with the female's estrus. One consequence of this competition is that only a small percentage of the available males impregnate almost all the females. A study of a group of elephant seals off the California coast showed that 4 percent of the males were responsible for 85 percent of the copulations during one breeding season.

By far the rarest mating strategy in the animal kingdom is pair-bonding. A pair bond is like a marriage. Males and females form into couples, remain loyal to each other usually until death, share in the parenting of offspring, and generally lead a stable domestic life. Because they mate for life, pair-bonding animals don't have to have bright feathers or threatening antlers. Among primates, the marmoset—a small, long-tailed, squirrel-like monkey that dwells in the trees of South America—is one of the species that mate by pair bonding. The term "two lovebirds" is based on the perception that birds, pair bonders, are a model for human couples.

And what about human males? If you watch too many soap operas, you might think that we're a mate-and-run tournament species, but in fact we're not. Of course, we're hardly perfect pair bonders either. In fact, unlike other animals that stick to one mating strategy, we humans tend to pick and choose among various strategies. Freed from the biological requirements of female estrus, we can combine the best—and worst—of many worlds. Although we usually form a bond with one mate, it isn't necessarily for life. Unlike the pair-bonding marmoset, we're all *too* capable of forming sexual attachments outside our bond or breaking our bond to take a new mate. But unlike the tournament species, human males sometimes take part in parenting their children—although not often enough.

So men have their choice of mating strategies just as women have their choice of when to have sex. Does that make things easier? Not at all. In fact, just the reverse. Our mating behavior is only complicated by our choices. It's the element of choice —the decision to do it or not to do it—that brings into play that source of so many complications, the human brain.

Clearly, only a diabolical mind could have devised such a scheme. Only a diabolical mind could make us want sex so much, make it so available to us, and then make it so complicated and frustrating to realize. Only a diabolical mind would dangle such a tempting bait so close and then snatch it away. Only one mind could

Unlike other animals, the human animal tends to pick and choose among various strategies of mating. Although we usually form a bond with one mate, it isn't necessarily for life.

play such a dirty joke—the human mind. No other animal is hung up about sex. Other animals may not enjoy it as much, but they enjoy it when they have it, and they don't feel guilty about it afterward. Only our human brain is capable of fabricating those deliciously frustrating romantic visions and those enticing images of degradation. How do we play this cruel joke on ourselves? How does the human mind take one of our greatest joys—a pleasure we're better equipped to enjoy than any other animal—and transform it into one of our greatest guilts?

We start by trying to keep our children in the dark about sex for as long as possible. For most of our 50,000-year history, adolescence was a time—a relatively short time—when kids learned from adults about human sexuality and its role in the society. Primitive tribes still conduct elaborate ceremonies, often centered on circumcision or first menstruation, that initiate teenagers into sexual adulthood.

What do we do? What kind of initiation ceremonies do we have? First of all, adults have very little to do with it. Most kids are initiated into the secrets of sex in the back seat of a car, or on the living-room sofa when the parents are away. Even before their first hands-on experience, most kids have undergone years of education by innuendo. They spend their weekends at movies like *Porky's* and their weeknights glued to MTV, and if they don't know all the jokes, they laugh anyway, because it's not cool not to know. They also learn the attitude: Sex is a hush-hush subject; something you don't mention around you parents; something you whisper about in the men's room, joke about in the locker room, giggle about in the powder room. It's a rare teenager indeed who learns anything when Mom or Dad finally takes the plunge—reluctantly, of course, and probably five years too late—and sits down to "have a talk with Junior about the facts of life."

Instead of discouraging our children from sexual curiosity—which is what we're trying to do—our reluctance even to *talk* about sex only succeeds in making them feel ashamed of their curiosity—and all the more curious. When we do get around to talking about it, we hem and haw and say as little of substance as we can get away with. After the awkwardness of the first "birds and bees" conversation, most parents communicate with their kids about sex only indirectly through disciplinary measures, curfews, and approval or disapproval of boyfriends and girlfriends. To make matters worse, our message when we do communicate is contradictory: one set of rules for boys, another set for girls. We tell our daughters, "Look, they're coming. Don't let them in." But we tell our sons, "Look, you're going to try, and that's normal—boys will be boys." We teach our daughters to avoid intercourse prior to marriage—to avoid boys who have "only one thing on their minds"—and then we teach our sons that somebody has to take the initiative, that someone has to have sex on the mind or else there will be no next generation. We end up lighting a fire under our sons while throwing cold water on our daughters.

Derelict in our duties as parents, we leave to the schools the hard job of sorting out the contradictory messages and letting kids in on the secret. That doesn't work either, because book learning is no substitute for education, especially on such a touchy subject. Says Dr. William Masters: "We're always in awe of the fact that all of the sex education and all of the contraceptive information available to them are rarely used by the young teenagers."

Is it any wonder that our kids grow up uneducated, frightened, confused—and, all too often, pregnant? "We turn teenage into disease," says John Money, "and we've certainly turned teenage pregnancy into an epidemic disease." One out of five girls today has had sexual intercourse by her first year in high school—almost six times more than in 1948. Each year, a half-million teenage pregnancies end in the birth of a child—often unwanted—and another half-million end in abortions.

We may be horrified by those statistics, but we shouldn't be too surprised. What else do teenagers have to do or think about? Back in the "good ol' days," as recently as two hundred years ago, the period between sexual coming of age and social coming of age was mercifully short. For reasons no one yet knows—but probably related to nutrition and exercise—puberty began at a later age, at about sixteen for girls and seventeen for boys. And because life expectancy was half what it is today, most people married by seventeen or eighteen. In other words, men and women—especially women—tended to marry almost as soon as they became sexually mature. There was no such thing as a delayed sex life, no need to repress or conceal sexual urges. In fact, just the opposite: there was social pressure to marry as soon as you were capable of reproducing. Some cultures have followed the practice of betrothal which required a woman to prove that she could become pregnant before she was allowed to marry. Instead of premarital sex, the taboo was presexual marriage.

What a change in two hundred years! Today, girls reach puberty at about twelve years and boys at about thirteen. Marriage is at least seven or eight years away and maybe ten or fifteen. Yet Mom and Dad and the local clergyman and everybody else say "Wait." Wait for ten years? How can anyone wait for ten years when the radio is blasting out songs like "I'm So Excited" and "What's Love Got to Do with It?"; when television is filled with steamy soap operas, "T-and-A," risqué humor, and

Can we expect our kids to put off sex for ten years after puberty begins when they're bombarded 24 hours a day on MTV with songs like Tina Turner's "What's Love Got to Do with It?"

music videos; when movies lump virgins and nerds together in the same category of undesirables; and finally, when that once-in-a-lifetime rush of hormones is lighting fires in all the wrong places? The body may be saying "go for it," but the culture is saying "don't do it." Later in life, our children will end up paying a high price for these contradictory signals when they try to put love and sex together in a meaningful relationship.

"Insofar as adolescence is related to the biological fact of puberty," says anthropologist Colin Turnbull, "I cannot think of a single culture I know that handles this crucial stage of life more abysmally than we do. The consequences of our folly are to be seen all around us in the violence, neurosis, and the loneliness of our youth, our adults, and our aged, some of whom never approach the fullness and richness of a life that could have been theirs had their adolescence been handled with more wisdom, understanding, and gentle respect. Our education process is a traumatically disintegrative process. It can and does lead to the split between body and mind that gives 'love' an exclusively physical, sexual meaning."

If some think that our children are not scarred for life by the repression of adolescence, there are hundreds of studies of sexual dysfunction, thousands of stories of ruined lives, to help them see the truth. Virginia Johnson suggests taking a look at the common problem of premature ejaculation. In most cases, says Johnson, "a man becomes a rapid ejaculator the first two or three times he ever has intercourse. For instance, if, the first time he's ever having intercourse, he's in his girlfriend's living room on the sofa and he hears her father get out of bed upstairs and start down the stairs—you'll admit there's a certain advantage in rapidity of function. Or if the young man's first sexual activity is a visit to a prostitute, obviously there's a certain value in speed to the prostitute. The faster she can turn the trick, the sooner she can make more money with the next man. Or the man is in the back seat of a car, worrying whether the police will arrest them or not. With any experience like that, the man is conditioned to rapid ejaculation, and he never learns anything different because nobody tells him there's anything different." The human brain has marvelous and merciless powers of retention. What we learn as teenagers may haunt us as adults.

Dr. John Money believes that most sexual "displacements," such as sadomasochism, transvestism, and fetishism, are the direct result of our children's sexual development. "The stakes are very high," says Dr. Money. "If a parent condemns a child for exhibiting proper heterosexual urges, all the parent does is create the conditions for distorted patterns of sexual longing." The argument is strikingly simple: "If we discourage sexual urges from developing normally, they develop abnormally—sort of like sneaking in the back door," says Dr. Money. A classic example of this process at work is little eight-year-old Johnny who's about to be spanked by his father, or any other authority figure. In anticipation of the spanking, he gets so anxious that his hypothalamus begins to work overtime. Because sexual signals are also transmitted to the body through the hypothalamus, Johnny gets an erection. Soon, the fear of being punished is all that's needed to produce an erection. By the time Johnny's grown up, he's capable of producing an erection *only* under threat of punishment. Johnny has become a classic sexual masochist.

By demanding that our kids defy their biological timetable, we force them into the sexual underground of secrecy and shame. "It is bad enough," says Colin Turnbull, "for a young girl to be so ignorant of her own body that the 'first blood' should fill her with terror rather than joy, with thoughts of sickness and death rather than of health and of life. Yet that is how it still is for many, and this kind of ignorance would be even more widespread if parental control were as inviolable as

OPPOSITE: *Two youths of the Xhosa tribe in Transkei province, South Africa, during maturity or marriage school.* RIGHT: *Initiation of young teens of the Dogon tribe in Mali.*

Unlike many primitive tribes, our "advanced" culture provides no preparation for the enormous challenges of love, sex, and marriage.

some parents would like. It should be a criminal offense that this natural, whole-some, and utterly wonderful signal of the transformation of a young body into some-thing else should be used to further that extraordinary argument that the body and all bodily functions, particularly those pertaining to sexual activity, are to be asso-ciated with dirt and impurity, if not with sin."

Sometimes it's enlightening to step back and compare the way our society deals with its problems and the ways other societies deal with similar problems. For example, other societies put their kids through hell, but some of them at least do so constructively. They take advantage of the opportunity to teach their kids something useful about sex, about human relationships, and about life. Colin Turnbull studied one such society, the primitive Mbuti tribe in East Africa.

The Mbuti refer to the passage from childhood to adulthood—what we call ado-lescence—as the *nkumbi*. Instead of lasting six years, the Mbuti adolescence lasts three months. During the *nkumbi*, the child learns the spiritual and moral values of the society that are the essential attributes of being an adult. Before it, the Mbuti male is a boy and the Mbuti female is a girl. After it, they are man and woman with full rights of adulthood. There's no extended puberty, no long period of sexual no-man's-land. "In other cultures, where each stage of life is seen as having its own contribution to make to the well-being of society," says Turnbull, "adolescence is no exception."

First, to symbolize the end of childhood, the boys are literally dragged away from their families by the elders. The boys in turn signal their willingness to leave child-hood by shaving their heads. Their families demonstrate their mourning for the loss of a child by shaving their own heads. The separation from family is celebrated when the boy ritually insults a member of his family, usually his father. This part of the ritual occurs in many Western homes, but the consequences are more ambigu-ous. When an Mbuti boy fights with his father and leaves the house, he knows he will return a man, an equal with his father. Some of our sons spend an entire lifetime trying to prove their worth to their fathers.

In preparation for their passage to adulthood, the boys are taken to an initiation camp—a symbolic place of death—where they undergo circumcision. To alleviate the pain of the operation, they are "beaten" and commanded to sing *nkumbi* songs. This procedure may seem savage, but in fact the beatings are more symbolic than hurtful and the pain doesn't compare to the emotional harm that more "civilized" adolescents often suffer in their struggle to break free of their parents.

After a long series of ritual dances and labors, the boys are forced to engage in women's tasks, such as planting corn, until they're "ready to drop." The idea is to make them "*want*, consciously, to become men," says Turnbull. Then they engage in a series of ritual events that educate them to the ins and outs of marriage at a level of sophistication that would be the envy of a New York marriage counselor. They learn about respect, responsibility, mutuality, and even conflict. At one point,

Virginia Johnson and Dr. William Masters. "The missing link is the failure on the part of responsible parents to let their young people know that they realize they are sexual beings and that parents appreciate that sexuality."

OVERLEAF: Surely our culture can devise a better initiation ceremony for our young than the long limbo of adolescence they now endure, one that would leave them more enlightened and less guilt-ridden about the urges they feel. Students at prom time.

they stage a mock battle with the young girls of the village, who have undergone a similar, although less rigorous, initiation ceremony of their own, using sticks and stones to remind them "that one of the major arenas of potential conflict is that of the male/female relationship."

Their ritual battles behind them, and armed with their new knowledge of life's complexities, the boys watch as the initiation camp is burned—another symbol that they're passing to a new stage of life. Their acceptance into the society is announced with a blast on a trumpet made from an elephant tusk. The boys are bathed, anointed with palm oil—a symbol of prosperity and continuity—and welcomed back to their village with gifts and jubilation. They return triumphant, walking on a carpet of plantain leaves to symbolize survival and success. Now each one is ready to build his own home, lead the independent life of an adult, and marry.

The Mbuti may not have microwave ovens, but when it comes to sex education, they're light-years ahead of us. By the time of the *nkumbi*, Mbuti boys already know the basic facts of life, so the initiation ceremony is used to teach them the more difficult lessons of sexual morality and the responsibilities of marriage. "Perhaps the most remarkable, and most important, thing about this rite of passage," says Turnbull, "is the way the boys learn the true significance of their approaching sexual maturity, the *full* meaning of 'love.'" For one thing, they learn that sex—*and* proper abstinence from it—is both a great responsibility and a great joy. "Dances and ordeals lend weight to what might otherwise be ineffective intellectual argument," Turnbull adds. Best of all, boys and girls—in their own similar rites—are taught that puberty is a positive experience. It's a celebration of their new power to endow their society with life.

Of course, no one is about to rush off to the jungle and forsake the cushiony life we've fluffed for ourselves over the last 10,000 years. Can you imagine trying to get a teenager to shave his head or to forsake her MTV for plantain leaves? But surely we can learn something from the *nkumbi*. Surely our species, with its clever brain, can devise a better initiation ceremony for our young than the long limbo of adoles-

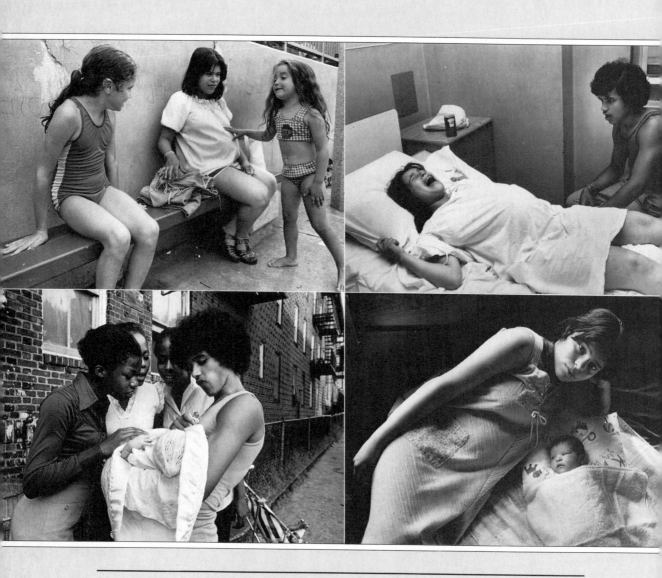

The question is not whether we can prevent adolescents from feeling sexual urges. Such urges are an irreversible biological fact and adolescents are going to feel them whether we want them to or not. The question is, how can we encourage responsible sexual behavior among adolescents and give them a healthy start at adulthood, unencumbered by shame, guilt, sexual distortions, or unwanted babies?

cence they now endure, one that leaves them more enlightened and less guilt-ridden about the urges they feel. Every adult was once an adolescent, so we should learn from our own experience: we know perfectly well that adolescents feel sexual urges, and are going to feel them whether we want them to or not. How can we begin to encourage responsible sexual behavior among our adolescents and give them a healthy start at adulthood, unencumbered by shame, guilt, sexual distortions, unwanted babies, ill-advised marital choices, or an inability to combine sex and love?

"The missing link," says Virginia Johnson, "is the failure on the part of responsible parents to let their young people know that they realize they are sexual beings and that the parents appreciate that sexuality. A parent needs to say something like, 'I know you have these feelings. I know you're going through this.' "

In other words, the first thing parents should do is face up to reality—and do it early. Forget the old routine of waiting till the last minute for a talk about the "birds and bees." If you turn a deaf ear, your children will pay the price. That's especially true if a child's sexual development is already going askew.

"I always say that some teenagers have a monster in their lives," says Dr. John Money, referring to adolescents with incipient major sexual problems, "and whatever that monster is, it's unspeakable. We need to make it easier for people who are harboring that monster in their mental lives to be able to go and say, 'Please give me some help.' We need an understanding society that would provide an opportunity for a terrified thirteen-year-old to share a painful secret with someone who understands and with whom she could form an alliance."

But is that the only answer? Is being able to talk about their sexual longings going to satisfy those longings enough to keep our kids out of trouble?

"We also need to become quite open," says Money, "about the fact that sex is a part of teenage life. I'm not talking about thirteen, I'm talking about middle to late teens. We need to make birth control available; we need to make it morally acceptable to go and ask for birth control, to admit to your mother and father and your grandmother and everybody else, 'I am now beginning my sex life, and I'm not going to stumble into the economic error of having children before I have proper support for them.' "

Are you advocating sex among adolescents in their late teens?

"I suggest that in addition to parents' reminding boys and girls that they are males and females—similar in feelings and desires and abilities, yet different in significant biological ways and roles—they must not interfere unduly with a child's interest in and activities with the opposite sex."

The next question, obviously, is "How early?" Are children ever too young to explore their sexuality? What about playing doctor?

"Playing doctor is not so bad," says Money. "Parents need to look with a little less terror, and a little more approval, on limited sexual activity among children."

In other words, playing doctor is "undress rehearsal" for a healthy adult sexual life, and juveniles should not be discouraged from engaging in sexual play. When confronted with the natural fact of your kid's sexuality, don't get crazy. *Relax.* You're not talking about free sex among adolescents but about an attitude toward sex that takes it out of the dirty magazines and distorted fantasies and into the healthier climate of acceptable family discussion and debate.

"I'm amazed at the extraordinary degree to which we can't accept normal heterosexual development in children," says Money. "By that I mean that if we see them engaged in what I call sexual rehearsal play we punish them for it, sometimes abusively—very abusively."

You mean little boys are told that, if they "play with themselves" their "thing" will fall off or they'll grow hair on their palms?

"Right," says Money. "If you look at all other primate species—the great apes, for example—you see that all the children engage in sexual rehearsal play. I think the most fascinating study in this regard was conducted at Wisconsin with monkeys. The study showed that if you raise monkeys in isolation and deprive them of sexual rehearsal play, then they never breed when they grow up."

Is that why some lovers are more successful at love than at making love?

"Lovers are mismatched on love above the belt less often than on lust below the belt," in Money's opinion. "Above-the-belt erotosexualism is less negated in childhood than is lust below the belt. Developmentally, therefore, it is less subject to eccentric distortion and circuitous expression. Lovers can imagine what to expect of each other at the above-the-belt stage of their encounter, and usually be correct."

What kind of sex play are you advocating? Certainly not sex play between adults and children? And what about play between two boys or two girls? Some parents think that kind of "doctoring" leads to homosexuality.

"Sexual rehearsal play," says Money, "is done with your own age group and your own playmate group. Nature should unfold herself: it's just like crawling before you can walk. You have to go through that stage if you're going to be able to develop normally for the rest of your childhood and adolescence and adulthood. Play makes eroticism a progressively familiar part of one's sense of well-being before extending it to become a familiar part of intimacy with the other sex. In this sense, self-sex and same-sex erotic play serve as a rehearsal for eroticism with the other sex."

But the question remains: how far is too far? Parents who believe that it's wrong to constantly besiege a child with "don'ts," "shouldn'ts," and "can'ts," who believe we've moved beyond Victorian repression, are no longer rare. The problem we're left with is how much freedom to permit.

"The problem is more difficult in the abstract than in practice," says Dr. Money. "In the very young, the sexual rehearsal is hardly even noticed as sexual, because it's close body contact. It's patting and smoothing. But, in children who are about three, you do see a lot of flirtatious play—and it's usually with someone in the family. Like the little girl who pirouettes and pulls her skirt up and flirts with her

In all other primate species, children engage in sexual rehearsal play. If they are deprived of such play, they simply can't breed when they become adults. Celebese crested macaques in the National Zoo, Washington, D.C.

daddy. And the little boy who becomes the little escort and goes to the shopping mall with Mommy. Most families know how to handle that, and they do it well."

So children grasp the notion that some activities are more private than others?

"From a *very* early age, they understand that you don't go into the supermarket and take your clothes off. So they assimilate very easily the idea that certain things are private within the family and that you don't display them when you're at school or when you're visiting."

According to Virginia Johnson, control is just as important to children's sexual education as accepting their sexual feelings or getting to know the anatomy.

"After letting the child know that his or her sexual urges are perfectly normal," says Johnson, "the child needs to be taught that it's also perfectly normal to *control* those urges. Parents already do a pretty good job of letting their daughters know where the limits are; where they fall down on the job is with their sons."

You mean fathers who tell their sons, directly or indirectly, "Go out there and prove your manhood"?

"Right." According to Johnson, "Too many fathers give their sons an implicit or even explicit license, bordering on encouragement, to act in ways they would never forgive their daughters. This is very much a woman speaking, but I think sons should be given less of a ticket to 'go be boys.' "

Under the present system, control is imposed. Kids aren't taught to control themselves, they're simply controlled. That kind of denial only whets their sexual appetites and makes them go crazy when Mom and Dad are away or as soon as they go off to college.

"If an adolescent addresses the issue of sexual control with expectation and hopefulness rather than a stern 'thou shalt not,' " says Johnson, "the overall sexual attitude and understanding will be much healthier in adulthood. Asking teens to control their urges is not inconsistent for our species. Sexual control is a tactic all human beings must learn. Unlike other animals, humans choose when to engage in sexual activity. Learning sexual control is part of the training our species must undergo. Although the teen's biological clock is spinning, only a part of our activities is determined by biology. The rest we learn."

Our attitudes toward sex are perhaps the most maladaptive solutions to the problems of mating we could have devised. We really haven't come very far from the caves of Mount Carmel where the earliest Adams and the earliest Eves must have wrestled with the same problems. We've made sex dirty and deprived ourselves of its pleasures. We've condemned our kids to ignorance and shame. It doesn't have to be that way. In Hindu culture, sex is worshiped as a route to paradise—not the sin that got us kicked out. It's a testament to the power and control of our brain that it could have denied our chemistry so thoroughly for so long. But we've paid dearly in the meantime in broken hearts and broken marriages and antisocial behavior. Our notions of sex are a dirty joke, and the joke is on us.

Once again, we need to call on our magnificent brain to extricate us from a mess that it's largely responsible for getting us into. We need to turn it around, persuade it to stop fighting our biology and start cooperating with it. True, some of our greatest accomplishments have been based on our refusal to be bound by biology. By defying biological constraints, we've been able to conquer our world and even begin to reach out to other worlds. But love isn't conquest.

Why can't our brain conquer love the same way it's conquered most of the rest of our environment? Because love isn't "out there"; it can't be manipulated like a stick or a wheel or a motor. Love hides in the deep recesses of the brain itself—the only place on earth where we haven't yet established our control. The brain is a master everywhere but in its own house. That's what makes love so special and so elusive. That's why when you love someone, you never feel really in control. It's the brain's greatest challenge and greatest exhilaration. It's a merging of two minds—and the bodies they command—on a level of consciousness we don't begin to understand. Of all the many mysteries of the universe, love is probably the only one we'll never solve.

8. Making History

What are little boys
*   made of?*
Snips and snails, and
*   puppy-dogs' tails;*
That's what little boys
*   are made of.*
What are little girls
*   made of?*
Sugar and spice and
*   everything nice;*
That's what little girls
*   are made of.*

Nursery Rhyme

Every time we fall in love, the roles we play are shaped by forces most of us are hardly aware of. It may not sound very romantic, but whenever you climb into bed with someone you love, thousands of years of history climb in with you. You may think, as Romeo and Juliet did, that you can leave the "rude world" behind, but you never really can. From the first time two people set eyes on each other, their efforts to combine sex and love are inevitably affected by their assumptions about men and women. "The status men and women have in a society," says psychologist Dr. Dorothy Dinnerstein of Rutgers University, "impacts the kind of relationship a man and woman share." As an example, Dinnerstein points to the effects of the woman's role as nurturer. "Children have been trained to expect one person, the mother, to satisfy all their needs," she says. "When they transfer those grandiose expectations of one person to one mate in adulthood, they are destined for disappointment."

What is the relative status of men and women today? We live in a culture that gave women the right to vote only sixty-five years ago. Although there have been changes, men's tasks and women's tasks continue to be sharply differentiated. When a woman does the same work as a man, she's likely to earn only about 60 percent of what he does. Until recently, it was almost unthinkable that a woman could be President, and still only a few women have made it into the Senate. Of

The historical distinction between men's work and women's work was that men hunted and women gathered. That was true, but the gathering accounted for far more of the family diet than the hunting. In most primitive tribes, she was the real breadwinner—and he knew it. TOP: Men of the !Kung tribe kill an elephant. LEFT: A !Kung woman tends her child.

OPPOSITE: These walls are all that remain of the ancient city of Arad, 65 miles south of Jerusalem. Four thousand years ago, Arad was the site of an early experiment in sex-role differentiation. Here, for the first time, women were left holding the baby.

---

course, as in almost all human cultures, women have been left holding the babies.

Most of us don't think of these assumptions about men and women as assumptions at all. They're just part of the natural order of things. Just as night has always followed day, and winter has always followed fall, women have always held the babies, taken care of home and hearth; men have always faced the world, "brought home the bacon," managed the store, run the country, etcetera, etcetera. Right? Wrong. There's nothing "natural" about this arrangement. In fact, there's very little about the human animal that's written in the biological equivalent of stone. After all, one of our unique talents has always been our ability to overcome biological constraints and shape our own environment.

We don't have to travel far in space or time to prove that the roles men and women play in our own society are not "natural." In her book *Nisa: The Life and Words of a !Kung Woman,* anthropologist Marjorie Shostak describes how the !Kung Bushmen of southern Africa have developed a different solution to the problem of dividing life's labors. Although !Kung males, with their greater speed and upper-

body strength, do the hunting, and females, with their breasts and wider hips, bear and nurse the children, that's where the similarity with suburbia ends. Mrs. !Kung is responsible for cultivating and collecting the staples of the !Kung family diet: nuts, roots, and plants. Only occasionally does Mr. !Kung get lucky and bring home the protein-rich but elusive game. As in most hunter-gatherer societies of the last 50,000 years, there's a lot more gathering than hunting going on, and women, not men, bring home most of what the !Kung would call "bacon."

Because both Mr. and Mrs. perform tasks that are vital to the survival of the family, they're equally respected in !Kung society. The clans within the tribe are oriented toward the women, not the men. Parents arrange most marriages, and a man leaves his own family to join his wife's clan. This, too, is the way it was during most of our recorded history. If the union doesn't work, it ends without recriminations—there are no divorce courts—leaving the individuals free to choose other mates on their own. By our standards, sexual activity among the !Kung is unrepressed. Virginity, chastity, and even lifelong monogamy are the exception, not the rule. Men may take "co-wives." Experimental sex play begins early and openly, but extramarital pregnancy is rare. Prevented from having large families by prolonged nursing and a subsistence diet, !Kung women bear only three or four children in a lifetime, spaced years apart.

Even in our own time, there are other societies that have evolved different roles for men and women. The Mbuti, for example, share more equitably, if not equally, *all* the work except for childbearing and nursing. That includes everything from hunting to baby tending. At the other end of the spectrum are tribes like the Yano-mamo Indians of South America who treat women little better than cattle. Any and all of these systems could be adapted to modern use. There's nothing inherently primitive about one system or inherently up-to-date about another. They all developed originally in primitive tribes thousands of years ago. So why did we end up with the roles we have? How did our system for dividing labor between men and women evolve?

It is metaphorically if not historically accurate to say that the battle of the sexes began in the area we now call the Holy Land. The first skirmishes were fought in towns very much like the ancient city of Arad, 65 miles south of Jerusalem. Life has been going on inside the walls of Arad for more than 4,000 years. Think of it as an early experiment in cohabitation. Things aren't as bad for women here as they are in other parts of the Moslem world. In Arad, they're allowed to show their faces and wear colored clothes. But as any visitor can see by the groups of women huddled around the cooking fires and serving their husbands, it was an experiment that has not gone well for women.

Before towns like Arad were founded, men and women in this area lived much like the !Kung, responding to the environment, exercising almost no control over it. The men hunted, the women gathered, both sharing their finds at the family hearth.

As in the !Kung society, male and female behavior were separate but equally valued. Then, about 10,000 years ago, a major change occurred. Someone—a woman probably—found that she could make her job easier and more productive by planting and waiting rather than roaming and gathering. The men and women who lived here began to harvest nature's bounty. Families we would call "farmers" began to appear among the old hunter-gatherers, and life on the surrounding plain would never be the same again.

Somewhere during this chapter of human evolution, someone—probably a man—looked down at one of these meager harvests and said for the first time, "This is mine." The concept of property was born. The new concept extended not only to the land and the early crops but to the family as well, where the human male, like all primates had always had an understandable interest in knowing which babies were his babies. The human emotion of jealousy was nurtured as these early residents shaped rules about what "he" and "she" were expected to do with their lives and how they would manage the most mysterious energy of all, sex. By the time Arad was founded, a man could say, with more or less certainty, this child is mine, this woman belongs to me.

A woman may have been property, but at least she was respected property. After all, her work was at least as necessary to an agricultural society as it was to a hunter-gatherer society. It wasn't until the Late Bronze Age—about 5,000 years ago—that women began to suffer second-class citizenship. It was a time of great terror; a time of war, famine, parasites, and plague—a time of catastrophic depopulation. Suddenly, fertility was urgently important. The situation was made more critical by the relatively small proportion of women in the population, women's shorter life expectancy—just the reverse of today—and high infant-mortality rates.

Sounding the battle cry, the Bible charged believers to "be fruitful and multiply" and condemned any sexual activity that didn't serve the cause of reproduction. Sex was no longer just a pleasure, it was a duty, and any sexual act that didn't promise children was an offense against the society. The biblical injunctions against masturbation, homosexuality, adultery, and prostitution date from this crackdown. Meanwhile, the role of women was increasingly restricted, while men assumed what had been the female job of farming. As the irreplaceable remedy for population loss, women were banished from public life, taken out of the temple, and forbidden to serve in any role that interfered with their child-rearing duties. They were a precious commodity that had to be preserved. By 1000 B.C., it had already been decreed: a woman's place—her only place—was in the home.

At first, all the to-do was a sign of respect, a recognition that women alone were capable of bearing children and that they were better suited to caring for them. It was the first of many times that women would be "put on pedestals" to be admired—and imprisoned. But in time, as the restrictions were codified and sanctified, they became a means not of freeing women for the purpose of having children, but of restricting them to that activity. Gradually, the priesthood and ruling groups became exclusively male. A matriarchal society became patriarchal. The subordination of the women had begun.

"It is indeed an irony of history," says Carol Meyers, a historian of the Jewish religion, "that this very tight channeling of female energies into domestic affairs, which was a liberating event in its own time, became, ultimately, the *raison d'être* for continued and exclusive confinement of female energies to that sphere. . . . Once the pattern of female nonparticipation in other spheres of life—the priesthood in particular—became established, society adhered to it in ways that became limiting and oppressive to women."

There are, of course, competing notions about the origins of sex roles in our society. Some scientists believe that male dominance in the Western world can be traced to an invasion that swept into the same area about 1,500 years before Christ. The marauders charged out of their homes in Russia and spread across Asia and Europe, from India to Ireland, changing the patterns of the societies they conquered. Today we refer to them as Indo-Europeans—although they didn't go by that name. If your ancestors came from *any* country in Europe except Finland or Hungary, they were probably Indo-Europeans. According to some experts, it was their notions about men and women that shaped our society.

The only word for the Indo-Europeans is *macho*. Where the people they con-

quered farmed peacefully, the Indo-Europeans lived by herding livestock and warring with each other for fun and extra animals. An economy based on herding and warring was, naturally, run by males, and gave women no opportunity for essential work. Women weren't partners, they were property, little more than childbearing slaves, secluded in their homes, barred from the male worlds of education and politics and frequently subjected to a sexual rite indistinguishable from rape.

"This was a major sweep of one male-dominant culture over a variety of cultures," says anthropologist Peggy Sanday, who points out that the Indo-European invasion was not the last time a male-dominated society imposed its values on other cultures. "We see this phenomenon repeated again in the nineteenth century when colonialism and the subsequent industrialization of larger areas by the European colonial powers changed the nature of marriage and the family throughout the world," says Sanday. "Colonialism imposed a European monogamous, nuclear, patriarchal family on cultures whose families had often been polygynous, extended, and matriarchal—the woman's authority greater than the man's."

Whether it was accomplished by invasion or by depopulation, the triumph of male-dominated culture a thousand years before Christ was complete. Even the religions changed to reflect the new sexual pecking order. Previously, the people in Arad had worshiped gods of both sexes. There were gods and goddesses just as there were priests and priestesses who served the pre-Judaic Canaanite faith ob-

OPPOSITE: "Yahweh," the God introduced by the monotheistic Jews, was definitely a male. In Orthodox Judaism, male worshipers regularly thank God for not letting them be born women. At the Western Wall in Jerusalem, male and female worshipers are segregated.

A thousand years before Christ, fertility goddesses like Astarte were replaced by a new idea of the divine: God—almighty, in His heaven, and always male. Unglazed fertility figure from 586–100 B.C.

served there. But by 1200 B.C., Yahweh, the God of the Israelites, was casting His long shadow over "mother" earth, replacing graven images and resident spirits. Gradually a new idea of the divine was taking hold: God—almighty, in His heaven, and always male.

Nowhere is the "masculinization" of religion more obvious than at Çatal Hüyük in southeastern Turkey. Çatal Hüyük is one of the oldest cities in the world and has been called the Vatican of an almost-forgotten religion—a religion that worshiped not a supreme God, but a Goddess. The excavators of the ancient city uncovered Her image everywhere. The people of Çatal Hüyük believed that the first Goddess had given birth to the world, or that the world was made from Her body. They worshiped Her amazing power to control the wild animals, nurse the seeds, and bring forth new life. For good measure, the people also prayed to a bevy of big-breasted fertility goddesses for good crops, rainfall, and protection from blight.

Among the various religions of the world, Çatal Hüyük is not a freak. From the deserts of Egypt to the hills of Rome to the jungles of Africa to the islands of the Pacific Basin and the plains of North America, gods have been both male and female, or even male and female at the same time. And yet in Judaism, Christianity, and Islam—three religions born in the Near East—there is only one *male* God. Some theologians argue in a weak rearguard action that the single God is really neuter. But explain that concept to the kids who grow up calling God "King," "Lord of Hosts," "Master of the Universe," and "Our Father in Heaven." God is never referred to as "Queen," "Lady," "Mistress," or "Mother."

The Talmud may dodge the issue by saying that "God sees but cannot be seen," but the proof is in the pronouns. Hebrew verbs have both masculine and feminine endings, but when they refer to the unseen God, the endings are always masculine. The product of all this subliminal training is right there in our unconscious. No matter how many times we hear that God has no human attributes, in our mind's eye we always see "Him" the way Michelangelo painted Him: old, white, stern, bearded—and male.

Of course, the Catholic Church grants a special place to Mary as the mother of Jesus, but like Western women in general, she derives her status from a male relative. There have also been splinter groups of Gnostic Christians who have treated God as both male and female, Father and Mother. One Gnostic prayer addresses Father and Mother, "the two immortal names, Parents of the divine." Among the Jews, a belief in fertility goddesses—a hedge on the bet—coexisted with the new Yahweh until the time of Josiah and was revived in a fit of nervousness after the destruction of the Temple.

No matter how many times we hear that God has no human attributes, in our mind's eye we always see "Him" the way Michelangelo painted Him on the Sistine ceiling: old, white, stern, bearded—and male. The Creation of the Sun, the Moon, and the Planets by Michelangelo Buonarroti.

Children learn sex roles even before they learn to speak. Studies have shown that mothers tend to hold their daughters closer and talk to them more. Sons get more rough play than daughters.

Despite these occasional deviations, there has never been any doubt where the Judeo-Christian heart is. Consider the last line of the secret Gospel of Thomas: "Simon Peter said to [the disciples]: Let Mary be excluded from among us, for she is a woman, and not worthy of Life." In a traditional prayer, male Jewish worshipers regularly thank God for not having let them be born women. Finally, there's the evidence of the Bible itself. To understand the Judeo-Christian view of women, we don't need to look any further than the Garden of Eden where Eve—formerly the revered goddess of fertility—is maligned as the originator of death and the dupe of evil. According to Elaine H. Pagels, a historian of religion, "The Judeo-Christian ethic based on a male God also raised men to a position of power and control over their societies and their women. These beliefs, together with industrialization, created today's male-dominant cultures."

What do fertility goddesses and *macho* invaders from Russia have to do with men and women today? What impact could such distant cultures have on our lives of commuter headaches, automated bank tellers, and video recorders? In fact, you don't have to look far to see their legacy. Just watch children at play.

Children learn the sexual roles they're supposed to play even before they learn to talk. By the time a little boy dons blue pants and a little girl models her new pink dress for Daddy—usually at about twelve months—they have learned that boys and girls are different because the world treats them differently. Studies have shown that mothers tend to hold their daughters closer and talk to them more, while sons get bounced on Daddy's knee or tossed playfully in the air more often.

"Little boys are encouraged to explore their rooms, and to play with toys by themselves," says Dr. Carol Malatesta of the University of Delaware, who has researched the interaction of mothers and their infants extensively. "Little girls are encouraged to stay close to their mothers, and to talk to them." Why the differences? Why do parents treat sons one way, daughters another? "I think we can say, unequivocally, that it has simply to do with our cultural values," concludes Dr. Malatesta. "We have decided to treat little boys as explorers and hunters and to treat little girls as housewives and care givers." The hunter-gatherer societies of our distant past are still alive and well and living in our nurseries.

In an experiment by Susan Goldberg and Michael Lewis in New Brunswick, New Jersey, one-year-old babies were confronted with a barrier of blocks separating them from their favorite toy. The boys tried to crawl around the barrier, climb over it, or knock it down. The girls reacted by crying. When the children were two years old they were put in the same frustrating situation again. Nothing had changed, except that the little girls now asked for help instead of crying.

Of course, there may be a hormone at work here—our old friend testosterone—making the boys more aggressive than the girls. But the researchers who conducted these tests didn't conclude simply that little boys are active and little girls are passive. In their view, each sex was actively seeking a solution to the barrier problem, but the solutions they reached for were determined by their learned sex roles. Boys reached for solutions that were "appropriate" for boys, and girls reached for

Dr. Michael Lewis of Rutgers University (above). In their famous barrier study, Dr. Lewis and Susan Goldberg found that one-year-old girls (near right) tended to cry when placed behind a barrier, while one-year-old boys (far right) tried to break through or find a way around the barrier.

solutions "appropriate" for girls. We bring up our boys to "go fetch" objects, to move actively and range far away from their parents. We bring up little girls to sit near their mothers, to ask questions, to communicate.

When these boys and girls grow up, they'll enter a society that's shaped by the same roles they learned as infants, a society in which male and female labor has become highly specialized—and, as far as wages go, highly unequal; a society in which women continue to be excluded from positions of power. They'll carry their training into relationships as well as careers—and pay the price. According to June Reinisch, females, as adults, "seem to be more interested in communication and in social interaction with other human beings, while males are more 'agentic-instrumental'—that is, they're more interested in the manipulation of objects in the environment." In too many relationships, these differences harden into "My wife nags" and "My husband won't talk to me."

In the 1950s, television shows like *Leave It to Beaver, Father Knows Best*, and *Ozzie and Harriet* immortalized on celluloid a world of male and female roles that a time traveler from the town of Arad 3,000 years ago would find soothingly familiar. The Cleavers, the Andersons, and the Nelsons represented images—still popular today—torn from the pages of history: the housebound woman tending to her children; the dominant father commuting to the modern equivalent of "the fields."

In those innocuous TV versions, the world of ancient sex roles doesn't seem too bad. But there's a dark side to that world that Hollywood never showed us. Statistics tell us that of those little girls who cried at the barrier, one out of ten will be raped when she grows up. This is another legacy of those seemingly distant events at Arad and Çatal Hüyük. "Our culture follows a pattern of behavior typical of rape-prone societies," says Dr. Peggy Sanday. "We tolerate violence and its images. We encourage our males to be tough, competitive, and aggressive. There are essentially two kinds of rape: that which is pathological and caused by an individual's particular illness—and the rape that we teach."

Again, it doesn't have to be this way. It's not written in the stars that men will rape women. Except in the rarest of cases, it's not the inevitable result of hormones, body chemistry, relative size, or sexual overload. There are societies in the world today where rape is virtually unknown. According to Dr. Sanday, the Minangkabau of western Sumatra are the largest matrilineal society in the world. Upon marriage, the Minangkabau male moves into his wife's house, leaving his mother and sisters in charge of the family property. Women occupy powerful roles in areas of customary law and domestic management. According to Dr. Sanday, violence is rare and war, unknown. The culture emphasizes courtesy, nonaggression, and a deep concern for the feelings and well-being of others. In 1983, among the 3 million Minangkabau people there were only 28 rapes. All occurred in areas that have regular contact with Westerners.

In sex roles as in science, we have made our own history. We are what we are

In the 1950s, television shows like Ozzie and Harriet *epitomized a world of male and female roles that had changed little from the time of Arad, 4,000 years earlier.*

not because biology dictated it, but because over thousands of years we have made millions of little decisions about what we wanted to be and those decisions have led us to this point. When the men and women of Arad decided that women should stay at home and have children to combat the threat of depopulation, it wasn't an act of male chauvinism, it was just a short-term solution to an immediate problem. Unfortunately, that short-term solution led to an even graver long-term problem: male domination and the subordination of women.

Slowly, we're beginning to undo this particular maladaptation. We're living in a time when the roles within the family are changing rapidly. Since 1970, the number of women who have returned to "the fields" has increased by 50 percent. Meanwhile, men have begun to return to the home. Although sometimes it may not seem so, surveys say that men are now doing almost 30 percent more of the housework than they did in the fifties when Ozzie and Harriet were playing in prime time.

But the cost of maladaptation is still unacceptably high. We're paying for it every day—in the workplace, in our families, even in bed. The man who tries to fill the powerful and controlling role society has cut out for him expects to be potent and ever-ready sexually. The woman has been taught to expect no less. Inevitably, both are disapppointed. "The man is incredibly handicapped," says Virginia Johnson. "The culture has deemed the male the sex expert. He doesn't know anything about female sexual functioning, at least subjectively. He can't be orgasmic for a woman. He can aid and abet her orgasm, but he can't have it for her."

Our children are paying for it. By their first birthday they've already learned enough to be limited by their identity as male or female. As they grow older, that identity may cause them years of suffering if it conflicts with their individual temperament—the unique style each of us is born with. "A parent's negative reaction to a child's inborn temperament," says psychiatrist Dr. Judd Marmor of U.C.L.A., "can have serious and lifelong consequences. Parents need to be very sensitive to

It's often difficult, but not impossible, to get a male to be maternal. Even the male rat, when given experience with pups, will start to engage in maternal behaviors. Here, a twenty-day-old male rat returns a pup to the nest.

who their child is as an individual and not become unduly angry if he/she doesn't conform completely to cultural assumptions."

This is the real, tragic cost of maladaptive gender roles: the waste of human potential. By forcing girls and boys into predetermined roles, we never get a chance to find out what they could achieve if they were free to create their own roles. Who knows what new way of getting over a barrier some little girl might have devised if she hadn't been trained to cry instead of try? The stereotypes under which we've labored for the last 3,000 years—the *macho* cowboy male and the defenseless, domestic female—have only prevented us from pursuing our own, individual solutions to the challenges of forming lifelong relationships. We've perpetuated the myth that men long for sex and women long for love, and then wondered why we have trouble fulfilling each other's needs. "Human beings are very flexible," says June Reinisch. "You cannot make generalizations about groups of human beings and then expect that to determine how a particular human being will behave. Males *are* more aggressive than females—in certain circumstances. But if a female is protecting her young, she makes male aggression look like potsy. By the same token, it's easier to get a female to be maternal, but it's not by any means impossible to get a male to be maternal. Even in the rat—which is a much lower form of mammalian life than we are—if you give a male rat enough experience with pups, he will start to engage in maternal behaviors."

Surely, if a rat can do it, we can too. The answer is to let every individual make his or her own history, just as we collectively make the history of our species. After all, the ability to shape our own destiny is perhaps our greatest distinction. It would be a tragedy to deny to the individual the best part of being human.

Who knows what potential would be unleashed? Dr. John Money, for example, sees a time when it will no longer be engraved in stone that men do the impregnating and women do the gestating: a time when men will bear children. "We will do it by regulating the hormone cycle and letting the baby grow on the external surface of the small intestine," Money explains. "There has already been a woman in New Zealand who, after a hysterectomy, had a baby that way. Her uterus had been removed, but the fertilized egg escaped at the time of the operation and joined itself onto the outside surface of her intestine and grew there like a normal baby. It was delivered by cesarean section and is now a normal child."

This may sound like a bad science-fiction novel or a banner headline from the *National Enquirer,* but it is, in fact, a logical step in our evolution. We've always been pushing against the bonds of biology that constrain us. We used a stick to extend our reach, a wheel to extend our range, a word to extend our thoughts. We are, by nature, overreachers, overachievers, overdoers. Is it any crazier to dream of putting a child in a man's body than to dream of putting a woman on the moon?

The human animal today may be at the beginning of one of the most important cultural advances in its history. The hi-tech, test-tube age is close to erasing the last lame excuses for a sexist society. Modern technology has made strength and aggression not only less necessary but perhaps even maladaptive. Men's larger size may be one reason for men's shorter life span. Today we need less muscle and more brain. A bellwether of the new age is the Kennedy Space Center in Florida.

Until recently, the American space program was basically an all-male club. In recruiting potential astronauts, the message had always been clear: No Women Need Apply. Then Sally Ride broke the gender barrier. The little girls sitting in front of the barrier crying for help would have been proud. On June 18, 1983, Ride, who was also married to an astronaut, became the first American woman in outer space—and she got there before her husband. Manned spaceflight had become human spaceflight. The Soviet Union had put a woman in space 20 years before, but many critics dismissed Valentina Tereshkova's ride as a propaganda ploy. She was an untrained, 26-year-old textile mill worker at the time of her space mission.

Very few adjustments had to be made to accommodate women in the space program. As for the spacecraft itself, only the on-board water closet had to be modified. Ride became an instant celebrity. Her adventure was made into a TV docudrama; her face appeared on the cover of *Newsweek;* she was interviewed on television and radio for weeks after her return. Inevitably, she was asked all the sexist questions: "Will you wear a bra in outer space?" and "Do you weep when you have a problem?" But the biggest news of the event was that sending a woman into outer space turned out to be no big deal.

In fact, if astronauts had been chosen from the start for their biological credentials alone, it would have been years before the first *male* astronaut made his "maiden" voyage. After all, women are smaller, they weigh less, they need less oxygen and less food, they live longer, they're generally healthier—despite the trauma of childbirth—and they bear up better under stress. Their eyes are better at picking small objects (like stars) out of a large field (like space); they can smell a broader range of odors and hear certain tones more clearly. Even the fifty-four American men who preceded Sally Ride would have to acknowledge that women, all else being equal, have more of "the right stuff."

With all these advantages, why haven't women pioneered in space from the start? "Because we think of men as the ones who should go off to conquer either California or the nearest star," says June Reinisch. "Therefore men were chosen to go into space. It was really a mistake on many levels." But all that is changing—slowly but inevitably. The artificial roles we inherited can't contain the human spirit indefinitely. We are drawn to the unexplored reaches of our potential as surely as air is drawn to a vacuum. Our irrepressible brain wouldn't have it any other way. That's why we will someday travel farther into space. A man may have been first to set foot on the moon, but the first human being on Mars may be a woman.

Women may have more of "the right stuff." Sally Ride.

PART THREE

WAR &
VIOLENCE

9. The Dark Side

We all have a dark side that loves violence. We may deny it, but we know it's true. The kids are in the living room watching "Tom and Jerry" knock each other around; Dad's at the neighbor's house cheering wildly as his football team beats up on this week's opponent; even Mom has slipped away to the bedroom to indulge her secret passion for Clint Eastwood Westerns. When the family gets together, they go see *Star Wars* or the latest "rock-'em, sock-'em" adventures of Indiana Jones. On the way to the theater, they pass the scene of an automobile crack-up. Dad slows down. Mom says, "I hope nobody's hurt," and the kids in the back seat crane their necks hoping to get a view of some ghastly carnage. Regardless of our age, social status, or education, we can't get enough of it. From the raucous fans at a hockey game to the black-tie audience

In our sports and in our entertainment, we are a culture obsessed with the fact and the fiction of violence.

"UNPARALLELED TERROR ...THE MOST HORRIFYING MOTION PICTURE YOU'LL EVER SEE!"
—Rex Reed

THE TEXAS CHAINSAW MASSACRE

A film by TOBE HOOPER • Starring MARILYN BURNS and GUNNAR HANSEN as "Leatherface"
Produced and Directed by TOBE HOOPER
© MCMLXXX New Line Cinema Corp. From NEW LINE CINEMA

R RESTRICTED
UNDER 17 REQUIRES ACCOMPANYING PARENT OR ADULT GUARDIAN

We like to think that the human animal is gradually losing its taste for violence, but the murder and mayhem business is still booming. Movies like The Texas Chainsaw Massacre—*"the granddaddy of slasher movies"—have given us popular images of violence more gruesome than anything in our past.*

for a closed-circuit boxing match, our dark sides are obsessed with the fact and the fiction of violence.

To excuse the appetite for mayhem in all of us, we like to compare ourselves with earlier cultures known for their bloodthirsty pastimes. See how civilized we are. Unlike the ancient Romans, *we* don't actually kill people for sport. *We* don't feed people to lions, *we* just pretend to. Of course, if the Romans had had the special-effects technology we have today, they too might have been satisfied with illusions. Certainly, we have invented illusions that are far gorier and more gruesome than anything the Romans cooked up in the Colosseum. Movies like the hugely successful *Halloween* series or *Friday the 13th* (Parts I, II, III, and IV) are filled with beautiful young girls and handsome young boys being systematically stabbed, impaled, burned, beheaded, and chain-sawed. All in close-up color and often in slow motion. The Romans were amateurs by comparison.

Not that all our violence is now confined to television, movies, and sports. If we could honestly say that we had replaced all real violence with illusionary violence, we might be able to justify our obsession with it. But the Nazi concentration camps like the one at Auschwitz bear chilling witness to the contrary. Modern culture is, in fact, the most violent culture in history in the number of crimes and in their brutality. In this century alone, between 80 million and 100 million people have been killed violently. Russia's famous and well-named Ivan the Terrible, who killed his son and butchered the entire population of Novgorod, the second-largest city in his empire, doesn't hold a candle to our own century's Adolf Hitler, who killed thousands of people every day for four years within the barbed-wire fences of death camps like Auschwitz. Throughout Europe, 50 million died by gassing, torture, starvation, and burning.

This isn't ancient history. Unlike the misadventures of the ancient Assyrian king Ashurnasirpal II, who gleefully beheaded his enemies and took a quirky delight in blinding and mutilating captive officers, Auschwitz is not an old skeleton rattling in the closet of history. It's a fresh corpse lying on the front doorstep. At the same time that Jews and Poles and Gypsies and homosexuals were being gassed in the Auschwitz "showers" and reduced to ashes in the Auschwitz ovens, Humphrey Bogart was starring in *The Maltese Falcon,* and a new electronic fad, television, was just beginning to catch on. As recently as the 1970s, as many as 4 million Cambodians were exterminated by their fellow Cambodians. The dark side haunts our lives as well as our illusions.

Why is our appetite for violence so insatiable? In the face of unanimous moral outrage, centuries of slaughter, and a heavy diet of vicarious thrills, why are we still addicted to violence? Do we have a basic physical need for it, the way we need air and food and water? If so, have we inherited that need from our animal past; is it a part of our genetic code? Or is violence something that we learn to like as children, the way we learn to like some foods more than others? It's one of the great mysteries of human behavior, one that puzzled even that great pioneer of the human psyche, William Shakespeare. "Is there any cause in nature," he asked, "that makes these hard hearts?"

These aren't just abstract speculations: they're immediate, urgent questions about life and death and the fear that each of us faces daily. Violence is not an abstraction, and it's not just entertainment, it's real people getting bruised, battered, maimed, and killed every day. In one generation, homicides in the U.S.A. have tripled. Three percent of all murders are committed by parents who murder their children. Reported cases of rape and wife beating have skyrocketed. Every year between 2,000 and 4,000 women are beaten to death, 162,000 report being raped, 19,310 people are murdered, and 1,092,000 are robbed. Finally, we all live with the constant knowledge and barely suppressed terror that a single nuclear exchange could kill us all. In the time it takes to read this book, the whole noble human experiment could go up in smoke, leaving the earth to a few hardy insects perhaps. The hard truth is that our dark side, our love affair with violence, may yet do us all in.

But surely, not *all* of us are violent? What about Grandma, who won't go to any movie that isn't rated "G"? What about conscientious objectors, Martin Luther King, Jr., and Mother Teresa? Who's the aberration, the saint or the sinner? Are violent people psychotic exceptions in a fundamentally peaceful species, or are they just an unvarnished version of the violent animal in all of us? Are we all candidates for assuming command positions in a place like Auschwitz? Are we basically peace-

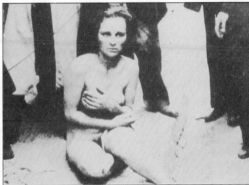

Under a sign reading "Work will make you free," millions of Jews died by gassing, torture, and starvation as did Poles, Gypsies, homosexuals, and political prisoners. We like to think that such atrocities are in our distant past. But camps like those at Dachau and Auschwitz are more recent inventions than television.

ful animals, trained by a violent society to become violent, or are we basically violent animals, prevented by a peaceful society from being ourselves?

What exactly *is* violence? By what strange biological process can a normal human being be levelheaded one minute and ready to kill the next? We all know the feeling, whether we express it with a harsh word, a clenched fist, or a long sulk. But where does it come from? There is, in fact, a chain of chemical reactions which produces anger—and often violence. It's called the arousal mechanism. When the brain is stimulated in the right way, it goes into a clearly defined physiological state called arousal. In that state, the body faces four choices: fight, flee, feed, or copulate.

Say, for example, you're watching television and a commercial comes on advertising pizza and suddenly you feel an emptiness in the pit of your stomach. Or an attractive person walks by you in the street and the smell of her perfume or his aftershave sets your mind to fantasizing. Or you're watching a horror movie and when the murderer jumps out of a shadow, you jump out of your seat. In each case, your reaction is so quick, so spontaneous, you may think it's automatic. But, in fact, a complicated chemical process has occurred in the split second between seeing the murderer and jumping out of your skin. Scientists can now trace much of that process in detail.

From your eyes, your ears, your nose, and your other senses your brain receives information about the world. When the murderer jumps out from behind the curtain, the image flashes along your optical nerve and into your neocortex, where it's broken down into electrochemical impulses and shot at speeds of 330 feet per second over to memory, where it's identified: "Aha, it's the murderer!" At that point, you *perceive* that the murderer has appeared, but you haven't reacted yet, you've just recognized him. But the image has also been identified as one that might possibly be arousing, so it's directed off to the *limbic system*—the seat of your emotions. In essence, one part of your brain is saying to another, "See what you make of this," although the two processes are essentially simultaneous.

In your limbic system, a region known as the hippocampus analyzes the incoming message by comparing it with previous "arousing" experiences stored in your memory. In essence, the hippocampus says, "Yes, this is definitely exciting. You should react." But *how* you should react is still undecided. From the hippocampus, the message is forwarded to the hypothalamus, a tiny bulb at the center of your brain. This is where the buck stops. The decision on how to feel is made in the hypothalamus—although such "decisions" shouldn't be confused with a conscious decision like what to have for dinner tonight.

The hypothalamus has two "consultants" in its decision making: the amygdala, a part of the brain that encourages arousal, and the septum, a part of the brain that discourages arousal. Like a judge, the hypothalamus weighs the conflicting arguments and then decides on a compromise: "This is pretty scary stuff and the appropriate response is to jump out of your chair!" This is the message that gets flashed down the spine to your muscles and your adrenal glands, located at the middle of your body. On command, these glands start pumping adrenaline into the bloodstream, and soon you feel very much "aroused": your muscles are tense, your heart is beating faster, your skin flushes, and your heart rushes extra supplies of oxygen-rich blood to selected muscles. It's been only a few seconds since you saw the murderer jump from the shadow or smelled the perfume or saw the pizza, but you're now fully aroused and ready for action: fighting, fleeing, feeding, or copulating.

But you don't necessarily act. You don't necessarily rush to the phone to order a pizza, or follow the attractive stranger, or flee the movie theater in terror. Arousal isn't action—it's just the state of preparedness, of physiological mobilization, that *enables* you to act. Once aroused, you can use the energy released by adrenaline to act aggressively in one of four very different ways: to fight, to run away from a threat instead of fighting, to obtain food, or to obtain sexual satisfaction. Why these four options? Because all four are important for the survival of the individual and the perpetuation of the genes.

"The classic experiment," says Dr. Melvin Konner, "is one in which the hypothalamus is stimulated. It was first thought that this was an area that would specifi-

In the twentieth century, the dark side has taken on a terrifying new dimension. We now live with the knowledge that a single nuclear exchange could reduce our beautiful blue planet to an insect-infested cinder.

cally make a rat eat, because early experiments showed that. Then it turned out that the stimulated rat eats because there's food around. But if you stimulate a mother rat when her pups are at hand, she'll collect the pups. If you stimulate a female in the right hormonal state when nesting material is available, she'll go and collect nesting material. What this part of the brain seems to be doing is making you say, 'I want' or 'I must do.' It's giving you that feeling of nervous energy, which takes on a direction according to what's around you at the time."

Have you ever wondered why you tend to eat more when you're sexually frustrated or after you've broken up with a girlfriend or boyfriend; or why some people need to be frightened in order to perform sexually? What happens is that the four arousal responses—fighting, fleeing, feeding, and copulating—get their wires crossed. So, instead of having sex when you're sexually stimulated, you reach for a candy bar. Someone who's a sexual masochist often responds to fear and the threat of punishment by being sexually aroused rather than fleeing. "One person might mistake anxiety or unfulfilled sexual desire for a desire for food," says Dr. Konner, "or might try to satisfy that desire with food and become very overweight. Another person might make the opposite miscalculation, and become promiscuous."

According to some scientists, this fallible, four-way arousal switch was built into us during the long years of fighting and fleeing other animals. It's one of those animal legacies that we just can't shake. "Every human being does inherit a basic capacity to become physically aroused when the environment presents the right stimuli," says Harvard professor E. O. Wilson. "Aggressive behavior is one outcome of arousal. Violent behavior observed arouses us. This is probably one reason that human beings find violence 'entertaining.' At a basic level, it excites us. Our organism becomes aroused, and we like that. And *no one* is immune to that."

Some scientists go further. It isn't just the arousal system that's inherited, they say, it's our whole disposition toward violence. So when we say that a criminal has acted "like an animal," we may be closer to the truth than if we tried to psychoanalyze him. One man who thinks our animal background accounts for a lot of our animalistic behavior is Dr. Paul MacLean, the man who defined the "triune brain." "If learning is such an overwhelming factor in human behavior," asks Dr. MacLean, "why is it that we so often do the same old things that animals do? Specifically with regard to aggression, human beings possess, attack, and defend territory just like other animals, and for the same reasons—access to vital resources necessary for life. We are animals, possessing animal brains; to say we are not influenced by 250 million years of evolution is pie-in-the-sky foolishness."

MacLean's theory—still highly controversial—is that we carry reptilian and mammalian aggression inside our brains just as we carry reptilian and mammalian brains inside our heads. Since 250 million years ago—long before the first mammals—reptiles have been fighting "border wars," disputes over territory. For many of them, defending territory from other animals is as important as killing for food because territory gives them access to food, as well as space to reproduce. To meet the need for aggressive behavior, many reptile species developed brains that were programmed from birth to mark off and defend a piece of turf. According to Mac-Lean, that preprogrammed part of the brain is still operating inside our heads somewhere, urging us on to aggressive and, perhaps, violent behavior.

Is human aggression really like two lizards fighting over a rock? Not exactly. In some ways, the lizards are a lot more civilized. A reptilian duel over territory is really more like a chivalrous joust from the days of Camelot and King Arthur. It's a test of strength rather than a to-the-death confrontation. Each combatant takes a turn testing the other's strength. After a few passes, the loser graciously signals his surrender by rolling over and urinating, and the victor magnanimously permits him to retire—defeated but unharmed. When two rattlesnakes duel, they wrestle with their necks intertwined to *avoid* sticking each other with their venom-tipped fangs. In vivid contrast to human violence, reptilian violence is seldom fatal. It's too bad we don't act *more* like lizards.

About 180 million years ago, a few reptiles broke away and developed into a new kind of animal, mammals. As their brains enlarged and became more complex, they depended more on learning and less on inherited behavior. A newborn mammal knows only a fraction of what it will know as an adult. A baby reptile, on the other hand, is born knowing almost everything it will ever know. Unfortunately, the ignorance of the young mammal made it more vulnerable to predators. In response to that vulnerability, a new form of aggression developed: fighting to defend the young.

According to Dr. Eibl-Eibesfeldt, long childhoods and an infant's need for protection led to the concept of "family," and the concept of family led inevitably to the concept of "stranger." The more advanced mammals, especially monkeys and apes, began to develop one form of aggression for relatives and another very different form for strangers. Among relatives, primates often ritualize their aggression. So fights over mates, food, or social status become elaborate dances filled with gestures, glances, screams, and threatening postures but little real violence. The scene is not unlike the scene in an American family when Junior asks for the keys to the car. Dad takes it as a threat to his control of the family, so he berates Junior for not taking out the garbage. Junior thinks he's too old to be humiliated by his father, so he provokes a fierce argument. Voices are raised. Dad pounds the table. Junior pounds the table. Finally, Dad proves he's still the boss by grounding Junior, and Junior, in an act of submission, goes to his room and sulks. As in primate families, the battle is usually decided without drawing blood. But when it comes to strangers, says Eibl-Eibesfeldt, primates have developed a very different form of aggression.

For a long time biologists had thought that primates were essentially peaceful animals, that they fought only for food and even then their aggression was nonlethal. Then, in 1974, at her research site in Gombe, Tanzania, primatologist Jane Goodall made a startling discovery. One day, for no apparent reason, a small group of chimpanzees separated from the main community and moved to a different part of the jungle. Not long afterward, as Goodall watched, a group of five chimpanzees from the splinter group "mugged" a lone male from the main community. They pummeled him, kicked him, and bit him for twenty minutes, then left him bleeding on the ground. Soon afterward, he disappeared. Within a month, another male from the original community was beaten up by the "thugs" from the rebel group and then disappeared. The attacks continued for three years until, by 1977, the main community, had been virtually wiped out—along with the myth of the peace-loving chimp.

Goodall soon made an even more shocking discovery about the lovable and all-too-humanlike chimpanzee. In the primate equivalent of a bizarre mass murder, Goodall found one of the female chimps, appropriately named Passion, and her daughter Pom systematically killing infant chimps and, often in full view of the distraught mothers, eating their bodies. Passion and her other offspring, whom she allowed to join her in these grisly feasts, "behaved as if the baby were normal prey," says Dr. Goodall. "They were quite calm. There was begging and sharing of the meat. They fed until they couldn't eat any more, then abandoned the remains." Three years after the first cannibalistic "crime," Pom herself had a baby, which she hid from her mother, Passion, for two weeks. "I think she was afraid," says Goodall, that "her mother would eat her baby." Between 1974, when Passion killed the first baby, and 1976, only one new infant survived Passion's terrible hunger.

News of the civil war at Gombe and Passion's crime rocked the scientific world. One of the truisms of animal behavior had always been that man was the only animal that killed his own kind. Confirmed by similar studies of baboons in East Africa by Joan Luft and Jeanne Altmann, Goodall's research forced scientists to rethink that dubious distinction. Intraspecific violence in other animals had never been witnessed not because it didn't exist but because no one had bothered to look long and hard enough. Suddenly, the human animal didn't look quite so bad. "One of the things we've discovered as biologists as we've undertaken long-range studies of mammals," says Harvard professor Irven DeVore, "is that they aren't better than we are. They're not organized to commit murder on a large scale, but they actually commit it more often than we do. In fact, compared to other mammals, we don't

Dr. Ashley Montagu: "Human violence . . . cannot be explained by reference to the behavior of animals."

OPPOSITE: Despite his fierce grimace, this lowland gorilla is basically peaceful. Other primates, like chimpanzees, however, have shown an all-too-human capacity for killing one another for no apparent reason.

come off so badly as a species."

But there are limits to what we can learn from other animals—even close relatives —about human violence. Ultimately, our decisions for violence, like our decisions for beauty or love or knowledge, are made by those parts of our brain that are uniquely human. "Studies of reptiles and other mammals are for them, not for humans," says Dr. Ashley Montagu. "Human violence, or any other human behavior for that matter, cannot be explained by reference to the behavior of animals. We are flexible, versatile, and created more by learning than by any evolutionary legacy."

Even if the brain of a lizard is still up there sending out signals to "fight or flee," even if a rush of testosterone is lighting fires telling us to defend our territory, compete for mates, or defend our young, the human side of us—the great big walnut —is still usually in charge. Except for your automatic activities (like heartbeat and breathing) and your reflex actions (like blinking when something is thrown at you), every signal your brain passes to your body goes through the neocortex, the uniquely human part of the brain, home of the "highest" intellectual functions. The brain may be divided, but it's no democracy. Control is from the top down, not the bottom up. In matters of behavior, including violence, the neocortex has the final say.

But if our animal past isn't at the root of our violent tendencies, what is? If the Mr. Hyde side of our personality isn't a distant evolutionary relative who's over-stayed his welcome, who is he and where did he come from? If we can answer those questions, maybe we can figure out how to control him. We don't want to get rid of him altogether—we'll always need him on standby in an unpredictable world. But we do want to make sure that he doesn't take charge of our lives and our destiny.

Most scientists attribute the violent streak in the human character to a combina-tion of biology and sociology. The best-known sociobiologist, Harvard professor E. O. Wilson, says, "unquestionably human aggression is the product of an interaction between genes and environment (culture). Like everything else human, it's *both* nature *and* nurture." Wilson's position is widely respected, but not shared by every-one in the scientific community. Dr. Ashley Montagu, for example, minimizes the role of evolution and genes in determining violent behavior in humans.

According to Montagu, "Human beings 'like' and are entertained by violence if their upbringing and the general values and attitudes of their particular culture teach them to value it. Human behavior is remarkably flexible and plastic, more so than that of any other animal. Whatever genes contribute to human behavior is far overshadowed by the postnatal influence of a particular culture. Our own cultural legacy is a violent one, and so we tend to encourage violent behavior and 'enjoy' it. There are other cultures which deplore and discourage violence, and their people don't find violence 'enjoyable' at all."

To prove their point that humans are not "born to be wild," scientists like Mon-tagu point to two tribes, the !Kung of southern Africa and the Yanomamo Indians of South America. The !Kung are a peaceful people who discourage aggressive behavior in their children and try to resolve disputes without resorting to violence. Anthropologists have called them "the harmless people," whose lives were free of war or violence. The Yanomamo, in contrast, are called "the fierce people." They bring up their children to believe that a man isn't a man unless he can fight, cheat, bully, and kill. And the Yanomamo teach their sons that the skill of killing another man is as vital to their survival as the skills of the hunt.

The !Kung and the Yanomamo have long been considered the Dr. Jekyll and Mr. Hyde of primitive societies. Scientists have used the !Kung to illustrate that societies free of violence and war could exist in the "primitive paradise" of the nomadic Stone Age. If the !Kung could *choose* a peaceful way of life, so could we. There was nothing innately violent about the human animal. Lately, however, there's been some trouble in paradise. According to Irven DeVore, we now know that the !Kung, despite their peace-loving ideals, have serious problems with homicide and other forms of personal violence. They would even fight wars if they had sufficient manpower, resources, and reasons to do so. According to the new view, the !Kung were pacified during a period of colonial rule before anthropologists arrived and began

The Yanomamo, or "fierce people," of South America bring up their children to believe that violence is an acceptable—even desirable—form of behavior. Most scientists now believe that the notion of nonviolent primitive societies is just a romantic myth.

Dr. Roderic Gorney, professor of psychiatry at U.C.L.A. On the average, American children watch 26 hours of television every week, much of it violent. This massive exposure to violence inevitably dulls their sensitivities and shapes their behavior.

OPPOSITE: According to experts, massive exposure to violence in the popular media plays a major role in shaping young people's violent behavior. Although media spokesmen continue to deny the connection publicly, savvy editors know how to boost circulation by appealing to their readers' fascination with violence.

their studies. Originally, the !Kung were probably more like the fierce Yanomamo, one of the few cultures that have been studied in a relatively pristine state.

Most scientists now believe that the notion of nonviolent primitive societies is as much a myth as Shangri-La or El Dorado. Every culture, from lost tribes to superpowers, has been forced to wrestle with the same problem that plagues us today: the human animal's tendency to transform aggressive feelings into violent behavior. But that's not to say that the situation is hopeless. There's still an important difference between the !Kung and the Yanomamo: one chooses to discourage whatever tendency toward aggression the human animal may have; the other chooses to promote it. Choice is still the crucial ingredient in human behavior. Aggression and conflict may be an inevitable part of the human condition, but the cultural values and ideals a society chooses *do* make a difference. "Culture clearly plays a crucial role," says Dr. Irenaus Eibl-Eibesfeldt, "in either discouraging human aggressiveness or promoting it into violence."

And what cultural values and ideals does *our* society choose? What do we teach our young? Unfortunately, *we*, meaning parents and other adult figures, don't teach them much at all. Most of what they learn comes from somewhere else entirely: TV. According to recent studies, the average American child watches 26 hours of television every week. In a year, that's 1,352 hours. Kids are like everybody else: one picture is worth a thousand words. In that 1,352 hours, they will see thousands of murders, robberies, and beatings. By the time they reach twelve, they will have sat in front of that cathode-ray tube for an average of 14,872 hours apiece—half as much time as they spend sleeping and far more than they spend in school.

According to psychiatrist Dr. Roderic Gorney of U.C.L.A., it's this massive exposure to violence in the popular media that determines primarily the shape of young

people's violent behavior. The television networks, of course, with more than a touch of self-interest, disagree. On one hand, they argue to advertisers that one minute of air time will induce little Johnny to go out and buy a G.I. Joe, but thousands of hours of violence won't induce him to go out and kick a playmate. Common sense has always told parents that watching violence can warp a young mind, but now there's an increasing amount of scientific evidence to prove it.

The most complete study ever done of the effects of violence on television was paid for by none other than CBS in the wake of Congressional investigations into the impact of televised violence. It was conducted by William Belson at the Survey Centre of the London School of Economics, and it involved 1,565 boys aged twelve to seventeen. Belson's report concluded that "long-term exposure to violence increases the degree to which boys engage in violence of a serious kind" as well as "swearing and the use of bad language, aggressiveness in sport or play, threatening to use violence on another boy, writing slogans on walls, [and] breaking windows."

The study also found that violent behavior isn't promoted by just any televised violence, but only by certain *kinds* of violence. The worst kind of violence for children to watch—the kind that's most likely to motivate them to go out and be violent themselves—is violence that's realistically portrayed; takes place not between strangers, but between people who have close personal relationships; is committed by the "good guys," not by the "bad guys"; or is "just thrown in for its own sake." According to the study unrealistic violence—the fantasy violence in movies like *Star Wars* or the slapstick violence in comedies—has less effect. Among sports, boxing and wrestling encourage violence among kids more than football, baseball, or most other popular TV sports.

For a long time, people thought that most of the violence in our country, like most of the crime, was simply a by-product of poverty. But scientists have recently begun to rethink that assumption. According to Jerome Kagan, a professor of developmental psychology at Harvard, it isn't poverty *per se* that turns people violent, it's the feelings of failure, frustration, and, inevitably, anger that poverty produces. "Aggressive behavior, delinquency, vandalism are communications," says Kagan. "They're messages. The perpetrators are trying to say something. And what do you think they're trying to say? They're saying, 'I'm angry.' Now, who commits these acts? Typically, they're committed by people who come from economically disadvantaged families, and who have failed in school. Those are two very good reasons to be angry. Very good reasons in a society where there is a larger class difference than we should have. If you feel that you are at the butt end of two very serious frustrations, and you don't have enough money or status, your home has peeling paint, and you can't make it in school, you have every right to be angry."

In other words, poverty of money is only one of many ways to be impoverished. There's also poverty of self-respect, poverty of fulfillment, poverty of hope. In our success-oriented, materialistic, and class-polarized society, the three often go together. It's hard to have self-respect when you're on welfare, and it's hard to have hope when you can't find a job. But it's the combination of poverties, not simply being poor, that leads to anger, and it's the anger that leads to violence.

We've already seen that there's plenty of violence in America—on television, in the movies, on the playing fields, in the streets. But there's another kind of violence that's far more common and far more destructive: child abuse. This is the violence that breeds violence. From run-down tenements to exclusive suburbs, this is our society's dark side. Scientists say it's wrongheaded to look for *one* cause of crime and violence, but child abuse is at the top of most lists. According to psychiatric reports, *90 percent* of all the inmates in American prisons were abused as children. In 1983 there were nearly 1 million *reported* cases of child abuse in this country. That was a 12-percent increase over the official figure for 1981—and, most experts

Violence breeds violence. A staggering 90 percent of all the inmates in American prisons were abused as children.

agree, only 10 to 25 percent of the actual number of abused children.

What's the effect of this epidemic of child beating? "We now believe that violence toward children, including cruelty, neglect, and other stresses related to a defective family," says Dr. Louis West, a psychiatrist at U.C.L.A. and a member of the president's commission on violence, "has a direct correlation with violent behavior by those same children when they grow up. And this correlation may well constitute a vicious spiral of increasing violence in America that feeds back into and contributes to our skyrocketing rate of violent crime since 1960." The testimony of experts like Dr. West should make us take a good, hard look at ourselves. The truth is not that poverty breeds violence or even that anger breeds violence. *Violence* breeds violence.

Most parents think of child abuse as something strange and distant, something they would never think of doing. But just as there are many kinds of poverty, there are many kinds of abuse. You don't have to hit a child to hurt it. Very few of us set out to be bad parents. Most often, if we hurt our children, we do it inadvertently or because "it's for the child's own good." There are some parents who think that children are essentially evil-spirited little monsters who need to be controlled at all times or they'll burn the house down. Their motto is, inevitably: Spare the rod and spoil the child. These are always the parents who feel the need to express their love in a variety of aggressive behaviors—spanking, scolding, punishing, etcetera. They're always saying to the child, "This will hurt me more than it does you." But, in fact, it never does.

Will sparing the rod *really* spoil the child, or is spanking just another form of child abuse that may encourage the child to resort to violence in his or her own life?

According to Ashley Montagu, a child who grows up with more hard spankings than soft words will behave toward the world in the same harsh way. "If you have been spanked as a child, you'll be a child spanker," says Montagu. "If your mother has been beaten by your father, you'll probably become a wife beater. We know this for a fact. These are not theories. More than eighty percent of the people who beat their children or beat their wives underwent this learning experience."

We're all familiar with the parent who spanks a kid not because the kid has done something particularly wrong, but because the parent has had a hard day at the office, a personal setback, an unpleasant phone call, or just a headache. Is that kind of abuse harder for a child to take?

According to Alice Miller, an expert on child raising, parents "*always* mistreat their children for psychological reasons," even though they *think* they're doing it because the child has done something wrong. Children, on the other hand, *want* to believe that their parents are perfect. They'd rather accept their own undeserved guilt than accept the idea that a parent might have punished them without a good reason. Usually, neither parent nor child is aware of the real reasons for punishment. Nor can a child understand it when a parent is just venting his or her anger

*Family violence is the most common vio-
lence in America. Statistics show that just
as spankers raise spankers, wife beaters
raise wife beaters. More than 80 percent of
the people who beat their wives or children
come from homes where such beatings were
common.* Battered wife.

and frustration at the world. Miller says that children's "tolerance for their parents
knows no bounds. The love a child has for his or her parents ensures that their
conscious or unconscious acts of mental cruelty will go undetected."

What about the loving parent who spanks the kids occasionally but makes it clear
that there's no anger or malice? Is a spanking less harmful if it's delivered in the
context of a loving relationship?

A parent who tells a child that the punishment is "for the child's own good," says
Miller, and who follows up the punishment with caring gestures and remarks is often
the most damaging. "If there is absolutely no possibility of reacting appropriately to
hurt, humiliation, and coercion, then these experiences cannot be integrated into
the personality; the feelings they evoke are repressed, and the need to articulate
them remains unsatisfied, without any hope of being fulfilled. It is this lack of hope
of ever being able to express repressed traumata by means of relevant feelings that
most often causes severe psychological problems."

Does that mean a loving parent can *never* resort to physical punishment? Is Junior
going to be scarred for life if Mom tweaks his ear for saying a bad word in front of
Grandma?

"One thing that we've learned from our basic research is that punishment is
painful," says University of Delaware professor Carroll Izard definitively; "that pain
elicits anger, and that this anger won't just dissipate. It won't just go away. The
child has to learn to do something with that anger. It may have to postpone action
in relation to the anger for a long time. But eventually it may come back to haunt
the parent who propagated the punishment."

So what is a parent to do? Does all this mean you should never spank your kids? You don't want them to grow up stealing hubcaps; but you also don't want them to grow up undisciplined. Is there any way to punish a child without leaving emotional scars? Are children so sensitive to physical punishment that the slightest slap on the wrist constitutes traumatic "abuse" and will ensure that the child grows up either delinquent or hopelessly neurotic? Is it possible to discipline a child physically without suffering from terminal guilt yourself if you do?

Not all behavioral experts agree with Miller that punishment, even if administered in the context of a loving relationship, is inevitably destructive. Harvard's Jerome Kagan, for example, thinks children are capable of accepting punishment without developing propensities toward violence as adults. He believes that, except in extreme cases of abuse, parental behavior is not as important as how the child interprets that behavior. "If the child interprets the physical punishment as unfair," rather than as a reflection of the "parent's desire to help him become a productive adult," says Kagan, "then you get delinquency, crime, drugs, and so on."

In fact, Kagan thinks that many scientists exaggerate the role of parents in causing violent behavior in their children. Although he's foursquare against parental beatings and sexual abuse, he has a lot of confidence in the ability of the human animal to survive a traumatic childhood and become a responsible member of society. The typical response of parents who discover their children engaging in some antisocial behavior is guilt. They wonder, "What did I do wrong?" According to Kagan, the answer is probably nothing. He thinks it's simplistic to assume, every time a youngster snatches a purse from an old lady, that his mother didn't love him enough.

What kind of sense can parents make of these mixed signals from the experts? Listening to advice on disciplining children is, like parenting itself, akin to walking on a waterbed—you're never quite sure of the next step. But this much seems firm: although it's hard to imagine when that little wiggling bundle comes home from the hospital that the day will come when you want to strike it, for most parents that day *does* come, and when it does most parents are woefully unprepared for it. All too often, they respond by doing what seems to come naturally—they lash out. "In the home, in church, and in school," says psychologist Dr. John E. Valusek, "we are taught the appropriateness of hitting as a means of problem solving. They don't call it hitting, of course. They call it spanking and disciplining. But essentially, it's hitting. And almost all forms of interpersonal violence—rape, murder, assault, child abuse, stabbing, shooting—involve some form of hitting." So when parents hit a child—even on the bottom—they are teaching it that hitting is an acceptable way to solve a problem, to demonstrate a grievance, or to express a frustration.

Some experts argue that parents and grandparents tend to exaggerate their role in determining whether a child grows up to be a responsible member of society.

Spanking opens a Pandora's box. If we permit spanking, we sanction hitting, and if we sanction hitting, where *do* we draw the line? When that unexpected but irresistible urge to strike out at a child finally comes, instead of "spare the rod, spoil the child," parents should be thinking that every time they use the rod, they're making it more likely that their child will grow up a "hitter." Almost inevitably, there will be times when the level of anger and frustration passes the breaking point. Even parents are only human. But the closer we come to eliminating those moments of weakness, the safer our children will be, the safer our streets will be, and the safer our world will be.

Sometimes, looking at the violence around us and the history of carnage in our historical closet, it's hard not to agree with those anthropologists, like Konrad Lorenz, who believe that aggression is at the core of the human personality, or like Lionel Tiger, who argues that our basic instinct is, in fact, warlike. Yet we shouldn't be led astray by a frank acknowledgment of our faults. For every violent person, every person who takes the life of another, there are thousands of profoundly peaceful people. There's the man who will run out of the crowd and pull a stranger out of a river, or the woman who will rush into a burning building to save a sleeping child.

As we've seen, for every scientist who says that aggression is inevitable, that it's built into the human biology, there's another scientist who says, "Hogwash—we aren't born aggressive any more than we're born talking." But whether the dark side comes into the world with us or ambushes us after we arrive, we're better equipped to deal with it than any other animal. We can choose how to respond. We can succumb to it, fight it, or compromise with it. The fact that we have a choice is both a saving grace and a terrible burden. Without a choice, we would never feel guilt.

If you're sorry you barked at your child, guilty about not writing your parents more often, or ashamed of having said something hurtful, take heart. Such feelings are far more common than crimes, and each one is a reaffirmation that we're making moral judgments. Even if we find ourselves falling short, at least we're asking ourselves the right questions. "Is it right or wrong?" That question—even if we choose to do wrong—is at least an indication that a human mind is at work, trying to mediate between instinct and behavior, trying to do what is right. Not to ask the question, to deny that guilt and remorse are important is to deny that we're human— and that, of course, is the ultimate surrender to the dark side.

Sensitive and loving parents can act as a buffer to help a child absorb the adversities of life and tame the dark side.

10. Anatomy of a Male

The sex organs actually secrete into the blood material that makes a boy manly, strong, and noble.

Boy Scout Handbook, 1911

When you're alone on a street at night and you see a woman, two women, or even a man and a woman, you breathe easier than if you see a man or a group of men. Why? Of the violent crimes reported every year in the United States—murder, rape, robbery, aggravated assault, manslaughter, and burglary—a staggering 89 percent are committed by men. Petty crimes tell the same story. If your hubcaps are stolen, your car broken into, or your house vandalized, you can almost be certain that a man, or a boy, was responsible. Why is crime essentially a male phenomenon? Is the male animal such a monster that if he could be somehow miraculously eliminated, the world would be a happier, more peaceful, and safer place? To answer those questions, we have to

Total U.S. Arrests, Distributed by Sex, 1983.

	TOTAL	MALE	FEMALE
Murder and nonnegligent manslaughter	18,064	15,653	2,411
Forcible rape	30,183	29,883	300
Robbery	134,018	124,159	9,859
Aggravated assault	261,421	226,088	35,333
Burglary	415,651	387,504	28,147
Larceny—theft	1,169,066	823,817	345,249
Motor-vehicle theft	105,514	96,108	9,406
Arson	17,203	15,099	2,104
Violent crime	443,686	395,783	47,903
Property crime	1,707,434	1,322,528	384,906

Some scientists argue that the male's body and brain developed in response to the demands of the hunt. !Kung hunter in search of prized meat.

OPPOSITE: "The young male has a biologically given need to prove himself as a physical individual," wrote Margaret Mead. "[I]n the past the hunt and warfare have provided the most common means of such validation." One of many Vietnam battlefields.

look inside a man's brain and try to understand what connections could make him commit a crime. Take rape, for example. As we've seen, humans are aroused when the senses send an image to the neocortex, which in turn alerts the limbic system that the image is arousing. The hippocampus compares the woman's image with all the stored images of women and decides that this woman is sexually attractive. If she is, the hippocampus signals the hypothalamus, the brain's clearinghouse for messages to the rest of the body. So far, there's nothing unusual. The same reactions would be set off in the brain of a woman if an attractive man had walked in.

The hypothalamus is where the initial reaction to the stimulation begins to form. Of the four possible responses—fighting, fleeing, feeding, and copulating—which one the man chooses will be determined by striking a compromise between the aggressive input of the amygdala and the passive input of the septum. This is the crucial split second that precedes every violent act. If, in that instant, the brain is bathed in testosterone, the decision-making process can be short-circuited—with disastrous results. The presence of enough testosterone throws the hypothalamus into high gear and causes the aggressive amygdala to fire like crazy. The effect is to muzzle the pacifying signals of the septum and "persuade" the hypothalamus to choose "fight" over "flight."

The fact that testosterone—the so-called "male" hormone—can short-circuit the normal arousal mechanism may be the chemical key to male aggression. "Testosterone appears to be one of the more important biological components of human vio-

lence," says Dr. Arnold Scheibel, neurologist at the University of California at Los Angeles. "Testosterone is produced by both sexes, but in greater amounts by one sex whose stronger anatomy and more aggressive behavior it influences—the male."

The chemistry of aggression, says Ashley Montagu, starts with the fact that women have two X chromosomes, men only one. "The male secretes a higher quantity of androgens, which are associated with the kind of hyperactivity" that men are known for. Although a flood of testosterone doesn't guarantee aggression, says Montagu, it does provide that rush of energy that "can be used for aggressive purposes." Most mothers notice this "hyperactivity," this excess of energy, early in a boy's life. "I can't keep up with him," "He gets into everything," "He won't stay still" are all just early symptoms of a masculine impatience and restlessness that can develop into more dangerous behaviors later in life.

Hyperactivity among males is hardly an American phenomenon. Even Margaret Mead, who spent much of her career trying to break down sexual stereotypes, believed that in *most* cultures men are the more aggressive sex. In *Male and Female*, she argued that "the young male has a biologically given need to prove himself as a physical individual . . . in the past the hunt and warfare have provided the most common means of such validation."

We can test Mead's observation by looking at one of the few societies that, until recently, relied on hunting just as our own ancestors did for tens of thousands of years—the !Kung. As late as the 1960s, !Kung men ranged through the savanna

LEFT AND BOTTOM: Even if aggression is in men's genes, that doesn't mean that violence is there too. Violence is a mode of behavior deeply influenced by our culture. We teach it and we learn it every day.

hunting wild animals while !Kung women gathered plants. Although women brought in most of the food, men did the "heavy" work of providing the tribe with meat—a scarce but essential part of their diet. (The !Kung and other hunter societies have two meanings for "hungry": "No food" and "Food but no meat.") Watching !Kung hunters go after a giraffe, it's easy to see why, over the course of evolution, at least one sex ended up with an extra boost of testosterone.

Evolutionists argue that the male's body as well as his mind developed in response to the demands of the hunt. For hurling spears or shooting arrows, he needed strong arms and shoulders. For stamina, he needed bigger lungs. For the chase, he needed strong legs. For the kill, he needed to tame his own fear. The short circuit provided by testosterone meant that at the crucial moment, he wouldn't hesitate from fear or run away and lose the precious protein. Hunting for meat was the job males did, the job evolution had shaped them for. They had no choice. The survival of their children depended on it. In a famous film, a group of !Kung hunters kill a giraffe with poison-tipped arrows after a grueling two-week chase. The tribe has been without meat for so long that the women can no longer nurse their infants. For the !Kung, at least, and probably for our own ancestors, male anatomy and male aggression were matters of survival.

According to Dr. Melvin Konner, hunting wasn't the only reason men developed into physical "hunks" and emotional firecrackers. Konner believes that competition for females may have preceded competition for game. "Other animal species—

OPPOSITE: Boys may engage in more rough-and-tumble play as a result of testosterone, but malice and meanness come from outside, not inside.

chimpanzees, for instance—have had males that are stronger and bigger than fe-males because they're competing with each other over females," says Konner. "When hunting came along, that only reinforced the differences in physique."

Whatever its evolutionary origin, most scientists think that some form of aggres-sion is built into the male system. Konrad Lorenz, author of *On Aggression*, for example, believes that every individual has a certain "fund of aggression" that must be expressed. Is that "fund" responsible for the thousands of crimes men commit? Are the male criminals who fill our jails just the slaves of a million years of hunting, the victims of a built-in short circuit in the male brain that they can't control? Are we doomed to high crime rates, wife beating, and rape as long as men are around?

Hardly. Even if aggressiveness is in men's genes—and there are many scientists who wouldn't agree that it is—violence is not. If men are more violent, it's not because they're overcharged with testosterone or overbuilt with muscles, it's be-cause they're *trained* to be more violent. Violence is deeply influenced by learned culture, the widely varying product of the human brain. The fact is, the human animal is violent or peaceful not because it inherits this as a character trait from the animal past, but because it *learns* to be violent or peaceful.

"Boys engage in more rough-and-tumble play than girls," says Jerome Kagan; "that's biological. But they do not necessarily intend to hurt. They're not malicious. A boy greets another by hitting him on the arm. We call that aggressive, but it's not aggressive in my book because there was not a malicious intent to hurt. The rough-and-tumble play is biological. But the hostile, malicious intention—the meanness—I don't think boys inherit more of that than girls."

Then where does the "hostility, malice, and meanness" that we see so often in men come from? Anthropologist Lionel Tiger argues that male aggression, in all its forms, is a direct response to the dynamics of men interacting with other men—an idea that won't surprise anyone who's been to a fraternity party. In his famous book on male bonding, *Men in Groups*, Tiger argues that when men get together with men they'll feel aggressive as surely as men and women together will feel sexual. A group of men will be drawn into aggressive interaction as inexorably as a mixed group will be drawn into sexual interaction.

"Men in continuous association aggress against the environment in much the same way that men and women in continuous association have sexual relations," says Tiger. "Put a healthy male and female or even several of each into a relatively isolated place and if they are members of a culture that sanctions or but mildly inhibits pre- or extramarital intercourse, there will be sexual congress. Similarly, put a group of males together and, once some dominance order is established, the group will either split into competing coalition units or seek some exterior object for collective 'masterful' action."

Have you ever wondered why, when Dad gets together with his buddies, they're more likely to be rowdy, but if the wives come along, the same men are more sedate?

WANT *ACTION?*

Join
U·S·Marine Corps!

APPLY TO NEAREST RECRUITING STATION

Want Action? Join U.S. Marine Corps! 1942. Collection Library of Congress.

According to anthropologist Lionel Tiger, wherever you find males together, you'll find "action." He suggests that women are excluded from the battlefield not because they can't fight, but because their absence permits males to fight without the inhibition they might experience were women to complain about the danger. Recruiting posters from World War II (left) and World War I (bottom).

GEE !!
I WISH I WERE
A MAN

I'd JOIN
The NAVY

BE A MAN AND DO IT
UNITED STATES NAVY
RECRUITING STATION

In the film version of William Golding's novel Lord of the Flies, *British schoolboys are marooned on a desert island during World War II. They quickly regress to a primitive state, hunting and killing one another until the last is "saved" by a passing warship that is on a hunt-and-kill mission of its own.*

Gang violence is the most prevalent and frightening form of urban violence, as well as a textbook example of what can happen to the male animal in groups. We should hardly be surprised. Gangs offer young males camaraderie, dignity, territory, group loyalty, even uniforms. What does our society offer them?

Or why coed college dorms suffer far less vandalism than all-male dorms? What pleasure do men get out of going to the Lodge or the Club or the Thursday-night poker game? For Tiger, aggression can show its head in the simple desire—common among men in groups—to dominate the people around you. The very purpose of fraternal organizations like the Elks and the Moose is the creation of a hierarchy. That's why there's such an emphasis on titles and rituals. Electing a man "Grand Pooh-Bah" or "Imperial Wizard" is a way of formally acknowledging his dominance. The same rules apply in college fraternities, where secret handshakes, initiation rites, pledging, hazing, and the rest are all part of an elaborate system of domination and submission.

To demonstrate just how low men in groups can sink, Tiger cites the 1954 novel of Nobel Prize winner William Golding, *Lord of the Flies*, in which a group of British schoolboys are shipwrecked on a desert island during World War II. Without adult supervision, the boys quickly revert to the primitive state. They form rival gangs and try—with some success—to kill each other. In the end, they're saved only at the last minute by the arrival of a British officer from a passing warship. According to Golding's allegory, man's basic instincts, if unchecked, would inevitably lead to murder and mayhem—much like what we see on some of our city streets. Is the officer who comes to the rescue at the end really any different from the schoolboys who are trying to butcher one another with homemade spears and knives? The only differences are that his brand of bloodletting is more mechanized and far more deadly; and instead of being left alone on an island, he and his fellow adults were left alone on a planet.

Tiger would also point out that if the boys had been stranded in a group with girls, they would probably not have turned murderous. It was the company of fellow aggressive males that led quickly to disaster. "Females tend to be excluded from aggressive organizations," Tiger says, "such as armies, where violence may occur, or even from the management of religious, commercial, or administrative groups in which aggressive mastery of various environments is the condition of persistence and growth. With only half whimsy, I suggest that one reason for the removal of women and children from the battlefield is that, as well as protecting them, the absence of women and children permits males to fight without the inhibition they might experience were children to cry and wander about, were women to complain about the danger to children, themselves, and their men." In support of Tiger's theory and Golding's book, the director of the film, Peter Brook, reported that his actors acted just like the characters they played. "My experience showed me," Brook said later, "that the only falsification in Golding's fable is the length of time the descent to savagery takes. I believe that if the cork of continued adult presence were removed from the bottle, the complete catastrophe could occur within a long weekend."

Maybe so. There are plenty of parents who are afraid to leave their sons alone in the house for a long weekend, fearing the catastrophe that might result. But Tiger's theory leaves unanswered the central question: is the aggressive behavior of males —alone or in groups—an immutable part of being male, or is it learned and therefore changeable?

It certainly isn't true that *whenever* men get together in groups, the result is brutality and wanton murder as in *Lord of the Flies*. Although the results are sometimes ugly and destructive—a bunch of high school toughs breaking into a schoolyard brawl or a group of fraternity "boys" gang-raping a young coed—they can also be harmless, even noble. Studies conducted during World War II showed that men usually fought most bravely—and often sacrificed their lives—not for ideological reasons but to protect their unit, the small group of "buddies" they were attached to.

Neither sex has cornered the market on humanity. The three most prominent female world leaders in recent years—Golda Meir, Indira Gandhi, and Margaret Thatcher—have all taken their nations to war. But there's no denying that we are a society, created largely by males, that teaches aggressiveness and sets it up as one of the key differences between men and women. We extol in men the virtue of violence and proclaim the inevitability of war. Ultimately, crimes like murder and rape start not in our chemistry, our evolution, or our groups, but in our definition of manhood. No boy is born with an evil thought in his head or a hacksaw in his hand. Hooligans aren't born, they're *made*—and we make them.

"Every human being," says Ashley Montagu, "comes into this world loving and trustful and devoid of violent aggression. A violent society like ours creates violent people by warping its children with lessons in violence. Children in societies have their love and trust crippled or destroyed by the institutionalized, approved role models for males that teach them to be aggressive, competitive, and violent by 'tough-minded' parents—parents that teach them to be warriors, fighters, 'winners' at all costs, and to despise those that trust or cooperate or show love.

"And then these crippled children that we raise grow up, and some of them become people of power and influence, who start wars to show the world no one's going to push them around, and others become the hoodlums who will beat up an old woman to steal her purse. And between the powerful leader and the petty criminal there is no essential difference. They are both products of the same social ethic, one that demands aggressive males."

We can see that social ethic at work all around us, turning babies into delinquent boys and boys into violence-prone men. Why do you suppose so-called "slasher" movies are the biggest box-office attractions in our culture, especially among adolescent boys? What are boxing matches, hockey slugfests, even baseball free-for-alls, but "lessons in violence" aimed directly at males—young and old alike—who are looking, consciously or unconsciously, for a way to release that pent-up, testosterone-induced "rough-and-tumble" aggression?

Extra testosterone may make men extra testy, but neither sex has cornered the market on aggression. The three most prominent female world leaders in recent years—Golda Meir, Indira Gandhi, and Margaret Thatcher—have all taken their nations to war.

"A violent society like ours," says Ashley Montagu, "creates violent people by warping its children with lessons in violence."

OPPOSITE: All around us, every day, our shoot-'em-up culture is turning babies into delinquent boys and boys into violence-loving men. Young guerrilla fighter in El Salvador.

"When Americans wring their hands about violence in their streets and the threat of nuclear war," says Montagu, "they should also think hard about the role models they accept for their male children—from *Star Wars* to John Wayne all the way back to the 'noble' knights of the Middle Ages. Our society sends a very clear message to its children to be tough, to be fighters, to be killers, and then throws up its hands in horror when they simply do what they're taught."

According to Dorothy Dinnerstein, a psychologist at Rutgers University, the process of transforming boys into hooligans begins even before they're exposed to *macho* models in movies and on television. She blames the typical family structure that leaves women holding the baby and men refusing to lend more than an occasional helping hand. Thousands of years ago, when there was hard labor for both sexes, it may have been adaptive for women to assume total responsibility for child care, she says, but not anymore.

In Dinnerstein's view, that old arrangement has become *maladaptive*. Because men rarely take the day-to-day responsibility for the care of their own children, they don't learn to take responsibility for the welfare of others. Caring teaches you not only how to care but also that caring is important and appropriate behavior, and that other people have needs as valid as your own. Isolated from caring for their children, men often don't learn these lessons. In the school of life, they skip one of the most important classes in the fundamental human value of compassion: child rearing. "It's an achievement," says Dinnerstein, "to recognize that other people are living inside their heads the way you're living inside yours." Without a solid grounding in compassion, men will always find it easier to ignore or abuse the needs and feelings of others, to dehumanize their victims.

And all too often, their victims are women. Dinnerstein argues that because their mothers assume all the responsibilities of child rearing, boys grow up with a skewed and ultimately dangerous view of all women. On the one hand, Mom is superhuman

because she gratifies all our needs and desires, but on the other, she inevitably disappoints us because she can't keep it up. Sooner or later, she's not going to gratify us as fully or as often as we'd like, and suddenly the perfect Mom is the pits. She's gone from superhuman to subhuman. "What the female-dominated early child care provides us with, as a way out of this challenge [to be compassionate], is a category of human being—the female—who is both more and less than human, but not a fellow creature."

So right from the start, males see half the human race as not entirely human. For the rest of their lives, men accept this as an adequate excuse not to treat everyone as human *and* to remain childish and self-centered.

If men took more of a role in child rearing, they might also approach life with less aggressive "hyperactivity." According to Dinnerstein, men feel frustrated because they don't have the capacity to bear children and, as a result, can make their mark on the world only by *doing* something—changing something, moving something,

In the school of life, men often skip one of the most important classes in compassion: child rearing. Without these lessons, men often find it easier to ignore or abuse the feelings of others.

OPPOSITE: Much has been made of Freud's argument that women suffer from penis envy, but not enough attention has been given to a related problem that afflicts men: "phallic obsession." The male preoccupation with size and potency pervades not only our culture but also our weaponry.

affecting something. Freud argued that women suffer from penis envy, but Margaret Mead added that men suffer from womb envy, a wish to exercise as much creative power as a woman exercises over her child. While this envy may underlie some of men's constructive behavior—achievements in the arts and ambition in business—it may also help explain why men tend to channel their innate aggressiveness into the effort to dominate people around them. "If you don't have the sense of efficacy that comes from helping another human being," says Dinnerstein, "making it possible for another human being to become human, to join the human condition, to change from a helpless infant into a competent child—if you don't have that power," you're more likely to want to go out and impose your will on other people, to prevail over them, to hurt them, to rape them, or even to kill them.

It's impossible to talk about male violence without coming finally to war. Of all our cultural institutions, none better embodies our society's ideals of manhood, crazy as they are. You may think that war and its values are remote from everyday

life, but scientists have discovered that the two worlds are closer than you ever imagined, that the concept of war not only haunts your nightmares, but affects your relationships with a spouse as well as your son's behavior in school. Dr. Beatrice Whiting, an anthropologist, and her husband, John, conducted a worldwide study to measure "the degree of intimacy between husbands and wives and fathers and children in societies around the world." What they discovered should surprise no one. "The least intimacy and greatest alienation between men and women and between husbands and children existed in those societies [that] practiced warfare to defend their territory and property, and . . . trained their young boys to be warriors, isolating them from women for this purpose. The warriors they trained were also indifferent to their wives and children, domineering over women, and socially hyperaggressive, in contrast to the more intimate, egalitarian, and less aggressive males of less warlike societies."

If we're looking for solutions to male violence, then one place to begin is with our society's attitudes toward war—undoubtedly the most maladaptive and destructive channel for our innate aggression we've ever devised. Irven DeVore suggests how we might get started: "I think we are deluding ourselves to say that aggression is only learned. On the other hand, I certainly do not agree with Konrad Lorenz and others who think of innate aggression as being something that can't help being expressed. Absolutely not. The propensity to be aggressive, to defend one's self and one's vital interests is at the heart of every species. . . . Either you can take this innate predisposition and you can glorify it, you can make the most of it, you can arm your young men, you can have them spend fifteen years learning the arts of war, or you can say, 'Yes, we know that you're angry today, but there are better ways to settle things. We are not going to do things that way anymore.' "

Although there's an unsettling amount of violence and evil human behavior in the world, the vast majority of the more than 4 billion human animals get through life without purposely hurting other people. Most of us adapt, cooperate, even sustain personal inconvenience by getting out of one another's way. Billions of us engage in countless unrecognized acts of care and, in many cases, love every day. So why is there so much violence?

Our look at the human animal, although brief, reveals that men have an evolutionary endowment of aggression, an arousal mechanism that predisposes us to what Jerome Kagan calls "rough-and-tumble" play. That much is certain—it's standard equipment. It comes with the basic model, like binocular vision, and warrants no apology. In the drama of survival, we wouldn't have come as far as we have without it. We wouldn't have been able to hunt for the protein we needed or protect ourselves from the aggression of other animals. Science also tells us that our arousal mechanism is relatively easy to trigger and that we like to have it triggered. That's why we raid the refrigerator, watch sexy people, and gawk at auto accidents. That's why Hollywood gives us so many violent movies.

Unlike the battling lizard, however, we're not hard-wired. We're endowed with a one-of-a-kind brain that gives us choices. When those options flash into the hypothalamus—fight, flee, feed, or copulate—we decide which it will be. We've even created a fifth option. Through that remarkable cultural achievement, language, we can negotiate, compromise, reason, adapt, and resolve conflicts in a nonviolent way. But the choices we make are inevitably influenced by the culture we create. Surrounded by violent imagery, pressed with ideals of manhood that associate potency with violence, trained to dehumanize others—especially women—and to expect too much of them, our boys and young men are more likely to push the "fight" button before giving it thought.

Why do we create a culture that can rise up and bite us if we're not careful? "Our culture doesn't bite us," says Dr. Melvin Konner, "it just stupidly lets go of the leash. It gives free rein—even encouragement—to the side of our nature that is most destructive. It takes the basic aggressive instincts of the animal on the leash and trains the animal to express those instincts more readily instead of less readily." In short, we are the animal on the leash *and* the trainer. If the animal inside loses control, we're to blame as much as the animal.

Whatever the current scientific squabbles, there's universal agreement that we —the most gifted life form on earth—now have the power to determine not only the shape of our future, but whether there will be a future at all. No religious doctrine is violated, nor is any scientific principle contradicted by the observation that we have been endowed by our Creator to do much better than we're doing. The mandate of the moment is to get on with the job of doing better. To know ourselves is to know that we can.

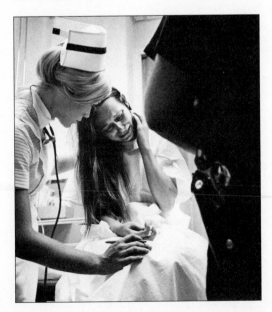

The rape victim is as much a victim of the society as of the rapist. Sociologists have found that warlike cultures also tend to be short on intimacy, long on alienation, and prone to domestic violence and rape.

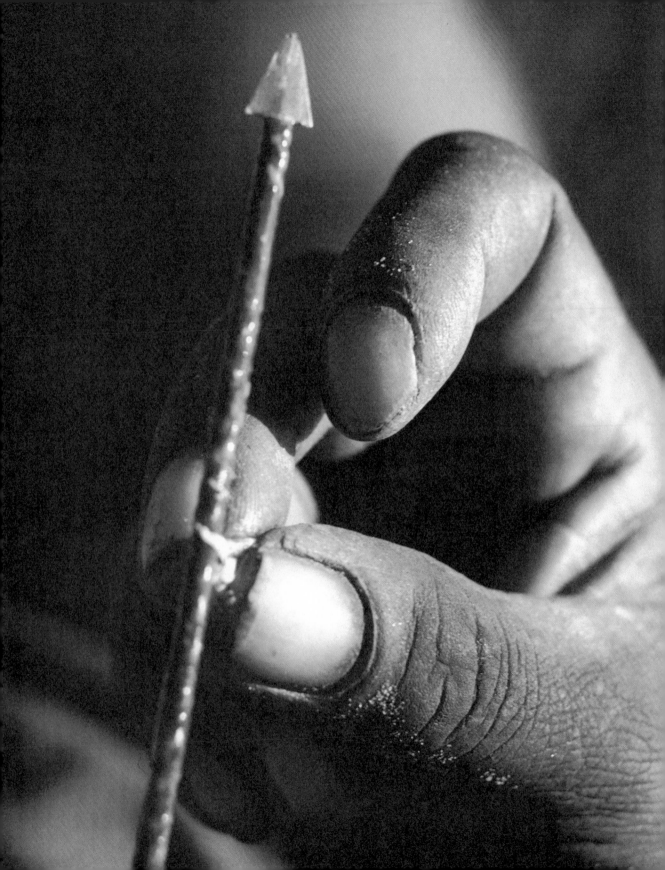

11. A Taste of Armageddon

*And there were flashes of
lightning, peals of thunder,
and a great earthquake
such as had never been since
men were on the earth . . .
and the cities of the nations
fell . . . and great hailstones
dropped on men from heaven,
till men cursed God.*

Revelation 15:1–16:21

In Washington, D.C., a severe black granite slab bears the name of every American killed in the Vietnam War: 58,014 men and 8 women. The Vietnam Memorial is the first attempt by any nation to remember, in one place, *all* the men and women who died in the service of their country during a single military conflict. The sea of names overwhelms visitors. Many of them come to find one name, and when they do, they leave a flower or a flag—and they weep.

Some nations go to war more often than others, but very few avoid war altogether. In our own century alone, the remains of 80 million people who died at war have been returned to the earth. Nuclear weapons have ensured that any future wars will be even more destructive. But war itself is a very *old* idea. A long list of historic figures became historic by engaging an enemy in battle and winning, or losing, big. And some of our greatest artists have devoted themselves to depicting history's bloodiest and most devastating wars. But, perhaps to protect us from war's true

War has always been hell, but because of technological innovations, hell is a lot hotter than it used to be. Submarine-launched Trident missile.

LEFT AND BOTTOM: The Vietnam Memorial is remarkable for its honesty. No flashing swords, no drums, no prancing horses, no glory. Simply the names of 58,022 human beings who died.

horrors, perhaps because we demand to be protected, the artist has often served up more romance than reality.

Our history suggests that we've always gone out of our way to protect ourselves from the truth of our own behavior. That talent for self-deception makes the Vietnam Memorial all the more remarkable for its honesty. Here there are no statues of heroic commanders, no prancing horses, no flashing swords, no drums, no pomp, no romance, no glory, no illusions. Of course, the honesty of it makes those people who prefer to be protected from reality uncomfortable. It's not surprising that during its planning, many Americans passionately condemned this memorial.

But of all humanity's monuments to its many wars, none comes closer to reminding us of questions that surely all of us have asked in our hearts at some time, questions so perplexing and disturbing that we don't even like to acknowledge them in public. With so much historical evidence of our ability to cooperate and to love, and with our unparalleled abilities to communicate and to reason, why do we time

OPPOSITE: In the past, we tended to glorify war. Many of our greatest artists, like Phidias, the sculptor of the Parthenon friezes, have devoted themselves to depicting, often in the most romantic light, the bloodiest pages of our history. Parthenon, North Frieze XXXVIII. The Acropolis, Athens.

and time again resort to violence one nation against another? Why does our species go so often and so willingly—even eagerly—to war?

For once, our fabulous neocortex seems to have failed us miserably. After millennia of slaughter and destruction, have we learned anything? Have we adapted our behavior to better ensure survival? Hardly. Except during the darkest days of two recent "world wars," the world has never been more violent or more dangerous than it is today. As of the first day of 1985, there were 41 wars being waged on our planet, from Cambodia to Iran to Nicaragua; more than 4 million soldiers were directly

engaged in combat; and 46 of the world's 165 nations were officially at war. Since the end of World War II, more than 16 million people have been killed in warfare worldwide.

What is the source of the human animal's insatiable appetite for war? We might feel better if we could blame this most inhuman of all behaviors on our animal past, but we would be doing our animal ancestors an injustice. Apparently, it is our species' dubious distinction to be the only creature that engages in the wholesale slaughter of its own kind. Although researchers have recently discovered that some primates are capable of murder, most animals vent their aggression in ritualized battles, a rudimentary form of war games, in which little harm is done. Only a few species—felines like lions, for example and the chimpanzees studied by Jane Goodall—resort to real violence, and none have an equivalent for war.

"Normally, fighting begins with a display," says Irenaus Eibl-Eibesfeldt, "and if the display doesn't lead to a spacing of the intruder, the animals will begin to fight, but after a few exchanges of bites" or other minimal wounds, "the animals are capable of separating themselves without doing further harm." Among wolves, for example, the weaker of two combatants will signal submission by rolling over and exposing his neck, saying, in essence, "I give up. You win. Let's quit." He offers himself to the victor "the way a puppy offers itself for grooming to the mother," says

Dr. Eibl-Eibesfeldt, "and then the attacker will start to lick him as if he were a puppy." Among the higher mammals, violence is often contained when a larger, higher-ranking male steps between two combatants and cows them both into passivity, like a daddy breaking up a fight between two rambunctious kids. It all seems so civilized by comparison.

Among our own ancestors, it used to be thought that war was a fairly recent invention. Experts figured that there had been no war until there was a reason to wage war, and the first reason, of course, was to defend property. Therefore, war must date from the invention of agriculture, about 10,000 years ago. "Human war-

OPPOSITE: *The killing goes on. Since the end of World War II, more than 16 million people have died in warfare. As of this writing, 46 of the world's 165 nations are officially at war.* Street fighting in Saigon. U.S. troops in Vietnam. Saigon during the Tet offensive. Refugees fleeing their homes.

When other animals do battle (unless they're killing for food), they tend to be more "humane" than humans. When two wolves fight, the weaker of the combatants signals submission by rolling over and exposing its neck. It's mostly for show; there is seldom bloodshed.

fare," says Ashley Montagu, explaining the traditional view in a nutshell, "is a tragedy of culture that resulted when food-producing cultures that shared resources and lived harmoniously with one another learned to be greedy and possessive of property, and established the complex, hierarchial, competitive social systems we now call, quite erroneously, 'civilization.' "

According to the old view, when people began farming their own plots of land, the population began to increase and the competition for basic resources heated up. Warfare developed, like any other social institution, as an adaptation designed to satisfy a basic need. Just as marriage safeguarded the vital resource of children, war guaranteed the essential resource of food-producing land.

Recently, however, scientists have begun to reject the old view that war was simply the dark lining in the silver cloud of civilization. As it turns out, settling down only *intensified* a penchant for warfare that had existed for as long as *Homo* had been considered *sapiens*. "The theory that war first developed in the Neolithic age with the development of horticulture and agriculture does not stand up to critical examination," says Eibl-Eibesfeldt; "there is evidence of armed clashes as early as the Paleolithic period." In the Saltadora cave in Castile, Spain, there's a crude painting of a man that dates from the Mesolithic era. He has been shot with an arrow. He drops to the ground, clutching his own bow as he goes down: the first recorded victim of our species' thirst for its own blood.

A clue to the real, warlike nature of even our distant ancestors can be found in the few primitive tribes that have survived into the twentieth century. Although scientists used to think that tribes like the !Kung were the primitive equivalent of "flower children," more recent research indicates that they can be quite aggressive in defense of their territory. Unlike more civilized societies that fight to defend their property, the Bushmen fight to defend their hunting and gathering grounds. But that's the only difference; the rest of the story is all too familiar. "The !Kung," says Irven DeVore, "are the most pacific people we know, but their murder rate compares to that in West St. Louis, Houston, and Detroit. The only reason they don't make war is that they live in such small groups that, even if all the males in one group went to war with all the males in another group, we wouldn't call it war because only twelve men would be involved."

The moral of the story is that life among our ancestors, even before they tied themselves down to the harvest and the hearth, was no picnic. That romantic nineteenth-century notion of the "noble savage" at peace in the wild, of Tarzan and Jane living in untroubled accord with native tribes and wild animals, is just wishful thinking, a longing for a paradise that never existed—at least, not here on earth. "In some instances," DeVore says, describing the lifestyle of primitive tribes, "you find the people living in an embattled atmosphere, in stockaded villages, frightened about the next raid, and extolling the virtues of manly war to their young men, and every young man growing up knowing that he will be a warrior, and that high status comes from being a warrior." Sound familiar?

Eibl-Eibesfeldt is quick to note, however, that many of these primitive societies take a cue from their animal cousins and turn their wars into ritual games. Not "games" in the Olympic sense, because people do get hurt and even killed, but games in the sense that the combat is stylized in order to *reduce* the chance of death. For example, among the Dani of New Guinea, who fight with bow and arrow, it's typical for warriors to use unfeathered arrows because they're less accurate, thereby reducing the number of hits. Among the Murngin of Australia, who fight with spears, a warrior is trained to lob his spear like a pop fly to second base so that everybody will see it coming and get out of the way. For variety, he may throw a low "grounder" occasionally, or simply remove the spear's stone tip. The purpose, after all, is just to determine a victor, not to spill blood.

The Tsembaga of New Guinea have perfected ritualized warfare games to such a degree that they serve as a model for more "civilized" societies. Their rare clan wars are usually sparked by a murder, following which the clan of the victim vows revenge on the clan of the murderer. But a strict protocol must be respected. As recorded by Eibl-Eibesfeldt, the "war" begins with a "skirmishing" phase in which "the aggrieved party sends a call over to the enemy, challenging them to present themselves at a definite battleground." Even if passions are running high, the fight is put off for several days while representatives from both sides visit the appointed battlefield to clear it of undergrowth. To avoid any pregame brawls, members of one clan withdraw from the field when members of the other clan approach. The delay itself is a way of letting tempers cool before the actual combat.

When the skirmish begins, warriors are allowed to bring only spears and unfeath-

Dr. Irven DeVore of Harvard University. "The brutal lesson of biology is that animals and individual humans do not on average work for the good of their species. They work out of more selfish shorter-term goals. That's why more than 99 percent of all species in the fossil record have gone extinct."

ered arrows. The combatants stand at a distance and hurl threats, not spears, at each other. The purpose is to allow the parties to vent their anger in a nonlethal way. If grievances aren't sufficiently aerated in the shouting match and mediation fails, the true battle begins. Spears and unfeathered arrows are replaced by battle-axes. But before going at it, the two sides must each sacrifice two pigs—a heavy price for letting the feud get this far. Then the warriors eat heavily salted bacon and refrain from drinking liquids. The effect is to dehydrate them, making them weaker and more apt to drop out of the coming battle. Finally, each clan's shamans proclaim the names of men among the enemy clan who, according to the spirits, can easily be killed. These hit lists, which are kept mercifully short, essentially establish a quota of killing. If the clan kills anyone not on the list, the spirits will be offended.

After the battle begins, every time a warrior is killed a truce is called so that the killer can carry out certain rituals. Before going back into battle, each side must sacrifice two more pigs. Before long, the clans begin to run out of pigs. And in the meantime, each truce gives both sides an opportunity to reconsider the wisdom of the feud and to turn a temporary lull in the fighting into a lasting peace. The entire ritual is a masterly psychological game designed to underscore the costs of war and make the alternatives to it more attractive.

The form of ritual combat practiced by the Tsembaga and other primitive tribes has come down to us. From the one-against-one of David and Goliath to the jousting of Lancelot and King Arthur, we have a tradition of champions' doing battle on behalf of their cause or clan or nation. The outcome decides the victor, and only one life, not thousands of lives, is lost in the process. Our modern sports teams and even the Olympics are in the tradition of these ritual battles designed to contain the devastation of war.

Another of our ancestors' adaptations that made war possible was the ability to think of other humans as essentially different from ourselves. Despite the millions of similarities in structure, function, behavior, and attitudes, we look at the people

TOP: The human animal has a built-in mechanism that prevents us from killing another of our own kind. But that mechanism can be short-circuited if we convince ourselves that the victim is less than human. That's the purpose of wartime propaganda. Scientists refer to this tendency to divide the world into "us" and "them" as "pseudospeciation." American and German war posters from World War II.

BOTTOM: Pseudospeciation can occur within a country as well as between countries. When it does, it's called prejudice. The Ku Klux Klan marching through Houston's gay community, June 9, 1984.

who differ from us only in the color of their skin or their shape of their eyes and say, "They're not our kind." This unique human tendency to make distinctions between people where there are no real differences Dr. Eibl-Eibesfeldt calls "pseudospeciation"—literally, the creation of false species.

"Separating into diverse cultures," says Dr. Eibl-Eibesfeldt, "provides the human species with a healthy genetic and cultural variety." But it also encourages people to treat groups other than one's own "as wholly other, alien, in effect a different species. It is a universal human tendency to label one's own social group as the only real 'humans' and everyone else as 'other.' This ability may explain why humans can kill their own kind. It's easier to kill a 'gook' or a 'nip' or a 'kraut' than to kill another person. It's easier to discriminate against a 'nigger' a 'honkey' or a 'kike' than it is to abuse one of your own." When we see other people as different, we don't need to obey the same rules of decency and fair play.

That's why pseudospeciation becomes so important in time of war. Propaganda machines busily transform our allies into saints and our enemies into subhuman monsters worthy only of death. During World War II, the Russians became our allies and the Germans were "Krauts." During the Cold War that followed, the Germans rejoined humanity while the once-friendly Russians were now "Reds" or "Commies." During the Vietnam War, it was common to hear from government spokesmen that "those people" in Southeast Asia "didn't value human life" as much as "we Westerners" do. Attitudes like that made incidents like the slaughter of civilians by American soldiers at My Lai possible. On one of his famous lithographs on the atrocities of war, Francisco Goya wrote: "They are of a different kind."

Pseudospeciation wasn't the only adaptation that made it possible for us to wage war from a comfortable moral and emotional distance. Far more important was an explosion in the technology of killing. It started with the invention of firearms—an invention that doomed the ritual combat of knights. Anyone could fire a gun from behind a bush and kill a man inside his elaborate suit of armor. That wasn't warfare, it was murder—a gross violation of the code of chivalry. We can only wish that the knights had been successful in their desperate attempts to outlaw the new weapons, but there was no holding back progress.

By 1914, the destructiveness of warfare—the power and efficiency of its deadly weapons—had moved from stone-tipped spears and featherless arrows to 16-inch mortars, mustard gas, and airplanes that spat bullets. For many people, World War I was a rude awakening to a battlefield that had been transformed from a field of honor into a killing ground. But those advances were nothing compared with what happened after the "war to end all wars." Today, sixty-five years later, we sit with our finger on the button of weapons that can annihilate worlds. With less effort than it takes to hurl a spear, we can kill hundreds of millions of people. Nowhere else has technology triumphed as it has in the business of war.

As warfare has become more mechanized, it has also become less ritualized. In the process, we may have lost our most important adaptation for survival. Ritualized warfare, like technology, permitted us to kill by insulating us from the horror of death, *but* it also prevented the killing from getting out of hand. As warfare became less ritualized, that crucial balance was thrown out of kilter. Guns and other advances in the technology of war allowed us to distance ourselves even further from the horrors of war; but, at the same time, they made it possible for us to kill almost without limit. The carefully circumscribed rituals that had contained our bloodlust for thousands of years suddenly went haywire, and it's still out of control. "A normal bomber pilot," says Eibl-Eibesfeldt, "is no pervert, but he can kill, in one raid, hundreds of civilians, including women and children. And he can because he's not completely aware of what he's doing."

Technology has allowed us to short-circuit our own protective mechanisms. According to Dr. Eibl-Eibesfeldt, the human animal, like all advanced animals, is endowed with an arousal mechanism, but this mechanism doesn't commit us to killing members of our own species. It comes with a built-in "governor" that should stop us short of murder. Just as the lizard is designed to retreat and the wolf to submit, we are *designed* to back away from death—our own or someone else's. The problem is that our brain has allowed us to develop instruments of war and death that are so quick that our natural inclination to end the dispute without killing never clicks into action.

"Weapons techniques," says Eibl-Eibesfeldt, "have to a certain extent circumvented our innate inhibitions. A rapid blow with a weapon can eliminate a fellow

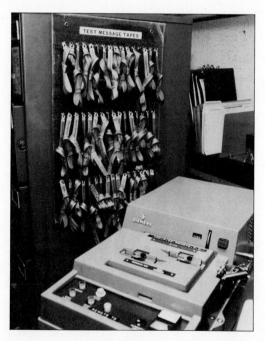

The "hot line" between Washington, D.C., and Moscow. Someone once likened it to "a twenty-pound-test line for a ten-ton fish."

human before he has a chance of appealing to our sympathy by an appropriate gesture of submission. This is even more likely to be the case if the killing is done from a distance: for instance, with an arrow"—or from an even greater distance, as from the sterile remoteness of a Minuteman silo.

We have taken the biological cork out of the bottle of warfare. The question now is: Can we put it back?

"A dehumanized hi-tech military of the future," says Dr. Eibl-Eibesfeldt, "will absolutely guarantee that more frequent and more destructive wars will be fought. Whatever control humans have over the violence of war comes from the actual experience of human suffering *on* the battlefield. As animal organisms, human beings have strong inhibitions about killing one another, which warlike cultures overcome by creating 'enemies' who are thought of as not human. For most of our history the actual physical contact of human beings in battle has to an extent mitigated such abstractions. But as modern war has become more and more distanced and technological, the inhibition against killing becomes easier to overcome. It's hard to look another human in the eye and shoot him. It's very easy to press a button and destroy an abstraction, a blip on a computer screen."

When people speak of the "technological imperative"—technology, itself, determining our fate—they must be talking about war. Nowhere is the human race more at the mercy of its own inventions. "Modern warfare," says anthropologist Dr. Richard Lee, "especially nuclear war, cannot really be classified as 'war.' The human species invented warfare as an adaptive social institution—one that would

MX "cold launch" test.

OVERLEAF: Paradoxically, the next "world war," if it comes, will be both the most destructive and the easiest that the world has ever seen. It will be "fought" here in the Emergency Conference Room at the National Military Command Center. Technology has distanced us so far from the horror of war that a button capable of killing millions can be pushed from an upholstered armchair.

WELCOME
to the
National Military
Command Center

help competing groups survive in the struggle for vital resources. This invention also worked because the males who fought found the physically arousing risk, the exertion, and the strategic contests of warfare satisfying. Obviously by these standards nuclear war is not war. The obliteration of the planet is of no use in an adaptive competition. Incineration can hardly be called a rousing good fight or romanticized into any myth of heroism."

Of course, the final and most terrifying move in what seems like an inexorable process is to remove humans from warfare altogether—except as victims. In a well-known episode of the television series *Star Trek* entitled "A Taste of Armageddon," computers from two planets fought simulated battles and issued casualty figures. People from each planet then reported to "disintegration chambers" in the appropriate numbers. It was clean, it was neat. No one looked an enemy in the eye; no one had to pull a trigger or see another human being bleed. Is such a world really a fantasy, or is it, like so much science fiction, perilously close to reality? "If we have a nuclear war," says Dr. Melvin Konner, "the guys who push the buttons are going to be in protected bunkers. They're going to be the *least* likely to get killed because they've got to be protected so they can push the next button, and watch the screen for the next set of missiles." The only step left is to replace the button pushers with computers.

At that point, the decision to kill will be made at computer speed, without human reflection, without even the possibility that at the last second, the image of a dead child or a childless mother will flash through a human brain, leaping from dendrite to dendrite until it sparks a question or a pause or a glimmer of regret, and then the brain in a burst of recognition will speed a message to the hand and the hand will move away from the button. The idea that we might give up that last chance to choose survival is the single most frightening development in current warfare.

War, like love, has *always* been a game, an exciting cerebral exercise invented by a uniquely talented brain that loves its games. In the beginning, the war game was also a highly ritualized one. As in much of the fighting within other animal species, the object of the game was to win, and to get thoroughly aroused and

The technology of warfare has changed radically since the days of the spear, but the purpose has remained the same: to kill. Australian aborigine demonstrates his killing technique to U.S. military personnel.

OPPOSITE: The next war may be the first in which front-line soldiers are more likely to survive than civilians at home. Both chemical and nuclear weapons will do most of their damage outside the battlefield. NATO exercise simulating chemical warfare.

excited in the process, without actually having to do much actual killing—if any. In fact, many battles among even the fiercest of primitive peoples, like the Dani tribesmen of New Guinea, end the moment a single warrior is killed.

Today we of the "civilized" world play the same game, and we have used our great gift for mental play to produce an unbelievably complex technology. A technology we operate in a state of cool detachment, without arousal, far from any battlefield, a technology that can kill a million people almost as fast as a Dani warrior can kill one. Our own brilliance has wrecked our inhibiting rituals.

According to the Bible, the end of the world will come at a dry, undistinguished place called Megiddo near Nazareth, the childhood home of Jesus. This is the site of Armageddon, a New Testament writer's vision of the final, universal battle among the nations of the earth. In biblical times, this city symbolized the horror of war. It was destroyed and rebuilt not fewer than twenty times in fighting over the fertile fields and the important trade routes in the valley below. And in our own century, two decisive battles were fought here: the first in World War I, the second during the 1948 Middle East War. Armageddon remains the symbol of apocalypse.

We haven't fulfilled the apocalyptic prophecy in Revelation—yet. But today our technology, coupled with our ideologies, is pushing us dangerously close. Our inventions have extended our power to hurt and kill beyond our natural limits. Just in the last century, we have moved from individuals fighting face to face to the faceless annihilation of the hydrogen bomb. And what do our leaders ask for? More and better missiles, more and bigger bombs. There is a Chinese saying that the fish are the last to see the water.

Is Armageddon inevitable? Millions of us think so. But against their resignation have gathered a growing number of us who find, in our power to cause the apocalypse, a hope we can ensure that the prophecy of Revelation is never fulfilled. "You can step back," says Irven DeVore, "and say that elephant seals should not be acting the way they do. That they should not be killing their own infants. You can say that humans should not be acting the way they do. That seventy million killed in warfare in the twentieth century is absurd. But the brutal lesson of biology is that animals and individual humans do not on average work for the good of their species. They work out of more selfish shorter-term goals. That's why more than ninety-nine percent of all species in the fossil record have gone extinct. We are the first species, in fact, to have enough cerebral power to actually begin to understand natural selection and evolution and to see that we may be the species that can overcome that problem and work for the good of the species."

Dr. Eibl-Eibesfeldt's solution is to make our aggressive tendencies, which have become destructive of human potential, constructive once again. Taking his cue from Freud's concept of sublimation, he suggests that we turn our aggressive energy to more peaceful pursuits: "There is a great deal in favor of the assumption that aggressive personalities are well able to put their dynamism to work in positive ways tackling problems. . . . Without man's attacking spirit, there would certainly be no worthwhile advances in either the intellectual or the social field." In fact, the most aggressive humans may well be the best suited to fighting the cause of peace: "I know many men who 'fight' passionately, but not destructively, for peace. Their weapons are arguments."

The real hope for the future doesn't lie in scientific advances or political rhetoric. The real hope is located in the same place as the real threat: inside each of us. Our exploration of other species and of our own primitive past reveals that we have, buried somewhere inside, a deep reluctance to kill another of our own—a pea of conscience that unsettles our sleep on the fat mattress of technology. If we can somehow recover and retrain that old, unused biological mechanism, perhaps we can stop the crazy, contrary motion of ascending threat and deadening conscience; perhaps by putting the horror back into war we can stop it before it starts.

Someone once suggested, only half tongue-in-cheek, that the President be required to cut open the abdomen of a living child to obtain the secret code number needed to order a nuclear strike. The idea sounds barbarous, but is it any more so

Seventy million people were killed in warfare in the twentieth century. We have to struggle to get behind the statistics, to understand that each of those 70 million was a unique, irreplaceable human being. Pulitzer-winning photograph of Vietnamese children fleeing napalm strike.

OVERLEAF: The biblical vision of apocalypse is now a real possibility. Technology and ideology are pushing us closer to it every day. The Great Day of His Wrath by John Martin.

The biological fact is that we have a natural aversion to killing our own kind. Although the male predisposition to war still survives, so does the basic instinct against killing. The instinct is our best hope for the future. Wounded American soldiers after the D-Day landings at Normandy in 1944.

OPPOSITE: We are touching, feeling, sensing animals. Distance—physical, moral, emotional—is what makes us monsters. Israeli soldier and Lebanese truck driver shake hands through a border fence.

than the instant incineration of millions? It's both a distressing sign of our times and a reassuring reminder of our best instincts that the image of killing defenseless children by stabbing is harder to accept—and harder to justify—than the image of a man in a pin-striped suit ordering a massive nuclear strike.

The biological fact seems to be that we hate war and have always hated it. We used to wage it as an adaptive necessity—and maybe we men occasionally got an adrenaline high out of it—but we tried from the start to limit the killing and to distance ourselves from it. Those are the basic instincts that still survive, not the instinct for war. "If human beings were in fact endowed with an innate proclivity for war," says sociologist Stanislav Andreski, "it would not be necessary to indoctrinate them with warlike virtues; and the mere fact that in so many societies, past and present, so much time has been devoted to such an indoctrination proves that there is no instinct for war." Love comes naturally to the human animal. Devotion to duty has to be drilled into us. We suffer not from a lack of love, but from too much devotion.

During World War I, French and German soldiers sitting in their trenches—sometimes only a few hundred feet apart—would begin to talk to each other during lulls in the fighting. Through years of living in neighboring countries, they knew each other's languages, so conversation was easy. After a while, during particularly long lulls, they would come out of their trenches and exchange cigarettes and food. These personal interchanges between men made them much less efficient as soldiers. It was very difficult for them to kill each other effectively after the lull ended. When military authorities heard what was happening, they established "nonfraternization" rules: soldiers on the front line must remember that the *enemy* is the enemy, not just another regular guy who smokes cigarettes and talks about his family back home.

We are touching, feeling, sensing animals. Distance—physical, moral, emotional —is what makes us monsters.

PART FOUR

NATURE & NURTURE

12. A Womb with a View

*It's a shame that a race
so broadly conceived should
end with most lives so
narrowly confined.
Why should we waste
childhood on the children?*

Terry and Renny Russell, *On the Loose*

Lyle Rosenbaum and Steven Leventhal had no reason to suspect that their lives were unusual until they were twenty-seven years old. Then a series of unexplainable events led them to a startling discovery. After taking several sick days, Steve Leventhal returned to his job at a department store in Queens, New York, and, out of the blue, his boss fired him. The boss insisted that he had seen Steve in the store the previous day—even though Steve had been home in bed. Some time later, Steve was sitting in a restaurant when a stranger walked over to him. "Hi, Lyle," the man said. "I'm not Lyle," Steve replied. But the man continued to insist that Steve was Lyle Rosenbaum, a relative. Not until Steve showed his driver's license did the man let him alone.

A few days later, Lyle Rosenbaum walked into the same room with Steve Leventhal and suddenly he was standing face to face with himself. It was like looking in a mirror—but there was no mirror. Steve and Lyle were identical twins who had been separated at birth. They hadn't seen each other since that first day in the hospital, and during all those years neither one had known that the other existed.

Over the next several months, Lyle and Steve learned that despite being separated from birth, their lives had been remarkably similar. Again and again they discovered identical interests, habits, and even quirks. Some were expectable. Both had done well in school, and both had prematurely gray hair. But some of the

---

Identical twins—individuals with exactly the same genetic material but different identities—help scientists answer perplexing questions about the relationship of nature and nurture in determining why we do the things we do.

similarities were almost spooky. When they held a glass, both "held their pinkies in the air." Both loved Donna Summer records, both owned the same make of car, both had been married since their late teens, both were nonsmokers despite having been raised in smoking households. Does that mean there's a gene that determines whether we like classical music or rock? A gene for glass holding? And a gene that tells us when to get married?

Hardly. What the case of Steve and Lyle and others like it give us is a rare glimpse into the relationship between heredity and environment, between nature and nurture, in the development of personality. Here we have two males with *exactly* the same genetic material but raised in different environments. If genes are more important in determining the way we are, then Steve and Lyle should be more alike than different. If environment has the upper hand, then they should be more different than alike. Maybe their case can throw some much-needed light on that old

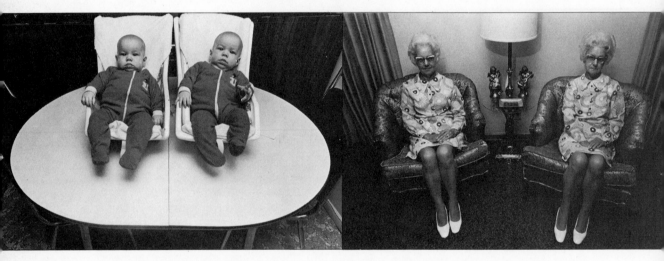

question, Are genes destiny?

The question is not just one for the scientists. Conscientious parents are constantly fretting about raising their kids properly, or feeling guilty because their kids turned out "wrong." Not surprisingly, parents want to know: "Is it my fault? What did I do? What *can* I do?" By looking at reunited twins like Steve and Lyle, scientists may begin to give us some answers to these and other questions that keep parents awake at night.

Unfortunately, the answers so far are not clear-cut. They're not about to put an end to the everlasting dialogue between heredity and environment. Although Lyle and Steve were startlingly alike in many ways, Lyle had three kids, Steve had none, and both said their wives were "very different." According to Dr. Thomas J. Bouchard of the University of Minnesota, who studied Lyle and Steve's case as well as dozens of others like it, "each of these twins is an absolutely unique person. It doesn't take a long time interacting with them to realize that each is a unique human being. When we talk about identical twins, we should always keep that in mind."

Not only did Lyle and Steve display some differences, but there was also an environmental explanation for their similarities. Both had been brought up in middle-class Jewish families, and in similar neighborhoods. Both adoptive families had been small, and both Lyle and Steve had enjoyed good relationships with their adoptive parents. Would their story have been different if one had been raised in a poor neighborhood and the other in Beverly Hills? "It's very rare that we find twins in dramatically different environments," says Dr. Bouchard, "so our results tend to look more similar than they might if these people were truly and dramatically separated. And when we do see twins who have undergone dramatic separation, we do find some large differences."

So all Lyle and Steve really do is pose the question in flesh-and-blood terms: How

much of the person we are is determined before we're born and how much do we learn afterward? Unfortunately, science can't tell us much more than Lyle and Steve can. We do know that some mental disorders, such as schizophrenia and manic depression, have a genetic factor. But these and other disorders are also affected by environment. For example, if Lyle were depressive, the chances are two out of three that Steve would be too. *But* that's not three out of three. Even with *identical* genes, it's not inevitable that both would have the same affliction. So maybe what we inherit is a *potential* for certain behavioral traits, a potential that isn't realized unless environmental circumstances trigger it.

Sigmund Freud was the first to suggest seriously that an individual's adult behavior could be better understood by examining his or her childhood experiences, and that notion became the basis of psychoanalysis. Although Freud's ideas were considered crazy by fellow doctors and scientists, all he did was transform the speculations of old wives and the poetic fancy of artists into a science. Every parent knows it's true: as the twig is bent, so grows the tree. What Freud did was to help us understand *how* the twig was bent.

You don't have to be around a baby long to see just how observant, how *absorbent* it is. A child's awareness is like a superfine screen that catches even the tiniest particle of experience, stores it, reworks it, and throws it back at you like a spoonful of creamed carrots. How else could a child learn something as complicated as language just by listening? Try to explain, in words, the difference between a desk and a table or between red and blue. Children can absorb these subtleties without a word being spoken. If such fine distinctions make a permanent mark on a child's awareness, imagine the impact of love, hate, fear, jealousy, anger, compassion, and longing. If the young twig stirs even in the soft breeze of language, how can it not be bent in the gale-force winds of emotion?

In fact, at some deep intuitive level, we've always been aware that what we are like and how we behave are profoundly—and sometimes tragically—shaped by our childhood ups and downs; that the child is truly parent to the adult. But only since Freud started asking questions—only since the beginning of this century—have we begun to study human childhood scientifically. It was Freud who convinced us that the relationship between childhood experiences and an adult's capacity for fulfillment can be studied systematically and, perhaps, altered. If Freud was right, then childhood, the morning of a human life, is the key phase in human development.

Our childhood world is an astonishing interaction between the perception of outer reality and an inner world of developing imagination. What we experience in childhood becomes the foundation of our later behavior and personality, of what makes us feel happy or sad or afraid—feelings that may remain with us a lifetime, even if we can't consciously remember how they came to be ours. They shape our attitudes,

Babies may seem like indifferent lumps of clay, but in fact they are little bundles of teeming senses hungry to be touched, taught, and loved.

OPPOSITE: Childhood is a constant interaction between the perception of outer reality and an inner world of developing imagination. Roulin's Baby by Vincent van Gogh, 1888.

our feelings about ourselves and the world about us. Experience gives a unique shape and form to our lives from the cradle to the grave. The forces that mold saints and sinners begin early. And they stay with us always. "There is a biology of learning," says Dr. John Money. "You can learn things so deeply, they become so deeply embedded, that—like your native language—you can't get rid of them by any known method except to have a neurosurgeon cut them out or to have a stroke."

In 1897, one year after Sigmund Freud coined the word "psychoanalysis" and about 120 miles from Freud's home in Vienna, an eight-year-old boy was sitting at the window of his house in Lambach, Austria, staring raptly at the austere facade of the town's great Benedictine monastery. The little boy knew something of the mysteries that took place inside. Because he was both an excellent student and a talented boy soprano, the monks had invited him to attend their choir school. It was the thrill of his young life. Years later, he recalled how "intoxicated" he had been with the "solemn splendor of brilliant church festivals." He idolized the monastery's abbot so much that he vowed that when he grew up, he too would become a priest. At home, he delivered what his relatives later recalled as "long and fervent sermons" to his family, standing on a chair in the kitchen, wearing the cook's apron over his shoulders as if it were a satin vestment.

This little boy's head may have been in heaven, but his life was pure hell. His father beat him and his older brother, Alois, unmercifully. Later, he described his father as "hard and determined." We would call him just plain cruel. His father once whipped brother Alois and then held him by the neck against a tree until he passed out. Relatives recalled that all the children in the family left the house as often as possible to escape their father's tyranny. Severe beatings were meted out for even the most trivial offenses against his authority. Alois ran away from home at age fourteen never to return, leaving his younger brother to bear the brunt of their

Above the arch leading to the Benedictine monastery in Lambach, Austria, where he was a choirboy, Hitler first saw the ancient symbol of the hooked cross that would become the emblem of the Third Reich: the swastika.

father's harsh, relentless discipline. Our studious eight-year-old with a gift for song must have been secretly overjoyed as he escaped his house every morning and set out for the monastery school. What a sense of relief he must have felt as he passed through the monastery's ancient gate and looked up at the coat of arms bearing an old mythic symbol, the swastika.

Not long afterward the boy and his family moved away from Lambach. But he never became a priest. He went into politics instead. But in quiet moments later in life he liked to reminisce about his happy days in Lambach. When he did, people listened with unusual interest. The boy's name was Adolf Hitler.

What, if anything, can we conclude about the mysterious human chemistry of a boy's fantasy of preaching to the masses, a tyrannical and abusive father, and the perhaps unconscious memory of an ancient mythic symbol? Maybe nothing. Maybe a lot. No one, including Sigmund Freud, has ever drawn a reliable map of all the specific connections between childhood experiences and adult character. Little boys with fervent piety, good singing voices, and abusive fathers don't all grow up to be Adolf Hitlers. There's no universal formula for human failure—or success. We are individuals with an unlimited range of potential. For every Adolf Hitler, there's an

NEAR RIGHT: Adolf Hitler as a young man. As a child, he "preached" to the family, standing on a kitchen chair and wearing the cook's apron as if it were a priest's robe. He wanted to be a priest someday.

FAR RIGHT: Hitler's father, Alois Hitler, Sr., routinely beat his sons for minor offenses.

Albert Schweitzer; for every Charles Manson, a Martin Luther King.

What accounts for the remarkable range of human personality? Other advanced mammals may differ in temperament and intelligence, as any pet owner knows, but their variations exist within a narrow range. Humans, on the other hand, are capable of monumental cruelty as well as total compassion, vulgar displays and exquisite sensibilities, seething hatred and consuming love. How can two animals that are biologically essentially identical develop in such different ways?

You may think that differences in personality are like differences in hair color or eye color—they're just part of our genetic makeup. Although there's support for the notion that each of us is born with a distinctive "temperament," most scientists

Given the enormous importance of human childhood, it's not surprising that most parents— even the illustrious—get a little anxious. The Prince and Princess of Wales with their sons Henry and William in the official portrait by Lord Snowdon.

agree that the conditions we grow up in exert a significant influence on the kind of person we become. But if that's true, one would expect to find very little variation within a community. After all, in most neighborhoods, the differences from one house to the next are very slight. Almost everybody's from the same social and economic class, they're part of the same culture, they share the same values. So why are kids on the same street so different? For that matter, why are two children from the *same* family so different?

This isn't just an idle question for scientists to mull over. For any parent or would-be parent, the question of why children develop as they do has a special urgency. We all wonder if we will make, are making, or have made mistakes in raising our kids, mistakes that we're not aware of, mistakes that we made for all the best reasons. It's a testament to the conscientiousness of most parents, *and* to the sensitivity of children, that we consider every move we make as parents to be important. We may forget occasionally and snap at them, lose our patience, or seem unloving, but we're almost always concerned about the consequences. Of course, no one wants to raise a "sad sack," or a child that grows up to be chronically angry. Most of all, we want to raise children who are capable of feeling happiness, achieving fulfillment, giving and accepting love.

What do we know about the early life of this extraordinary creature, the human infant? What do we know about how it grows, what it needs? What do we know—and what don't we know—about the consequences of how we care for and nurture it? When you think about the enormous importance of childhood, about how much is at stake in the fundamental human act of raising a child from helpless infancy to successful adulthood, you begin to realize what an awesome challenge it is. And if you're a parent, you get a little weak in the knees.

We can begin to understand the variety and the potential of human behavior by looking closely at the newborn baby. Although it will eventually grow into the most intelligent and the most powerful animal that has ever existed, you'd never guess it by looking. When a baby comes into the world, it is more helpless and dependent on parental care than any other animal. It will also remain in that precarious state longer than any other animal. Some animals are prepared for their own survival at the moment of birth. Not this one. Baby will take most of a year just to stand erect, and several more years to perfect walking and talking. The "tribe" to which it belongs, still confused about what's reasonable to expect of children, won't even consider it an adult for twenty-one years.

Compared even to other primates, human infants come into the world as small lumps of barely formed clay. Most of the shaping—both physical and mental—has yet to be done. Only about 5 percent of human growth takes place *in utero*, leaving a full 95 percent for after delivery. "Humans are born at an earlier stage of physical development than apes," says Dr. Ashley Montagu, "and as they develop remain more like the immature infant than does the ape, the latter pursuing a more specialized developmental path." Human infancy is a womb with a view.

The human infant is slightly larger than an infant ape, but the proportion of head to body is pretty much the same in both animals. As they mature, however, the ape's body begins to grow much faster than its head, while the human remains in roughly the same proportions. The result is a mature ape that's practically a pin-head. A quick glance at comparable photographs shows that humans and chimps look much more alike as babies than they do as adults.

The differences in the development of humans and chimps are probably best seen with the help of computer graphics. As infants, a human and a chimpanzee have skulls that are generally the same shape, with much more space devoted to the brain than to the structure of the mouth. If you've ever seen baby chimps close up, the similarities can be startling; so startling that some scientists believe that an ancestor of the chimp—similar to the pygmy chimpanzees of Zaïre—may have been a close relative of the earliest humans. For support, they point to the surprising similarities in the structure of the chromosomes in humans and chimpanzees.

But even if chimps are a not-so-distant relative, says Montagu, "they remain closer in form and behavior to apes than to humans." The differences begin to show up as the two infants begin to mature. Humans tend to retain their infantile physical characteristics throughout adult life. Although both the area of the skull devoted to the brain and the area devoted to the mouth expand, the proportions remain roughly the same as in the infant. The chimpanzee, on the other hand, goes through a radical change as the brain-devoted space remains relatively constant while the mouth and

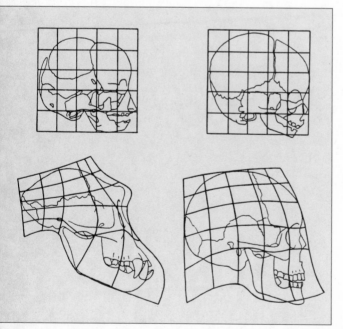

The relationship of brain area to jaw area remains roughly the same in the human skull from infancy (upper right) to adulthood (lower right). In the chimpanzee skull, however, the space devoted to brain remains relatively unchanged, while the jaw grows to exaggerated proportions (upper and lower left).

OPPOSITE: According to the principle of neoteny, we retain our childlike behaviors and appearance throughout our lives. Unlike the chimpanzee, whose face and skull change radically as it ages, we remain more or less baby-faced into adulthood.

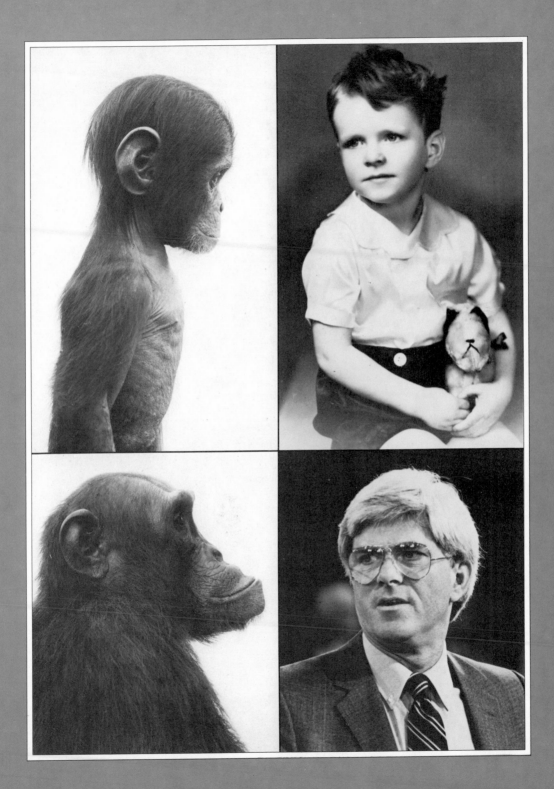

jaw grow to their exaggerated proportions. These changes are even more striking in other primates, especially the gorilla.

The same story is repeated throughout the infant human's body: every system is barely at the threshold of working order. We think of babies as little adults, but nothing could be further from the truth. "The enzyme systems of the newborn, the digestive system, the immunological system, the body-temperature-regulation system are all markedly deficient," says Dr. Montagu. The same is true of bone development and growth of the legs. "No other mammal grows at so slow a tempo as *Homo sapiens*," says Montagu. "There is none that takes so long to grow up after birth, none with such prolonged developmental periods."

In only one area has Baby reached a relatively advanced stage by birth: brain development. At two months after conception, a fetus's head is half its body length. At birth, the baby's brain is at more than one-quarter of full adult weight, while its body is at only one-twentieth of adult weight. Even though the human brain is well advanced at birth, it still has a long way to go. During the first six months of life outside the womb, it will double in size. In other words, most of the development in a human brain takes place after birth.

By contrast, in rhesus monkeys and gibbons, 70 percent of brain growth takes place in the womb, and the rest is completed within six months. Great apes take a little longer: full brain growth is not completed until eleven months past birth. A human will be three or four years old before its brain has reached full size.

Is it just because our brains grow so big that we're such good learners as children? Not according to Ashley Montagu. "The behavior of which an animal is capable," says Montagu, "is determined more by the size of its specialized areas than by the overall size of the brain." In other words, you could have a brain the size of a 21-inch television screen, but if the area dedicated to controlling your mouth, larynx, and tongue were tiny, you'd have trouble saying your name. The size of the specialized area in the brain corresponds not to the size of the corresponding body part, but to the complexity of the skill which it controls. That's why we humans have a large area of our brain dedicated to control of the tongue, the hand, and the eyes, and a relatively small area dedicated to the legs. Some scientists have speculated that people who try to teach chimpanzees to speak are attempting the impossible: the area in their brain that controls the use of the tongue and the larynx just isn't big enough to do the job.

Finally, the important process of myelination—the completion of the fatty sheaths of nerve fibers in the brain which makes connections more efficient—is not achieved until fifteen months after delivery. "The microscopic structure of the newborn human brain," says Ashley Montagu, "more closely resembles that of the fetus than that of the adult." So both in body and in brain, the human baby has a long way to go. Birth is only one milestone in a long process.

"Not only is the period of immaturity in humans absolutely longer [than in animals]," says Montagu, "it is also proportionately much longer in relation to total life span than that of any other creature. There is no placental mammal that remotely approaches the human in duration of infantile immaturity—not even such animals as the elephant, rhinoceros, camel, and wild ass, whose fetuses spend a longer time in the womb. The newborn of these animals are able to run with their mothers or the herd shortly after they are born."

The fact that Baby does so much of its developing after leaving the womb has convinced many scientists, including Montagu, that "the human infant when born has completed only half its gestation, the other half being completed outside the womb." John Bostock of the University of Queensland says that if you define gestation as complete only when the child begins to crawl—the point at which a human infant, like his animal ancestors, "walks" on all fours—then human gestation continues for eight to ten months after birth.

After all, life during this period of gestation on the outside is really rather like life on the inside. As any parent knows, a newborn spends most of its day sleeping and being carried around, interrupted by periods of feeding. "Babies," says Bostock, "must live in an atmosphere very different from that of ordinary everyday living, and its main principles of isolation and security closely resemble gestation itself. It is indeed an exterior gestation." If these scientists are correct, then the period of human gestation is not the nine months we think it is but really more like nineteen. Why is Baby forced to confront the world of light and noise before it's "finished"? Once again, the difference between humans and the other animals appears to be in the brain. The head of a fetus is so large that if the child were born any later than nine months after conception, it simply wouldn't fit through the birth canal.

Why does the human animal stay young—both physiologically (in body) and psychologically (in mind)—for such an inordinately long time after birth? How does it affect our development to be booted out of the womb before we're ready just because it's getting crowded? Wouldn't it be more efficient if we waited and popped into the world ten months later as fully developed miniature versions of our adult selves? Hardly. In fact, leaving the womb so early in its long growth process may be the best thing that happens to Baby in its entire life.

If there is a single characteristic unique to the human animal, it is adaptability. How well could you adapt to your circumstances if you couldn't change from the moment you were born? More than any other animal, we learn from experience. In the womb, the only kind of growth that can take place is biological. It's *because* we're forced to cope with experience at such an early age that we learn to learn. We're the best students on this planet partly because we have the faculties to see and understand and manipulate our world, but also because we start "school" a lot sooner.

"In humans," says Ashley Montagu, "genetic channeling of behavior is almost completely superseded by learned responses to environmental messages. Human behavior does not proceed in predestined grooves, which in many animals produce a fixity of instinctive reaction but which in humans are replaced by the flexibility and experimental nature of intelligence." Montagu attributes this unique capacity for learning to our extraordinarily long "babyhood," or what he calls *neoteny*.

"Whatever the precise origins of the human capacity for educability and intelligence," he says, "the hypothesis that best accounts for the mechanism of their evolution is neoteny—the retention of the fetal-juvenile traits of plasticity, flexibility." According to Montagu, the most important "neotenous" childhood trait is simply "play." Yes, the simple activity that occupies all of our childhood and a surprising amount of our adulthood. "Play" is nature's instinctive vehicle for learning—a combination of imagination, creativity, and curiosity that is purely a creation of the neocortex: our thinking brain. In play, says Montagu, we can find the "roots

of our adult capacities to think creatively and flexibly, to innovate, adapt, change. We are playful mammals all our lives, and that has been the reason for our remarkable adaptability and achievement as a species."

Scientists have discovered that other mammals play in childhood, but humans never *stop* playing. Throughout our long lives, we retain the ability—however underutilized it may be—to experiment and learn. "It's like learning language," says Montagu. "A kid can learn languages, as we all know, with the greatest of ease—many languages. But as you grow older, it becomes increasingly difficult to do so. It's the same, really, with any other potentiality." That's one reason why what we teach our children when they're young has so much impact on their adult personalities. But parents never have the last word; no one does; there is no "last word" for the human animal. At no point does the human mind shut off and stop absorbing. It

For all mammals, play is the most important learning activity. For the human animal, it is a renewing source of joy and creativity. Our lifelong capacity for play is partly responsible for our species' phenomenal record of adaptation and achievement.

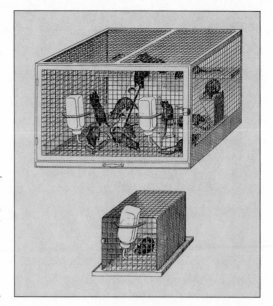

As adults, we tend to overestimate the value of work and underestimate the value of play. But recent research indicates that the brain can continue to benefit from play throughout life. Even old rats, when placed in an "enriched" environment (above), showed substantial brain growth, while rats placed in standard cages (below) showed no growth.

may take more conscious effort to learn new things as an adult than as a child, but the capacity for learning never abates. "It's like a muscle," says Montagu: "the more you exercise it, the stronger it grows." You might say that humans are the only old dogs that can learn new tricks.

It used to be accepted wisdom that old age was accompanied by mental disintegration. We often surrendered our old folks to nursing homes, assuming that their fuzzy thinking and poor memories were just the price of long life. But scientists are now correcting that cruel view. Strong evidence that the brain can continue to grow throughout life, no matter how advanced the age, has recently come from Dr. Marian Diamond of the University of California at Berkeley. "I have spent most of my life," says Dr. Diamond, "dealing with the question Will the brain continue to change in response to the environment at any age? And essentially within this last year, we've been able to show that the extremely old animal's brain *will* still change in response to a stimulating environment."

Diamond separates laboratory rats into two groups. One group she puts in what she calls an "enriched environment" and the other into a standard cage. The enriched environment is something like a country club for rats: a spacious cage, plenty of stimulating company, and lots of interesting "toys" like mazes and wheels and ladders—"anything that they're curious about, that they will climb on, and look at, and explore." Every "country-club" animal has a littermate, a genetic relative, who goes into the "rest home" for rats, what Diamond calls the "standard colony environment": a small cage, just a few deadbeat cellmates, and no toys.

"The animals live for varying periods of time, in either enriched or standard-colony conditions, and then we study their brains," Diamond reports. "What we find is that the brains of the enriched animals have grown significantly in comparison to those in the standard colony. And we found that this occurs not only just after birth, but with young animals, middle-aged animals, and more recently with animals that are nine hundred days of age—extremely old rats." Diamond's experiments have very important implications for the way we treat our elderly citizens. "We're trying to challenge the isolation of the elderly," says Diamond. "The way we put them in little standard colonies, little boxes, without many stimulating influences. Once we show that we can change an old brain, I think people will take a different look at aging. It doesn't *have* to be all downhill—*if* you keep your brain stimulated."

What does it all mean? How does the ability to "play" and learn, even as an adult, affect your daily life? It may not change what you do, but it should change how you do it. We adults have a tendency to overestimate the value of work and underestimate the value of play. Maybe it's because we have to do so much of the former and get to enjoy so little of the latter. Sometimes we convey that attitude to our children: "When are you going to stop playing around and do something constructive for a change?" Sound familiar? In fact an activity as simple as window-shopping or as complicated as chess is an exercise of the biological equivalent of a divine right. No other animal can go fly a kite. No other animal can throw a surprise party or play a practical joke or tickle or tease or go up on the roof on a starry night to find the Big Dipper. We need to let ourselves be *really* human more often.

But neoteny is more than just an endorsement of play. It's a reassurance that although early experiences are influential in our development as people, they don't put our feet in cement. Our ability to learn throughout our lengthening lifetimes gives us hope that we can both build on early positive experiences and unlearn early negative ones. Never underestimate the power of learning. It is, after all, our first life experience. From the moment we enter the world, still half-asleep and half-formed, vulnerable and profoundly teachable, we learn to learn.

That is the delicious irony of human life. Our weakness at birth makes us much stronger as we grow. Unlike the animals that develop more fully in the darkness of a womb, we can incorporate the ever-changing outside world into our development. We don't come into the world saying, "Take me as I am, world." We enter saying, "I'm ready to learn, world. Teach me." That's why we continue to master our environment, rather than be mastered by it. "There is no reason," says Ashley Montagu, "to believe that either the quality or the duration of man's capacity for learning will not be subject to further evolution." We may think well of our own intelligence compared with that of our ancestors even a few dozen thousand years ago; but there's no evidence that we've fulfilled our potential, or even that complete fulfillment is possible. We are vessels that have never been full. As far as we know, the possibilities are limitless.

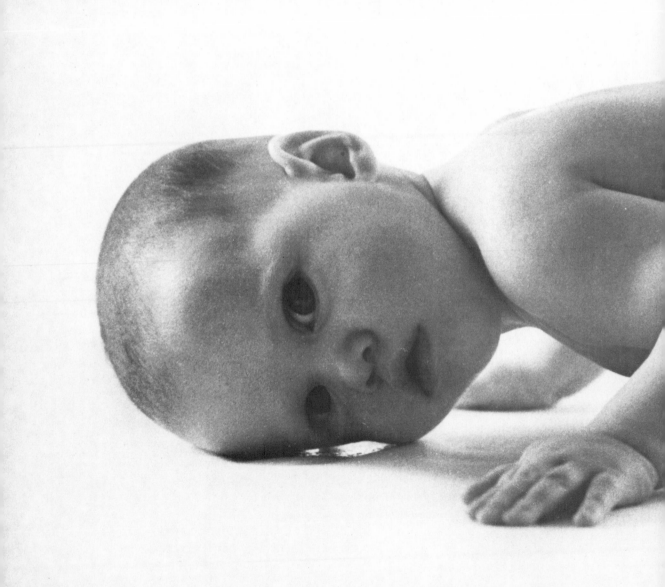

From the moment we're born, the learning wheels begin to turn. Human infancy is a womb with a view.

13. Born to Learn

Sow a thought,
and you reap an Act;
Sow an Act,
and you reap a Habit;
Sow a Habit,
and you reap a Character;
Sow a Character,
and reap a Destiny.

Anonymous

We come into this world a barely formed lump of clay, helpless and vulnerable, carrying a great big brain with virtually nothing in it. How do we get from there to here? How does a babbling baby grow up to be an Einstein or a Beethoven?—or just to be the everyday miracle of a thinking, speaking, conscious human being?

The learning process happens so slowly that we tend to take it for granted. We lose sight of how much of our behavior is learned. Take, for example, that morning cup of coffee so many people couldn't begin their day without. There it is, sitting on the kitchen table or the restaurant counter. We reach out to pick it up. That action requires sophisticated eye–muscle coordination, spatial judgment, and motor skills. We grasp the handle—something no other animal can do; even a human infant isn't capable of such advanced muscular coordination until it's at least nine months old. Then we bring the cup to our face and smell. Recognizing the familiar aroma is another complicated, *learned* skill. We drink and immediately decide if this is a good or a bad cup of coffee. That's a sophisticated judgment that requires bringing to bear past experiences. If we decide it tastes good, we're glad we drank it. If it tastes bad, we put it down in disgust. Both reactions—gladness and disgust—are extraordinarily complex mental activities that scientists are only beginning to understand. But we learned them. How?

First, although we learn almost everything we know, we don't come into the world a blank slate. We start off with a few basic reflexes that are genetically carried survival mechanisms from our earliest ancestors. For example, at birth we have no

What happens inside a baby's head to produce that big smile? The process of face recognition may seem automatic, but it's really a complex, learned behavior.

OPPOSITE: The grasping reflex is only one of the survival mechanisms with which a baby is born. Most of these innate reflexes disappear after several months.

fear of water. A young baby will instinctively hold its breath and contract its throat to keep water out. In fact, a newborn infant is instinctively afraid only of loud noises and of falling. If a newborn falls, it will instinctively reach out for support, a reaction called the Moro Reflex. If you touch it on the palm, it will automatically grasp your finger. When a newborn is hungry, it will naturally root for its mother's breast. It even has a stepping reflex that gives it the rudiments of mobility.

But even these few basic survival gifts from evolution disappear after the first three to four months of life. It's as if they were intended only to help us survive until we can learn. They're replaced by a set of secondary reflexes that involve rolling, balancing, and protecting the body in a fall. For example, if you lower a four-month-old baby into a playpen, it will stretch its legs out to prepare for the landing—a maneuver called a "downward parachute." If you tilt a baby forward and try to put it down flat, it will extend its arms and fingers to prepare for a landing on all fours. This is called a "forward parachute." Over the first year, these secondary reflexes will become increasingly sophisticated as key areas in the brain mature and fine muscle control becomes possible. For example, the newborn's reflexive grasp will be replaced by deliberate grasping at six months, use of the thumb at eight months, and finally the delicate "teacup" grip at one year. These and other secondary responses are not learned—they're hard-wired into the basic model. So are some less delicate reflexes like belching, coughing, sneezing, yawning, and vomiting. But such standard features are the exception, not the rule, for the human animal. In most cases, we do things the old-fashioned way: we *learn* them.

Every moment, no matter how ordinary, can be a learning experience for a developing child. It experiences the world through an extraordinary network of senses, evaluates the input, reacts to it, stores some of it, and discards the rest. Although we're used to thinking that there are five senses—sight, smell, taste, touch, and hearing—in fact, these are just the most obvious features of this phenomenal learning mechanism, the human body. The newborn's body contains specialized nerves that respond to light, sound, touch, pressure, heat, cold, hunger, thirst, pain, fatigue, and other forms of stimulation. Information about the "outside" world—and about the baby's own body—is picked up by these sensors and transmitted to the brain, giving the baby up-to-the-minute coverage of everything that's happening to it, inside and out.

Of the many senses, touch plays a crucial role in the first months of life. Later, vision will be the most important mode of interaction with the world, but at birth, a baby's field of vision is narrow, shallow, and blurred, so touch is its primary form of communication. Messages can come to the brain from three kinds of nerve endings. Exteroceptors ("outside sensors") monitor what's going on in the outside world—heat, cold, the feel of Mommy's breast or Daddy's shoulder. Interoceptors ("inside sensors") monitor the inside story—if Baby needs to eat or it's time to burp. Proprioceptors ("self sensors") help Baby keep track of arms and legs and, later, fingers.

The skin—the boundary between organism and environment—tells the human infant much of what its brain is learning about life through subtle messages, both physical and emotional. The message of a parent's touch is picked up by some of the hundreds of thousands of sensitive exteroceptors spread over the surface of a baby's body. Because exteroceptors are concentrated on the lips, the tip of the tongue, and the pads of the fingers, some touches mean more than others. A kiss or a tiny fistful of hair are unusually rich learning experiences. A pat on the shin or the shoulder will hardly be noticed.

Pain can also be a very powerful learning device. How much pain a baby feels also depends on which area of the body is stimulated. You might think that the areas with the most touch receptors are also the most sensitive to pain, but that isn't always the case. The fingertips, for example, are very sensitive to touch but twenty

times more resistant to pain than the abdomen. This combination of touch discrimination and pain resistance helps make the fingertip an ideal investigator of unknown objects, from building blocks to hot stove tops. It has been suggested that a parent who wants to spank his child should use his or her bare hand instead of a paddle or belt. By using the hand, which has far more "pain spots" per square inch than a child's bottom, a parent can put some real meaning into that old phrase, "This hurts me more than it does you."

The child with a sore bottom may not believe it, but pain travels more slowly through the nervous system than almost any other kind of signal. The system is made up of fibers that vary in thickness, each of which is dedicated to a particular "sense": pain, heat, cold, or touch. The largest and fastest nerve fibers are reserved for registering light touch and vibrations, while pain is relegated to the slower "back route" of small fibers. That's why pain has nothing to do with the size of the nerve affected. Stimulating even the largest nerve that's dedicated to touch will produce no pain, just a rubbing sensation. But stimulate even the tiniest nerve fiber dedicated to pain and you'll definitely feel it. Between these two extremes, there are a variety of levels of stimulation with which a baby quickly becomes familiar. Tickling, for example, is produced by just barely stimulating the touch receptors. Stimulate the pain receptors in the same way and the effect may be an itching sensation

OPPOSITE: By six weeks of age, sight replaces touch as a baby's primary sense.

Beauty is not in the eye of the beholder. Like everything else, it's in the brain. Before we "see" anything, signals have to travel from the eye to the visual cortex at the back of the brain where the complex job of "seeing" is actually done.

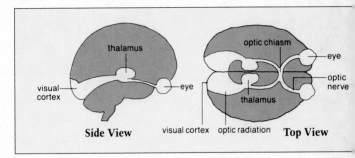

—which may explain why one of your first reactions when you're tickled is to scratch.

Whatever signals the skin receptors send to the brain move along the spinal cord, where they're subjected to an initial "editing" process, then channeled through the thalamus, which is the system's editor-in-chief, sorting out important messages and passing them on to the brain while disregarding the unimportant ones. For example, if the same signal persists for a long time, the thalamus will start to ignore it. This convenient screening device allows you to forget that you're wearing clothes or sitting in a chair.

At six weeks, a baby can focus both eyes on one object, but has only about half the field of vision of an adult. If you make funny faces while Baby is looking off to the side, you're wasting your time. But even at this early age, sight has already replaced touch as Baby's primary sense. The best indication of how important sight will be for the rest of its life is that more of the body's billions of nerve cells are devoted to sight (approximately one-third) than to any other sense. It's our most detailed, most instructional contact with our environment.

What happens when Baby sees Mommy's face? What goes on inside that little head to produce such a big smile? First, the light rays bouncing off Mommy's face enter the jelly-filled ball on either side of Baby's nose—the eyes. They enter through the pupil. an opening in the iris that can be adjusted like the aperture of a camera lens to let in more or less light. In the eye, the image is inverted by a lens so that it appears upside down on the retina at the back of the eye. The retina is really a highly specialized extension of the brain made up of a remarkable, complex web of nerve cells, primarily photoreceptors ("light sensors"). Think of the retina as the opposite of a television screen: instead of converting electrical impulses into a picture, as a TV screen does, the retina converts an image, made up of light waves, into the "brain language" of electrochemical impulses. The retina "screen" is made up of 6 million color-sensitive "cones" and 125 million "rods" that can't distinguish colors; the rods enable us to distinguish objects in low light, but only in shades of gray.

The journey from the retina to the brain, where the electrochemical impulses are unscrambled, is astonishingly complex: through the optic chiasma, where the sig-

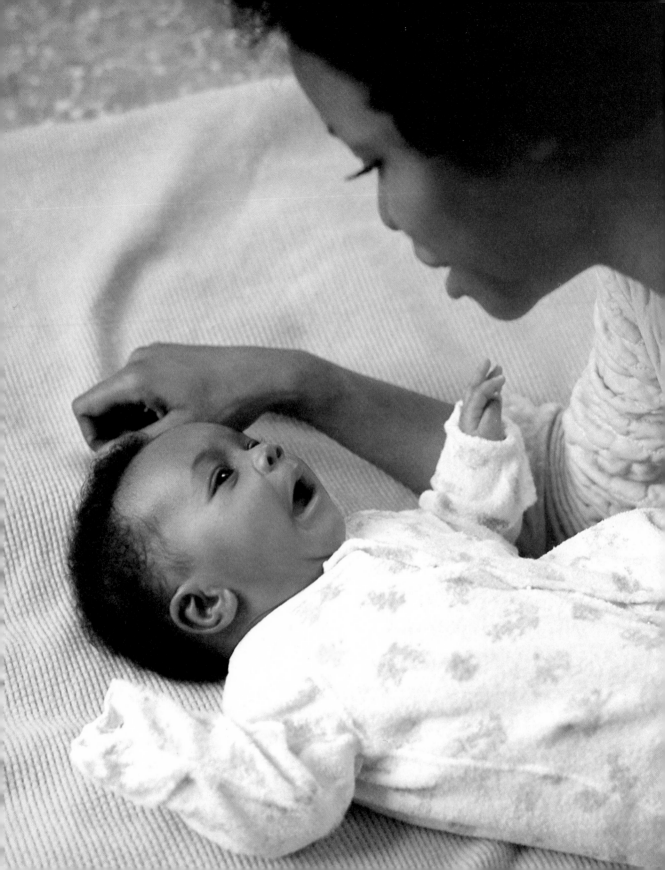

nals from both eyes are mingled, to the thalamus, then through the optic radiation, to the visual cortex on the rear inside edge of each cerebral hemisphere. Here the image of Mommy's face is painstakingly taken apart to be identified. Different areas are assigned the task of recognizing different pieces of the puzzle. For example, one area recognizes that the image is in the shape of a face; another reconfirms that it's a face by recognizing the pattern within the shape—the eyes, mouth, nose. Another area inverts the image; another recognizes that it's close up, not far away. When the pieces are reassembled, the visual cortex informs the hippocampus of the details of the image, and the hippocampus matches those details to images stored in memory. After a brief calculation, it responds: "This is a familiar face." Messages flash through the "feeling" limbic system, then to the hypothalamus, which in turn orders a shot of adrenaline—so arms and legs begin to wriggle—and sends a happy message to the muscles of the mouth: "Smile. It's *Mommy!*"

And all of it happens in the blink of an eye—so fast it appears instantaneous.

The other senses—hearing, smell, taste—are important to the learning process, but the newborn infant relies less on them to learn about the outside world than on touch and sight. Unlike vision, the baby's hearing mechanism is fully formed at birth. The more complicated process of localizing sound, however, takes almost a full year to develop. A baby's sense of taste is actually more acute than an adult's. Where adults have only about nine thousand taste buds, babies have considerably more. That creamed corn that tastes so bland when a parent tries it is a taste sensation to Baby. The newborn's sense of smell is also highly developed, thanks to its remarkably sophisticated, if underused, olfactory membranes. These two membranes take up only about a square inch, but they're packed with as many as 20 million olfactory-nerve endings, each one bristling with sensitive filaments. The total area of exposed olfactory receptors is equal to the skin surface of your body. All that exposure enables Baby to detect 32 *trillionths* of an ounce of musk.

All of these signals, from exteroceptors (fingertips), interoceptors (stomach), proprioceptors (muscles), photoreceptors (eyes), chemoreceptors (mouth), olfactory receptors (nose), and the rest, eventually end up, by a variety of routes, in our old friend, the human brain. How does the brain make sense of this bombardment of sensory input, these thousands of messages pouring in from millions of receptors every second? How does the brain synthesize this chaos into what we call "experience"? With all that noise, it's a miracle that anything gets understood. Yet the brain not only understands this blizzard of sensory data, it can organize it, respond to it, and even sort out the important bits and pieces and store them for later use. This, after all, is what learning is all about.

To understand how the brain makes sense of our senses, we need to look at the way the brain itself is organized. When Baby reaches out and touches Mommy or Daddy, receptors in its fingertips fire. Every scrap of sensory input begins its journey from receptor to brain in the form of a chemical floating across a tiny gap, or synapse, that separates the receptor and the next nerve cell. Once across the synapse, the chemical message becomes an electrical one and travels through a forest of brambly fibers called dendrites toward the nucleus of the nerve, the neuron, the basic building block of the human nervous system. The neuron functions like a switchboard. It gathers incoming messages from the dendrites and then sends out a message of its own in the form of a series of electrical impulses that journey along a long string of fiber called an axon to the next synapse, where the message is again transformed from electrical to chemical so that it can cross the gap to the next nerve cell, where the process begins again. This is the arduous journey every message makes on its way to the brain, island-hopping from nerve cell to nerve cell, changing form from chemical to electrical millions of times, all in fractions of a second. In the brain of a newborn infant, some 50 billion to 100 billion neurons wait to receive and process messages from throughout the body, including the signal from the fingertips touching Mommy's cheek.

As remarkable as it is, the system has its flaws, especially in the beginning. Like any electrical system, the human nervous system is subject to short circuits caused by crossed wires, static caused by electrical interference, and loss of conductivity due to poor insulation. When a child is born, the axons responsible for conveying information through the nervous system are thin and bare. As a result, messages are more vulnerable to interference, more likely to get jumbled or garbled or just plain lost on their way to the brain. If the message does get through in roughly accurate form—"Fingers are now touching Mommy's face"—the messages that the brain sends in response are just as vulnerable to interference as the incoming signals. So Baby may be thinking, "Grab Mommy's nose," but by the time the instructions arrive at the hand, they're so garbled that Baby sticks its finger in Mommy's eye.

To solve these problems, the nervous system begins almost immediately to develop insulation. If all goes well, through the next months and years—until age ten or later—nerve fibers will be enveloped by a sheathing material called myelin that virtually eliminates static and interference along the axons. Myelin works sort of like the rubber that insulates the electric cord on a vacuum cleaner or any other home appliance: it speeds up the passage of signals along the axon. Faster signal transmission means that the brain is capable of faster perception, more refined analysis, and quicker, more accurate response. Myelination permits the crude grasping mechanism of the newborn to become the sophisticated "teacup" grip of the morning coffee drinker. It permits a five-year-old to hold a pencil and an organist to master the fugues of Bach.

Myelination is only one of the genetically programmed processes that sculpt and resculpt the infant's brain and nervous system. Connections between nerve cells will re-form to create new pathways for faster communication with each other. Some neural connections will disappear as involuntary reflexes like grasping and rooting

The brain of an infant is like a new house in the final stages of construction. The business of childhood is to make that house a home.

are replaced by voluntary movements. This natural neural sculpting gives the infant more control over itself and its environment. It marks the beginning of the critical transformation from a feeling, reacting animal to a thinking, learning animal.

The sculpting of neural pathways is a critical process in human development. For the infant, it can also be a dangerous process. As old reflex connections disappear, the brain has to form new ones to take their place or important jobs don't get done. For example, Baby is born with a head-turning reflex that prevents it from smothering. But at about four months, the neural pathway of that reflex begins to change. If a new pathway isn't sculpted to replace it, the infant may smother as it sleeps. Some experts believe that sudden-infant-death syndrome—so-called "crib death"—may be the result of just such a lag between a lost reflex and learned behavior. Although the result is tragic, the message is clear: we must learn to survive.

The brain of a newborn human is like a new house in the final stages of construction. Most of the rooms are finished, but they haven't been decorated yet. It's not yet a home. All the fixtures and appliances are installed, but they're not necessarily hooked up. The two cerebral hemispheres are fully formed, but haven't yet begun to perform their individual functions. The cortical neurons aren't yet completely wired. The intricate webbing of dendrites and axons that will soon lace the cortex—giving Baby its uniquely human gifts of thought, language, and human consciousness—won't begin to grow until the brain is stimulated by experience. And the upper thinking areas of the neocortex, the newest part of the brain, may take as long as twelve years to be fully connected with the limbic system, the old mammalian "feeling" brain.

Let's return to the infant and her mother. How does Baby know to smile? How did it select delight as the appropriate response to the visual and tactile stimuli of

Mommy's face? There's no doubt that an infant's earliest emotional responses influence actual brain growth, and therefore affect all of its future behavior. As Baby learns how to get its needs satisfied, behavior patterns, in the form of neural pathways, are literally formed in the brain, connecting stimulus with response. Crying, smiling, and cooing are good examples. Crying is the infant's natural alarm system. It goes off like a jackhammer, any time of day or night, when Baby's basic needs aren't being met. It's a simple behavior, involving only a few muscles and less thinking. If it works—if Mommy or Daddy comes running into the room, groggy but affectionate—the brain will make the appropriate connection: crying in the middle of the night brings Mommy or Daddy running. A stimulus—discomfort—hooks up with a response—crying—to produce the desired result—Mommy or Daddy. Likewise with smiles and coos. If they work, neural patterns in the brain will specialize for them in the form of new dendrite branches. As experience presents more complicated stimuli—"Mommy doesn't love me enough"—the possible responses become more numerous and more subtle—"I won't smile at her"—and the dendritic connections gradually become a thicket of possibilities. Experience is the teacher, and its lessons are reflected in the actual physical structure of the brain. The result is an organ—and an organism—of subtlety, sophistication, annoying unpredictability, and infinite possibilities.

The moment when Baby looks at Mommy, reaches out to touch her cheek, then smiles and coos with pleasure, is a moment of extraordinary achievement, a triumph of the human animal. It celebrates the joining of the motor reflexes of the brain stem—the oldest, "reptilian" part of our brain; the feelings of the emotional limbic system; and the learning capacity of the neocortex. It may be a small reach for Baby, but it's a giant leap for humankind.

Meanwhile, the developing brain is storing experiences in the form of memories. Exactly how memory works remains one of the unsolved mysteries of science, but we know enough to be in awe. The human animal can remember an essentially unlimited amount of information. The boundaries of our storage capacity have never

LEFT AND OPPOSITE: The process of myelination—the formation of the fatty sheaths along the nerve fibers in the brain—helps a child to accomplish more and more complicated tasks, to go from crawling to walking to running. This is only one of many ways in which early experience and brain growth interact.

even been glimpsed, much less tested. Although some people remember more than others, all of us store a lifetime of memories that form the basis of our identities.

There are a number of theories that seek to explain the mechanism by which we remember—and forget. According to one, all messages from the senses pass through a quick editing procedure on their way to the brain. Located somewhere in the limbic system, almost certainly involving the hippocampus, this "immediate" memory selects certain items and passes them off to short-term memory, which can hold only five to ten items at a time and only for ten to thirty seconds. In this temporary-storage area, the brain decides what to do with them. Some are "rehearsed" for a while in the short-term memory; some are sent directly on to long-term memory. Almost everything has to be compared with previous messages, categorized, and "filed" in the appropriate place.

According to some recent research, short-term memory is geared to the sounds of words—unlike long-term memory, with its unlimited capacity for images. So if you pass a store that has a sale on, your short-term memory doesn't remember the fact of a sale or the image of the storefront: it remembers the word "sale" and,

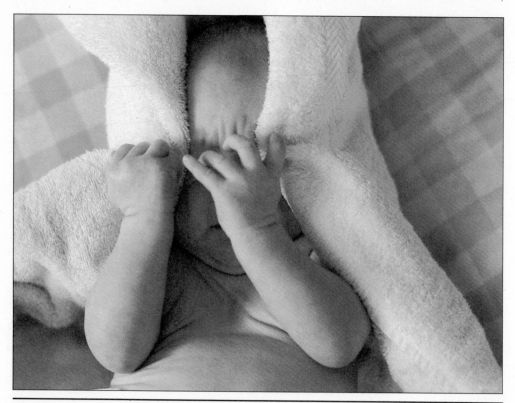

A simple game of peek-a-boo is an extraordinary achievement. It combines the motor reflexes of the brain stem, the feelings of the limbic system, and the learning capacity of the neocortex.

perhaps, the name of the store. If an item—like a telephone number you call frequently—is repeated often enough in the short-term memory, it's transferred to the long-term memory.

Scientists think there are three kinds of long-term memory. Stimulus–response memory allows you to "remember" to smile when someone smiles at you, to be angry when someone is rude. Event memory is the primary repository of all those wonderful memories of childhood, friends, vacations, and special occasions. Located probably in the hippocampus and the frontal lobes, this kind of long-term memory is remarkable both for its accuracy and for its capacity. Finally, abstract memory is the brain's dictionary. All the objects, all the concepts that you know are stored here. It's the part of memory that allows you to remember what "red" looks like and what that piece of flat wood with four legs in the middle of the dining room is called. Like event memory, abstract memory has an almost unlimited capacity.

The real miracle of memory isn't that we *store* so much information, it's that we can *retrieve* it so quickly. Scientists aren't sure what the filing system looks like, but they know that memories that don't come immediately to mind can be retrieved by using cues. You may not remember the name of the first person you ever kissed, or your sixth-grade teacher or the hotel where you stayed on your honeymoon, but if someone mentions the name of another teacher at the same school, or starts to reminisce about your wedding day, then the missing pieces of information will sometimes pop up from long-term memory. The implication is that memories are arranged in related groups and that once you establish a path to a particular group, it's easier to retrieve other, "forgotten" items from the same group.

Ironically, forgetting is as important to learning as remembering. Few people complain about remembering too much—the opposite is usually the problem—but there are people with exceptionally retentive memories who complain that they can't rid their minds of the thousands of trivial occurrences and images that speed through the mind every minute. Part of learning is discarding information that's unimportant or irrelevant, and the brain accomplishes this by replacing old memories with new or by simply erasing the memory trace altogether—the difference between replacing the tenant and tearing down the house. Although we may sometimes disagree with its selection, the brain does a remarkably good job of picking and choosing.

Memory allows an infant to divide its experience into known and unknown, the familiar and the alien. Although an important learning tool, this ability to distinguish friend from stranger has its dark side. At about eight months old, the formerly trusting infant suddenly begins to be afraid of strangers. The same thing happens to infants throughout the world, in every culture, at every economic level: When Uncle Charlie visits Baby buries his face in Daddy's chest. Mommy and Daddy spend the whole visit frustrated, saying, "Say hello to your Uncle Charlie—let him see your big smile," which, of course, Baby never does.

Brain experts believe that this sudden onset of shyness has its origins in the memory function of the hippocampus. According to the most recent theory, as each moment passes, Baby's brain draws a kind of instant cartoon of the fleeting present and compares the current cartoon to the ones "on file" in the memory area of the hippocampus. If something in the latest cartoon doesn't match the previous ones (that is, doesn't fit with our previous experience of the world), the hippocampus registers the discrepancy between the familiar past and unfamiliar present, and, as a result, Baby feels anxious and uneasy.

By this same mechanism, the basic processing of experience into memory by the hippocampus may contribute to human prejudice: our fear and dislike of the unfamiliar. Is this why Arabs and Jews, blacks and whites, Hindus and Muslims have such a hard time getting along? Are there biological facts—immutable facts—underlying the economic, sociological, and political causes of xenophobia, racism and discrimination in the world? Facts? Perhaps. Immutable? Never. Even if human prejudice gets a subtle biological boost—and we're not sure that it does—it's not insurmountable. The key fact about our emotional, limbic, mammalian brain is that it doesn't have the last word when it comes to human behavior. Part of the miraculous process of learning in the human animal is learning to use our thinking neocortex to regulate rudimentary, untrained emotions like fear of the unknown.

By the time Baby is no longer a baby—two years old—brain development and integration are well under way. The number of dendrites has increased five- or sixfold; the number of nerve connections is well into the billions. If we were to duplicate in hi-tech hardware the number of potential connections in Baby's brain, we'd have to build a computer the size of Chicago. And even then, it wouldn't be an equal in every way. But to reach this level of sophistication, Baby's brain must be stimulated. Only the barest connections are "born"; the vast majority are made, in the never-ending learning process. For the human animal, using your brain cells is no idle luxury. The house rule appears to be, "Use 'em or lose 'em."

Science is only beginning to understand the learning process in the human animal. It's still something of a secret that the brain guards jealously. One of the problems is that we're still not sure how much of our behavior *is* learned and how much comes through the birth canal with us. How much of what we become is influenced by those important others who nurtured us through childhood? "I owe it all to you, Mom and Dad" isn't just something we say to be nice—we mean it. But recent studies can't help but make us wonder: Do we really owe it *all* to our parents? The boundary between "nature" and "nurture" is no bright line; it's a wide and vaguely defined no-man's-land where scientists continue to research and dispute.

For example, Dr. Carroll Izard, professor of psychology at the University of Del-

---

The onset of shyness, which occurs in almost all children at about eight months, has its origins in the hippocampus. The same mechanism may play a role in human prejudice.

Emotions like anger, sadness, and surprise may be wired into the newborn infant, awaiting only the proper stimulus to be expressed.

aware, is looking into babies' faces for evidence of an inborn set of basic human emotions. Using videotape and computers, Izard analyzes the tiniest movements of infants' faces as they react to common experiences of childhood. He will hand an infant an ice cube; give it a favorite toy, then take it away; or put a ticking clock to its ear—then photograph its response. "A picture may be worth a thousand words," he says, "but a picture of an infant is worth ten thousand."

Each facial pattern is photographed, then coded according to an intricate system developed by Izard: the Maximally Discriminative Facial Movement Coding System, or Max for short. The careful codings enable him to distinguish between, say, an expression of anger and one of pain, which involves only one small difference in the area of the eyes. From his observations, Izard concludes that at least six human emotions—joy, surprise, sadness, anger, disgust, and fear—are inherent in the human being at birth and that another five—interest, shame, shyness, guilt, and contempt—can be observed by the middle of the second year. "I suspect," he says, "that emotions are preprogrammed on a biological clock." If you inoculate an infant at two months, it will express pain; if you inoculate it seven months later, it will have developed the capacity for anger as well. These responses, says Izard, "are the primary colors, as it were, that evolution puts on our behavioral palette, colors that experience and socialization then mix and blend into subtler hues of feelings."

Other scientists dispute Izard's conclusions, arguing that words like "anger," "sadness," "shame," and "guilt" are loaded with adult meanings and adult under-

standings no child is capable of. Anger, in their view, requires a certain cognitive ability. For you to be angry at someone, you have to be able to reason in a way that newborns aren't yet equipped to do. You have to conclude that the person has done you wrong. A baby can't do that—it hasn't yet sculpted the necessary neural pathways to make those connections.

Right or wrong, Izard's work is valuable because it encourages us to look more skeptically at the assumptions we've always made about ourselves. If human infants aren't the blank slates we used to think they were, perhaps other human feelings also have biological origins. An ongoing twenty-year study by Jerome Kagan suggests that each of us carries a unique, inborn "style" or temperament—from timidity to boldness—that's tied to our autonomic nervous system, a temperament that we display from the moment of birth.

Do studies like this give new meaning to old sociological observations like "born free," "born to be wild," "a born leader," "to the manner born"? No. Science is a long way from proving that nature has the upper hand over nuture in determining who we are. But these recent studies do make us stop and rethink some of our sixties, where-did-I-go-wrong? notions about the influence parents have on the development of their kids. Perhaps the most conscientious parents have been too hard on themselves when their youngsters "go wrong." Perhaps we've overestimated our power to help—or hurt. Certainly, children are phenomenal learning machines, but we're not the only teachers.

14. Love's Labor

Before mammals evolved, parenting was almost a nonexistent profession. The giant dinosaurs mated pretty much the way reptiles mate today—businesslike, at best—then laid their eggs and forgot them. Their survival strategy was to produce huge armies of offspring and count on a few of them to survive. The baby dinosaurs popped out of their eggs with everything they needed to get by—essentially miniature adults, ready to make a run at survival. They never saw their mother, or if they did, wouldn't have recognized her—just as she wouldn't have recognized Father. Then, at least 150 million years ago, mammals revolutionized the parenting business with a system that *began* with intercourse, instead of ending with it.

As the paragon of mammals, we've carried the idea of parenting to its most sophisticated—if not always its most admirable—level. Because the human infant remains dependent far longer than any other animal, the human adult ends up parenting far longer. All the advantages of neoteny, of learning about the world *after*

Child-rearing practices vary from one society to another and even from year to year. Some of the advice in the first editions of Dr. Benjamin Spock's Baby and Child Care, *a widely used child-rearing handbook in the 1950s, has changed with the passage of time.*

DR. BENJAMIN SPOCK

BABY AND CHILD CARE

The most widely recommended handbook for parents ever published—Authoritative, illustrated, indexed

Over 19,000,000 copies sold

birth, place a remarkable burden on the parenting process, making it not only longer, but more complex, more difficult, and more open to abuse. To push such an unformed, vulnerable, impressionable, and potent bundle of joy as a human baby out into the world, nature had to have a great deal of confidence both in the baby's ability to learn *and* in the parents' ability to teach. Anyone who has ever been a parent often wonders if they deserve that confidence.

Any thinking parents have to wonder if they're making mistakes in raising their own children, mistakes they're not aware of, mistakes made for all the best of reasons. Just by way of example, for a long time many child-rearing experts stressed the importance of teaching children from the earliest age not to cry. They suggested that parents practice "a little hardening of the heart," and, by age five or six months, to avoid picking up a child *every* time it cried. But when anthropologist Melvin Konner informed a !Kung woman of this piece of well-intentioned advice, she responded: "Don't they realize it's only a baby? It has no sense—that's why it cries. You pick it up. Later on, when it gets bigger, it will have sense, and it won't cry so much." Now scientists are beginning to agree more with the !Kung mother that children aren't fully developed, and aren't physically or emotionally prepared for prolonged separation from the adult, until about ten months. Trying to force independence five months too early may be counterproductive.

Child-rearing experts used to advise parents to avoid picking up a child whenever it cries. Among the !Kung tribe of Africa, however, babies have always been considered too young to understand such "lessons." Today, experts tend to side with the !Kung.

OPPOSITE: Lest there be any doubt that parents have a profound impact on their child's development, recent research indicates that in the first six months of life, the typical infant has more than 32,000 interactions with its parents.

That an uneducated woman from a primitive society may have more insight into an aspect of child care than our best child-care experts is enough to make any parent pause and take a deep breath. Perhaps we're doing our children the most damage just when we think we're doing them the most good.

A parent's first, worried question at a time like that—although it's seldom expressed—is, "How much can I hurt my child?" We all know that the emotional bond between parent and child runs deep, but how deep? Dr. Carroll Izard and his team of researchers are studying parent–infant interaction to discover just how soon, and how much, infants are shaped by interaction with their parents. The answers, according to his research, are, very early, and, quite a lot. One of Izard's students, Carol Malatesta, estimates that from the third to the sixth month, an infant has about 32,000 emotion-laden experiences with the adults who care for it. That's 32,000 opportunities to learn from Mommy and Daddy—even though Mommy and Daddy may not be aware of what they're teaching.

In a long-term study of children with chronically depressed parents, Dr. Izard found "a clear correlation between the parents' personalities and their kids'. The way a parent expresses emotion may help determine how a child learns to cope with life's stresses. Through socialization and the interplay of communication between parent and child, the child learns to take on the parent's emotional state." What

about more subtle parental behavior? What are the effects when parents feel joy, or fear? If children learn to learn long before they learn to speak, if indeed we communicate with them in thousands of nonverbal ways—posture, breathing, facial expressions—how self-conscious should we be around that wide-eyed little tyke in the crib or playpen? Does every scowl become a lifelong scar?

Because parents are understandably reluctant to let scientists test the effects of emotional deprivation on their babies, the answers to questions like these come mostly from research with animals. The famous and tragic exception to that rule is the research conducted in a Swiss orphanage by psychiatrist René Spitz during the 1930s. Spitz found many of the orphans starving to death even though they had all the food they could eat. They had been separated from their parents at the critical age of eight months, and no amount of nourishment and competent medical care could keep them from physically wasting away. Dr. Spitz called this condition "marasmus," which means "wasting away." Infants can literally die for lack of love.

The tragedy of Dr. Spitz's orphans testifies more powerfully than any experiment to how deeply linked each of us is with those who from our earliest days have nurtured us through life. It seems that in childhood we are open receivers tuned continuously to those who nurture us, and the nurturing messages of love and attention they send lay the foundation for our later capacities to feel joy and fear, to love ourselves and extend love and compassion to others—to live as healthy and fulfilled human beings. But if, as Dr. Spitz discovered, that attention is lacking, if what is communicated isn't love but indifference, the impact on a child can be every bit as devastating as physical abuse.

And that discovery raises some questions: Given the human frailties of even the best-intentioned parents, and the inevitable perils and problems of even the most fortunate childhood, how long-lasting are the effects of our childhood experiences? Are the influences from nurturers that made us what we are subject to modification if as adults we find ourselves to be maladjusted or unhappy? Or are we locked in, without hope of change, to a personal fate that, for better or worse, became ours before we had anything to say about it? Will the blessings of a healthy childhood sustain us all our lives? Can the handicaps of an unhealthy one be overcome?

The questions are easy to ask, but the answers are as subtle and elusive as the interaction between parent and child. Scientists have been collecting evidence toward those answers, however, evidence so compelling that it persuaded the National Institute of Health's Child Development Division to fund Dr. Stephen Suomi's experiments on rhesus monkeys. Why fund monkey studies to learn about human children? Because Dr. Suomi's work carries on the earlier research of psychologist Harry Harlow, whose experiments reproduced for the first time in the laboratory the equivalent of an emotionally deprived childhood.

In the 1950s, Harlow proved systematically how devastating parental indifference can be for a child. In his classic experiment, he separated infant rhesus monkeys

Our capacities as adults to feel joy and fear, to love ourselves and extend love and compassion to others are shaped by the adults who nurture us as infants with love and attention. The Boating Party by Mary Cassatt, 1893–1894.

Dr. Stephen Suomi, director of the Primate Research Facility of the National Institute of Health's Child Development Center in Maryland, says, "We have learned that there are strong parallels between humans and nonhuman primates in the ways that poor mothering, environmental stress, and the lack of social supports affect their children. Special attention in the form of a stable social setting, available peers, and access to adult nurturing can reverse early deficits."

OPPOSITE: In a classic experiment, infant rhesus monkeys were given a choice between two artificial surrogate mothers—one made of terry cloth, the other of bare wire. Even when the wire surrogate was equipped with a milk bottle, the infants chose the terry mother. Softness and warmth, it seems, can be more important than food.

from their natural mothers. He gave one group a choice of two artificial surrogate mothers—one a heated cylinder covered with terry cloth, the other an equally warm, bare-wire tube. He discovered that the baby monkeys clung to the warm terry-cloth surrogate, even when the bare-wire surrogate had a milk bottle attached to it, providing the infants with their only source of food. They needed the security of warmth and touch as much as they needed food. When they were confronted with a frightening object, they ran right back to the cloth-covered surrogate—not to the milk-providing wire one—to be comforted. Touch was more important than food.

The group of Harlow's monkeys that had grown up with artificial mother surrogates behaved abnormally enough. But a third group, raised by Harlow in complete social isolation, without anything remotely resembling a mother, turned out to be a group of utter misfits, withdrawn and bizarre. The results were catastrophic. The males were abnormally violent toward other monkeys. Neither males nor females could perform sexual intercourse. If artificially inseminated, the females had babies they ignored or even brutalized. In some cases, the deprived monkeys were reduced to spending whole days banging their heads against the cage. All because they had been deprived of a mother's touch and of other baby monkeys to play with.

In the "jungles" of the Primate Center at the National Institute of Health's Child Development Division in Maryland, Dr. Suomi is taking Dr. Harlow's research one step further—one crucial step that ought to have all of us on the edges of our seats in anticipation of the results. Here in his lab, Dr. Suomi studies monkeys which as infants had been deprived of normal nurturing, just as Dr. Harlow's monkeys were; but then he devotes himself to experimentally healing the behavioral scars that deprivation has left. And his results so far indicate that, within limits, you can teach an old monkey new tricks, that the very same unfinished openness that makes our children so dependent on us and vulnerable to deficient nurturing may also be their salvation from permanent psychological damage.

According to Dr. Suomi, "We have learned that there are strong parallels between humans and nonhuman primates in the ways that poor mothering, environmental stress, and the lack of social supports affect their children. But we have learned with these monkeys, who were themselves parented in abnormal situations, that extra care later can rehabilitate them. Special attention in the form of a stable social setting, available peers, and access to adult nurturing can reverse early deficits. We don't know if everything can be regained. But we do know we can help. And I am optimistic about the capacity of human beings to overcome quite a lot. That's the nature of the human brain—more flexible and resilient than any other."

Harlow's and Suomi's research has concentrated on what happens when Mom isn't there to do her job. But what about *Dad?* There were two parents at conception; where's the other one now? Did nature intend for Mom to be left holding the baby? How much of a role does Dad really play, after conception, in the long and arduous process of teaching and nurturing this vulnerable but precious little creature? After all, most males in the wild are—they should excuse the expression—

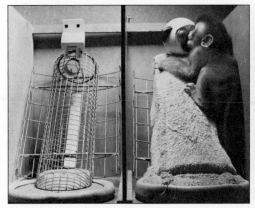

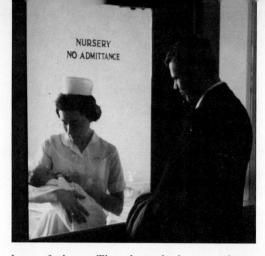

A father in the 1950s and '60s usually saw his child for the first time through a window of the maternity ward—an arrangement that didn't exactly encourage bonding between father and child.

lousy fathers. They have little or nothing to do with their offspring. Is this also the natural state of the human male? "We give birth to highly vulnerable infants," responds Irven DeVore. "Their brain development and social development take years. Just as in other species with vulnerable infants, there comes to be an advantage in having a male participate in intensive care of the offspring, so it has come to be true in our species."

Has it? Or are most of us still stuck in the old mammalian routine of nurturing mother and wandering father? Certainly, we still recognize that there's something very special and unique about a mother's relationship to her children. "I think there is a mammalian basis," says Dorothy Dinnerstein, "for the female passion for infants. There's no doubt about it. Only a woman knows what it feels like to have milk spurting out of her body when she hears a little voice crying. Only a woman has the intimate tie to somebody who grew up in her body and whom she feeds from her own body." Dr. DeVore agrees: "In mammals, the ultimate caretaker must be the mother, because she is doing the breast feeding. And in our own species this was also completely true until just a few decades ago. It was really the invention of efficient nursing bottles and contraception that released women in this species from their status from time immemorial as baby-bearing machines."

It appears to be a simple, immutable fact of nature that even the human brain can't overcome or ignore: women make better mothers than men. But the biological excuse that women bear and breast-feed isn't the whole story. Fathers are, by and large, *capable* of caring for their young. If Dad's not helping out with the kids, don't let him plead biology. Laziness, indifference, insecurity, perhaps, but not genes. A decade ago, William Redican of the University of California at Davis raised a group of infant monkeys in a laboratory setting with adult males but no adult females. The males—typically—tried to ignore the problem at first, but when no females came to the rescue, they bit the bullet and started providing "maternal" care. "Under those circumstances," says Stephen Suomi, "the males did a pretty good job. And the infants became attached to the males much as they would become attached to a real mother."

No, the issue isn't whether fathers are *capable* of caring for their young under unusual circumstances, the issue is whether the culture will *encourage* fathers to share parenting—not only because it offers priceless benefits to the child, but because plain old-fashioned common sense says any animal that takes this long to mature will be best served during the agonizingly slow process of growing up by *two* parents. As Grandma used to say: "If you're going to have kids, get some help." While there may be some excuse in the evolutionary scheme of things for animals like the rhesus male who spends less than 5 percent of his time with his infants, the human animal, it may be said, should know better. But a look at the lonely nurturing life of females like the rhesus monkey makes it clear why the human female who fights for equality appears to be fighting an uphill ethological struggle.

But things aren't as bad as they look at first. "The study of animal behavior," says DeVore, "suggests that in the greater evolutionary scheme of things, human fathers do play an important role in the nurturing of their children. If you arrange mammalian males on a continuum line of the interest they take in their mates and offspring, from the least interested to the most, you'll find that the human male is very close to the 'most nurturant' end."

Because Dr. DeVore's statement may come as something of a surprise, let's do what he suggests. Let's put the human male on a lineup of mammalian males, from the least nurturing to the most nurturing. It's an interesting collection, starting with our two-ton aquatic cousin, the elephant seal; then moving on to the baboon, whose behavior has long been compared to man's; then to our closest kin, the chimp, who but for *1 percent* of its genes would *be* a man; then to the wolves and dogs, whose

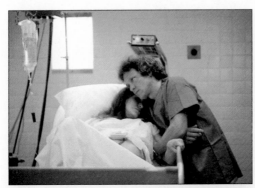
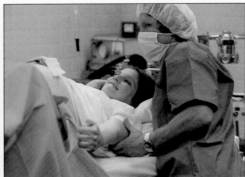
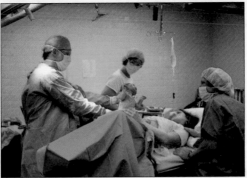

Today, it's not unusual for a father to be present in the delivery room when his child is born.

bonding in packs is often compared to our social behavior; and finally to the tiny marmoset, a monkey that puts every human father to shame.

Holding down the "least nurturing" end of our lineup is a real bruiser, the elephant seal. An impressive fellow, sizewise, but a real dud of a dad. The male elephant seal is an extreme example of a tournament species. Tournament males have one and only one goal when their mating season comes around: to impregnate as many females as possible. "He puts all of his energy," says DeVore, "into fighting for status, fighting for territory, fighting to keep a group of females all to himself. His reproductive strategy is simply to get as many females pregnant as possible and leave all the care to them." Among elephant seals only 4 percent of the males are responsible for 85 percent of the pregnancies. And once the job's done, it's "Goodbye. Don't get up." The tournament male couldn't care less what happens next. Like the permanent denizen of some singles bar, he never forms a bond and never plays father. In fact, during the next mating season he sometimes carelessly crushes his own offspring to death in his blubberous effort to get at yet another female.

The male baboon, who stands somewhere in the middle of our lineup, has a lot more tolerance for parenthood than the elephant seal. He will let an infant ride on him, or sit in the shade he makes under the hot African sun. He'll share his food with it, even protect it from other baboons that threaten physical harm. And best of all, he'll provide these services not just to his own infants, but to any infants that belong to his female companion of the moment, even though they were sired by some other male. He's like a watchful human father making sure that none of the neighbor kids run into the street. In the animal world, the baboon would make a great second husband.

At the "most nurturing" end of our lineup, we have a truly inspirational dad, one that puts the high-and-mighty *Homo sapiens* to shame. This is the marmoset, per-

All in all, compared to most other mammals, the human male scores surprisingly well on the fathering scale. LEFT: Marmoset father with young. *OPPOSITE: Beach Scene* by Malcolm Morley, 1968.

Despite the rising divorce rates, marriage is more popular than ever. In a ceremony in New York's Madison Square Garden, the Reverend Sun Myung Moon joins 2,500 brides to 2,500 grooms in the largest mass wedding on record.

haps the most responsible father in the mammalian world. Marmosets are the best example of what biologists call a "pair-bonding" species—animals that mate and cooperate in raising their young. The concept may sound very human, but the execution has no parallels in our society. In marmoset bonding, there are two males for every female. This group of three bonds for life. The single female presents one of her two mates with twins (marmoset females always bear twins). Although nobody knows for sure who the real father is, nobody seems to care. Each of the two husbands happily puts one of the twins on his back, where it remains until grown, returning to Mom only at feeding time. Marmoset males literally shoulder their responsibilities. And the two males and one female live happily ever after in something very close to our nuclear family: a male-female team dedicated to nurturing the young.

The fathering behavior of other mammals falls somewhere between the noble marmoset and the hell-raising elephant seal. Human parental behavior—like most human behavior—is all over the lot. The human father takes less of a role in raising his young than a marmoset, but more than a wolf. Like an elephant seal, he spends a lot of time competing with other males for access to females; but, like the baboon, he conscientiously protects his own offspring and even those of his neighbors. He also occasionally helps with their care. All in all, on our mammalian fathering scale, the human male comes out looking pretty good.

Another way of gauging how good the human father is compared to other animals is to look at his relative size. Scientists have determined that where an animal falls on the continuum between tournament strategist and pair bonders is closely related to the differences in body size between the male and female of the species. The experts call this sexual size difference "dimorphism." At one end of the scale, tournament strategists are highly dimorphic. The male elephant seal, for example, is twice the size of his mate. By contrast, pair bonders are often identical in size. Male birds are often indistinguishable from females in size, and the pairs they form tend to last a lifetime. Greylag geese mate only after an elaborate courtship, grow lovesick if separated, and sink into depression or even death if a mate dies.

How does the human male score on the dimorphism scale? Are we more or less nurturing than our relative size would dictate? According to Dr. DeVore, the human male isn't much bigger than the female in terms of height, "but if you test the strength of the biceps and triceps, the fighting muscles, these may be two or three times the strength of the muscles in a female," says DeVore. "In certain respects, humans are a comparatively highly dimorphic species." So, given the patterns of animal behavior, it's probably surprising that men take as much care of their kids as they do. We score better than our biology.

The human male also looks pretty good if you compare him to his closest relatives in the primate family. "In our very closest relatives like the orangutans," says DeVore, "the males and females are together for only a few hours every four years. This isn't exactly your 'Good Housekeeping' nuclear family. And in gorillas, chimpanzees, and our other closest relatives, there is very little male parental care."

Not only is the human male comparatively caring, he's also comparatively devoted. According to research, there's a lot of precedent among other mammals for the marital wanderlust we call the "seven-year itch." Other animals have mate problems and suffer from a similar malaise; in fact, most do. And when they do, most other animals simply pick up and walk out. It might be more reassuring if anthropologists would tell us that monogamy and lifelong bonding are consistent with our nature, but that doesn't seem to be the case. Apparently, in opting for monogamy, we are going against our biological nature, rather than conforming to it. But that, after all, is one of the prerogatives of being human.

Of course, it's considerably more difficult to generalize about human "pair-bonding" behavior than it is to talk about marmosets. We humans are a messy lot, tending to wander all over the statistical landscape, and nowhere is that more true than in our relationships. Our pair-bonding behavior varies enormously from couple to couple, especially in the level of male participation in child raising. On any one block in any neighborhood, there's probably one male who outdoes the marmoset for fidelity, another who's unaffectionate but responsible like the baboon, and even one who outphilanders the elephant seal.

"In most human societies," says DeVore, "males try very hard to be polygynous —to have a series of wives, to garner as many women around them as possible." As an extreme example of this kind of behavior, DeVore points to the flamboyant rock

Mating behavior among human males runs the gamut from rock stars with their pha-lanxes of female groupies to the men in the three-piece suits with their wedding bands, mortgages, and college tuition payments. LEFT: Mick Jagger performs with the Roll-ing Stones at a concert in Philadelphia, 1981. BOTTOM: Executives wait for a bus home.

stars who gather around them phalanxes of female groupies. "They're sending off a very different message to the world from the man in the gray flannel suit on the five-twenty to Westchester," says DeVore. "*He's* basically saying, with his gold wedding band and drab clothing, 'I'm into investing in my offspring,' which may be literally true. I mean, if they're going to college, he may be spending fifty to a hundred thousand dollars on them."

Of course, rock stars—even if their mating behavior is more consistent with our biological heritage—make up only a tiny piece of the male pie. The man in the three-piece suit—even if he wears a blue collar or a white coat—is much more typical of human fathers who have overcome the model set by our primate ancestors. He may not be demonstrative, but at least he's loving. He should do more of the hard work of nurturing, but at least he's there as an example. Is this the best we can do? The average human father may be more caring than his biology requires him to be, but is that enough?

Dr. Dorothy Dinnerstein, professor of psychology at Rutgers University, thinks not. "Human infants need to be raised by a nurturing team," says Dr. Dinnerstein. "One parent, even if it's the mother, isn't enough. But we should be less concerned about the growing number of single-parent households in our society—as long as they can provide the child with an involved parenting figure of the missing sex—and

OPPOSITE: In the Norman Rockwell days of stability and small towns, nuclear families were surrounded by relatives who were available both for everyday nurturing and for help in a crisis. This model of family life, which millions of people long for, is a thing of the past for many of us. Freedom from Want by Norman Rockwell, 1946.

more concerned about our many 'traditional' families which dump all the child-rearing responsibilities on the mother, without much participation from Dad. By tolerating such families as 'normal' we are cheating our children of the nurturing team they need."

At one time, recruiting a "nurturing team" to care for children was relatively easy even if Dad was preoccupied. As in marmoset groups, there were always a few surplus males around. "In many cultures children are raised quite successfully with the mother's uncle or brother playing the role the father traditionally plays in ours," says Dr. Dinnerstein. "What's important is that a male parenting figure be involved." But times have changed, and the role of father has been dragged to center stage by another critical change in the nurturing process: the disintegration of the extended family.

To ensure proper nurturing, most animals tend to spread the responsibility for raising the young to the whole community. This is nature's form of day care. Flamingos on Lake Naivasha, Kenya.

In the Norman Rockwell days of stability and small towns when Aunt Harriet lived down the street, nuclear families were surrounded by relatives—parents and grandparents, brothers and sisters, aunts and uncles—who were available both for everyday nurturing and for help in a crisis. Now, with airplanes and travel trailers, families have scattered apart to the point where sometimes not even Mom and Dad live in the same city. "In earlier days," says Irven DeVore, "we lived in big extended families and in settled communities. You grew up all of your life with friends and relatives around you—very much more like the way people live in other societies."

We may think that the extended family went the way of the Studebaker, the 10-cent cup of coffee, and home milk delivery, but it's still the rule, not the exception, in most human societies. "If you look at a world sample of, say, thirteen hundred societies," says Irven DeVore, "you find this highly mobile nuclear family—husband, wife, and children—only at the two extremes. You find them among hunter-gatherers and you find them in the industrial world, and for the same reason: they're chasing dispersed resources, game and food, and they must be able to move, and the only economic unit possible is the nuclear family."

Does that mean the new nuclear family is really just a throwback—way back—to primitive societies? Hardly. There are some significant differences. When a Bushman's nuclear family moves from one camp to another, they're moving to another group of friends and relatives, people they've known all their lives. When our nuclear family in the United States moves from Des Moines to California, they're moving into a strange town, into a strange apartment building, often into an indifferent, if not actually hostile environment. Yet we somehow expect people to go on operating in an effective way, in a loving, caring way, without the emotional support that the species has had throughout history.

Even the apes know better. In primate societies as in human societies, small nuclear families are the exception to the rule. Communities of gorillas and chimpanzees ensure the proper nurturing of their young not by relying exclusively on two parents, but by spreading the responsibility for raising the children to the whole community. "There's no question," says Stephen Suomi, summarizing his years of research into the behavior of rhesus monkeys, "that solid and stable community support is an essential part of a healthy social environment in which to grow up."

So the tight little family group we're all so used to isn't just unnatural. By dumping all responsibility for child rearing on two parents—and sometimes even just *one*—it actually overloads the nurturing capabilities of even the most loving mother or father. "I don't know where we got the notion," says DeVore, "that you can take a man and a woman and their children and their dog, Spot, and move them across country, and that they can go on operating and that they can get all the psychological support they need from each other. When the mother is alone, when the baby's crying and she's at her wits' end, she has no one to turn to. In that pressure-cooker kind of situation, it would be peculiar if we didn't have enormous strains and enormous problems."

DeVore points to the communes that were established by disenchanted young people during the late sixties and early seventies as an attempt to get back to a nurturing environment more appropriate to our species. "We called them radical," says DeVore, "but I think they were reactionaries. They were saying, 'This isolated family life just doesn't work.' " In other words those ambitious young executives, male or female, who leave Hometown, U.S.A., for a better-paying job should be aware of the possible consequences. By spinning off from their community, they're putting a lot of additional pressure on relationships within the family—between parents and child *and* between husband and wife. According to Dr. DeVore, all that good Norman Rockwell support, psychological and economic, that used to come from family and friends now has to come from one person: the spouse. In a world of two-career couples, that kind of total support is becoming more and more difficult to muster. The result shows up in the statistics on divorce as more and more marriages collapse under the weight of unreasonable expectations.

What does this mean to that increasingly common phenomenon in our society, the single parent? He or she has to cope both as a parent without a partner and as an animal without a mate. Especially when there's no extended family to fall back on, single parenthood just may be the worst possible nurturing situation in the entire primate world. And what about the working mother? Do so-called "latchkey" kids grow up emotionally deprived because Mommy isn't there to greet them when they come home from school? Is the mother who has to work robbing her kids of emotional support in order to give them financial support?

"I think the book is still out as to what the long-term consequences of [separation] are," says Suomi, "and it's certainly not going to be the same for every individual. We now know that some individuals are more vulnerable than others to the availability or lack of availability of a nurturing figure or other social support. But we also do know that when that support is provided, it need not be there twenty-four hours a day. Sometimes a little bit of intense love will go a lot further than a large amount of very little love."

It may be that the quality, not the quantity, of love is what counts. "The data so far suggest that if the mother comes back from work and has the time and energy to provide support and spend some close time with her offspring when she is not otherwise occupied, then there are few long-term consequences. If, when she comes back, she is so tired that she has neither the energy nor the patience to deal with the child, so that their relationship is tense, then you are going to have some problems. We know that the potential for difficulty also depends on what else is going on. If she comes back to a stable situation, where there is not a lot of strife and rivalry and challenge, then her being gone is not crucial. If she comes back, and a lot of terrible things are going on, then her absence may turn out to be disastrous."

If there's a consensus of scientific opinion, it's this: that extremes of parental behavior—intense love or unrelenting neglect—can override whatever characteristics a child has been endowed with by its genes. Nurture can override nature. Between the extremes, in the vast middle ground where most of us raise our children, both nature and nurture play their eternal game of one-upmanship. In ten years—maybe more, maybe less—there may be more agreement among scientists about the relative influences of natural and nurturing forces. But as Jerome Kagan points out, perhaps the question, not the answer, is at fault. Instead of thinking of the child's development as a football game between Nature and Nurture and always asking ourselves questions like, "Can a good nature win out over a bad upbringing?"

we should regard the development of a human "as if it were the shape of an offshore sandbar over a twenty-year interval."

"The wind and waves, which we might consider as analogous to the environment, are constantly changing the shape of the sandbar. That does not mean that there will be no preservation of form. It depends on the number, and especially the duration, of those storms. If a child has a set of qualities that are either pathological

Day-care centers appear to solve some of the problems created by the decline of the extended family, but many parents are concerned about the effects of prolonged separation. Some experts believe that the right kind of love and attention can make up for the effects of separation.

or maladaptive, and the environment that produced them remains the same, the child is likely to be in trouble as an adult. But if the environment becomes benevolent, the available data suggest that changes are likely to occur." Given the right change of circumstances, even the most emotionally deprived youngster is resilient enough to change.

So the parent who struggles with the guilt of a failed child, or an antisocial child —a child who can't make friends, turns to drugs, or steals hubcaps—is both right and wrong in asking the question, "What did I do wrong?" Kagan's prescription for parental anxieties and guilt is a heavy dose of realism. Parents think they can do more than they can, says Kagan, and as a result, they end up assuming more guilt than they deserve if something goes wrong. "The most important task for the concerned parent is not to train the child but to avoid too much training. Parents who want energetic, independent children—the kinds of children who will succeed at school and on the job—must give them a certain amount of independence at home, even—and this is the difficult part: even if it means standing by and watching as the child makes mistakes." The human animal is a learning machine, after all, and it learns from its mistakes. But it has to *learn* to learn.

Fortunately, the newborn baby is both the most vulnerable *and* the most resilient creature on earth. Nature trusted us as parents to take care of this helpless lump, but not completely. A baby may take in all our worst qualities, all our bad moments —our impatience, our harsh words, our raised voices—but also, in the same great gulps of curiosity, it takes in everything else—the quiet moments, the whistling in the hall, the whispering at the door. In the end, it all evens out. "For the majority of children in the world," explains Kagan, "probably ninety-five percent, they're all treated within a relatively narrow range. Some children are kissed more than others, some children are pampered more than others, some children are spanked a little more than others, but the evidence indicates that these differences are not preserved." In other words, an active toddler doesn't always end up an active twenty-

year-old, an irritable two-year-old isn't necessarily a whiny teenager, and so on.

That kind of hands-off attitude toward parenting may make a lot of parents breathe easier, but it means risking a lot on a bet we can't afford to lose. It may be that children are resilient, but what conscientious parent wants to test the limits of that resilience? It probably is true, as Kagan says, that we don't have to tiptoe through parenthood constantly in fear that the slightest miscalculation will destroy a child forever, but that doesn't mean that we shouldn't do everything we can to give our children a chance at a happy, successful, fulfilled life.

It would be reassuring to think that children are hearty little creatures that will take care of themselves, but the history of the human animal tells us that it just ain't so. Children are evolution's gift to us. For hundreds of thousands of years we have gone out of our way to accommodate the needs of these phenomenal creatures. Our bodies, our roles, our social structure, our emotions, our life span, our reproductive cycle—all of them have been shaped to serve our children's enormous needs for learning and for love. If they are the most needful creatures on the planet, then surely we are the most giving.

The question is, will we continue to give? Or has our cultural evolution left us with a society that no longer gives their needs a high priority? One thing is sure. They will do as we do, not as we say. If we cheat them, they will cheat their children. If we give to them, they will give to their children. Whatever dreams they may have, only we can make them come true.

15. "Goo-Goo" and "Ga-Ga"

In the beginning was the Word . . .

John 1:1

If there is one behavior that separates the human animal from the rest of the animal world, it's the ability to communicate. Gorillas may pound their chests, birds may trill their mating calls, whales may sing their plaintive songs, but even a simple conversation over lunch sounds articulate by comparison. Language allowed us to create a social environment that produced literature, law, art, religion, and science. In its complexity of information, depth of emotion, and range of ideas, our language is the masterpiece of that master craftsman, the human brain.

Recently, scientists have uncovered evidence that we actually think in words, that the currency of short-term memory is words, that at birth the brain is wired to learn to speak words. Despite the inroads of television, our social, intellectual, moral, religious, and perhaps even our emotional lives are still organized around words. We may have invented language, but we've reached a point where creator and creation have become almost inseparable.

How did we acquire this magical ability to speak? Is it part of our inheritance as members of the human race, something that we bring into life like opposable thumbs and bifocal vision? Or is it something our parents teach us? People have been asking

Language, the ability to communicate our thoughts and feelings with others, is among the greatest gifts we give our children. RIGHT: The Rosetta Stone, discovered in Egypt in 1799, enabled archeologists to decipher hieroglyphics. OPPOSITE: New York University library, New York City.

Evolution has built into us the potential for language. That potential just needs the right stimulus to come along and hook the system together so it works as it was designed to work.

this question at least since the thirteenth century, when Holy Roman Emperor Frederick II decided to satisfy his curiosity in a particularly cruel way. Being in a position to do whatever he liked, Frederick decided to experiment on a group of children. And being even more stupid than he was powerful, Frederick posed the question this way: What language would children speak if no one ever spoke to them? He selected some newborn infants for his experiment, trained people to care for the infants without speaking to them, and then waited to see what would happen. Unfortunately for both science and the infants, the experiment was a failure: all the children died.

If Frederick's experimental infants had lived, chances are that they wouldn't have spoken any language, and Frederick would have concluded that language was entirely an acquired skill, without any basis in biology. In fact, that's exactly what experts believed until very recently: the mind of the newborn was a *tabula rasa*—a "blank slate"; the only skills written on that slate were put there by experience. In the past few years, however, the scientific view has grown far more subtle and sophisticated. You might say that instead of a blank slate, scientists are beginning to think of the infant's mind as more like a game of "connect the dots." Evolution has built into us certain potentials, just waiting for the right experiences to come along and hook the system together so that it works as it was *designed* to work.

Even behaviorists like B. F. Skinner have always agreed that *some* activities are programmed into our genes, but they thought the list of inborn skills was very short —little more than the basic sensory activities like hearing and seeing. But now prominent experts on language think the list ought to be expanded to include human speech. Like the other fundamental human skills, they say, language is a biological pattern waiting to be filled in with experience.

Noam Chomsky, professor of linguistics and philosophy at the Massachusetts Institute of Technology, argues that language, like most of human behavior, is as much a matter of nature as it is of nurture. We come into the world as children with what he calls a "language organ"—a language-specific biological system, not unlike the circulatory or respiratory system. According to Chomsky, this system is highly specialized and can function independently of other parts of the brain.

If this "language organ" functions like the heart or the lungs, why can't we see it on an X-ray? So far, not even Chomsky has been able to *find* such an organ buried in the brain's complexities, but he does make a convincing argument for its existence. There's no way a child could learn the complex rules of English grammar, says Chomsky, unless the brain were programmed to accept such knowledge.

Just consider the seemingly simple English sentence "John believes he is intelligent." Chomsky says this is a perfect example of just what a miracle the brain performs in learning to speak. "We all know that *he* can refer to John or to someone else, so that the sentence is ambiguous: it can mean either that John thinks he, John, is intelligent or that he thinks someone else is intelligent. But consider the sentence 'John believes him to be intelligent.' Here the pronoun *him* can't refer to John—it can refer only to someone else. Now, did anyone teach us this peculiarity about English pronouns when we were children? Nevertheless, everybody knows it —knows it without experience, without training, and at quite an early age."

Although by no means universally accepted in the scientific community, Chomsky's ideas do help us focus on just what a miracle human speech is. Learning to speak is one of those human processes—like walking or seeing or remembering— that seem so natural we hardly ever think about them. We're so thrilled when the first "mama" appears in the midst of all that babbling that we don't stop to think about what made it possible. The simple process of connecting a sound—"mama" —with an object—the person holding the bottle—is a triumph of the human brain. We can get a sense of just how much of a triumph it is by looking at similar processes in people who can't speak at all.

In January of 1882, in Tuscumbia, Alabama, Arthur and Katherine Keller were horrified to discover that their two-year-old daughter, Helen, had been left deaf, blind, and mute by a severe illness. By the time the little girl was seven, she was terrified of a world she couldn't hear or see. At the suggestion of Alexander Graham Bell, her parents hired a tutor from Boston named Anne Sullivan to try to break through the wall of isolation and fear created by her handicaps. In a harrowing process—later re-created in the play and film *The Miracle Worker*—Sullivan tried to teach Keller the names of objects in the outside world by spelling the names in sign language, forming the letters in the girl's hand so that she could "feel" the names. Up to that point, Keller had been unable to relate to reality; she couldn't

Dr. Noam Chomsky, professor of linguistics and philosophy at the Massachusetts Institute of Technology: "The language organ interacts with early experience and matures into the grammar of the language that the child speaks."

hear or see objects, she could only touch them. Nothing had a name, not even her own parents. The hard part was getting the girl to understand the *connections* between the signs and the objects. Not until Sullivan held Keller's hands under a stream of water while frantically signing "W-A-T-E-R" did Keller finally connect the symbol—the series of hand signs—with the physical object.

That triumph of understanding—along with the innate capacity of her own brain —unlocked the world for Helen Keller. Within two years she had learned to read and write in Braille. She learned the rudiments of actual speech by placing her hand on Sullivan's larynx and duplicating the vibrations she felt. In 1904, with the aid of Sullivan, who accompanied her to school and "spelled" the lectures into her hand, Keller graduated *cum laude* from Radcliffe College. She devoted the rest of her eighty-eight years to writing, lecturing, and advocating aid for the handicapped.

In fact, a very similar triumph of understanding takes place in the mind of every baby. From the "babble" of adult conversation it gradually begins to comprehend that particular sounds relate to particular objects; that "Mama" is different from "Dada," "bed" is different from "crib," "toy" is different from "bottle." The family eats dinner at a four-legged object called a "table," but the four-legged object where Mama does her work is a "desk." At the astonishing rate of about ten words a day,

The writings of William Shakespeare are undoubtedly works of genius, but even the simplest sentence is a miracle of comprehension unparalleled in the animal world.

OPPOSITE: Helen Keller, left deaf, blind, and mute by a severe illness at the age of two, had to make the complicated associations between words and objects with only a sense of touch to guide her. Helen Keller (left) with her teacher Anne Sullivan in 1897.

MR. WILLIAM
SHAKESPEARES
COMEDIES,
HISTORIES, &
TRAGEDIES.
Published according to the True Originall Copies.

LONDON
Printed by Isaac Iaggard, and Ed. Blount. 1623.

Children learn language in stages. By one and a half or two, a child can speak simple phrases. But it takes another year or two to learn the meanings of concepts like colors, and still longer to comprehend and express more abstract ideas.

without the benefit of a dictionary for checking, Baby starts to name the objects in its world, just by hearing the sounds once. And, according to Chomsky, it can imitate the pronunciation of these words with "fantastic precision."

As a child becomes more sophisticated, it begins to understand that sounds can also refer to ideas or concepts. When "Dada" points at a rattle and says "red," he means something different than when he says "rattle." "Red" can apply to a dress as well as a rattle, and "rattle" can apply to a white rattle as well as a red one. Dada can be "happy," but Mama can too, yet "Dada" is always Dada. The concepts are so complicated that it would take pages and pages to explore them like this, but yet that little bundle of "goo-goo's" somehow manages to sort out all the fine distinctions and, eventually, makes itself understood.

Chomsky's idea that children learn the "universal grammar" in stages won't surprise any parent. Anybody who has ever had a child remembers when Baby said the first word—usually at ten or eleven months; when Baby said the first phrase—"Daddy go bye-bye"; and when Baby said the first complete sentence—"I want to go to McDonald's." Each event is celebrated like a moon landing. What most parents don't know is that the stages in the development of speech are very specific and the whole process takes a lot longer than it appears.

For example, Baby may be saying complete sentences like "I want the red ball" by one and a half or two, but he won't really understand what the word "red" means until three or four. "Two-year-olds will use color words to 'dress up' a sentence," says Chomsky, citing a study by Dr. Lila Gleitman of the University of Pennsylvania, "but they don't really know what they mean. There's a certain age, around three or four, when they start using the words denotatively, so that 'red' means something red—and so on. Blind children use the color words too, to dress up their discourse, until the same age; then they stop using them. Their linguistic system is ready to use the proper words denotatively, but of course they don't have the necessary information." So we have a stage for learning names, a stage for understanding concepts like color, and, later, stages for more advanced abstractions and more complicated grammar.

The idea that children learn in stages was first advanced by Jean Piaget, the great Swiss child psychologist. He argued that at successive stages a child is capable of more and more complicated activities, and that the order of the stages is the same in all children. But Piaget never really explained *why* we learn in defined stages.

Chomsky says that biology is the reason. He says learning a language is just like going through puberty. It happens in biologically determined, chemically controlled stages. No one argues that we *learn* how to go through puberty, says Chomsky. "Everyone takes for granted that the fundamental processes controlling puberty are genetically programmed." The only difference is that we understand a little bit about the mechanism of puberty while the mechanism of language is still much more of a mystery.

Because Chomsky's "language organ" is still a mystery, scientists tend to talk about it in metaphors and analogies. Chomsky likes to compare this built-in predisposition for language to an automobile waiting to have its accelerator pushed. "If you don't push the accelerator," he says, "you're not going to be able to drive it—but it's *never* going to be able to fly." This "triggering stimulation," Chomsky says,

Although children don't understand what the words for colors—such as "red"—mean until three or four, they often use such words to "dress up" their conversation as early as age two.

happens "in a parallel way for all children. It happens under rather severe mental deficit; it happens under severe physical constraints—and pretty much in the same way, and as far as we know, in all societies."

If this sounds far too complicated to be true, we don't have to look far for a precedent. According to ethologist Peter Marler at Rockefeller University, newborn birds come into the world prepared to sing the song of their species. They need only to listen to it a few times early in life and then practice it before they can sing it as well as their parents. They're not born with the song in their hearts, but they don't exactly *learn* it either. Hearing it triggers a kind of biological recording mechanism that can then be played back. Or to put it another way, they're predisposed to learn some song, at a certain time, in a certain way. So it is with humans, whatever their native language. All languages have enough in common, according to Chomsky, that they have have the same effect on this inborn recording system.

If an animal is *not* biologically ready to learn a language, says Chomsky, then nothing on God's green earth can make it learn. If there's no tape recorder, nothing can be recorded. That's why Chomsky thinks that researchers who spend years trying to get chimpanzees to talk are wasting their time. He's not at all surprised by the pitiful results of such experiments. "Nim Chimpsky"—a trained chimp that is Chomsky's namesake—can combine a few simple word signs to form new signs, but after years of private tutoring, he still can't compete with any normal two-year-old. An ape can't really learn to speak for the simple reason that it just doesn't have the basic requirement: the "language organ." "Another organism is as likely to develop language," says Chomsky, "as we are likely to develop wings." Not all scientists agree with Chomsky, however, about the prospects for chattering chimps and babbling baboons. "We *have* developed wings," says Dr. Melvin Konner, "through learning, culture, and technology. The returns are not all in yet on how much apes like Nim Chimpsky will be capable of when given more training."

What happens if an animal that has the ability to learn a language is never exposed to that language? What becomes of the bird that never hears the song of its

So far, all attempts to teach apes to speak complicated sentences have failed. According to Noam Chomsky, our primate cousins will never learn to talk because they lack the necessary "language organ." Gorilla at the San Francisco Zoo.

OPPOSITE: If birds like the seaside sparrow don't hear their songs a few times early in life, they never learn to sing. In a similar way, humans must hear others speak by a certain age in order to develop a full command of language and grammar.

Plant. Rosa Carolina
Vulg. Wild Rose.

Nº 19.
Plate 93.

Sea side Finch.

species? Colin Blakemore, a scientist at the Physiological Laboratory at Cambridge University, England, performed experiments with the visual systems of cats. He isolated kittens, from the age of three weeks until three months, in rooms painted with horizontal lines, but no vertical lines. Later in life, these kittens had no problem jumping from one horizontal surface to another, from table to floor; but when they encountered a vertical in their environment, they were completely stumped. They would bump into table legs. Horizontals they could handle because they had grown up with them; verticals they just couldn't *see*. Blakemore concluded that the cells in their brain responsible for responding to vertical images had never become functional because they had never been used. The tape recorders were in place but because they had been given nothing to record, they simply stopped functioning.

The same is true of the human animal's ability to learn language. If a child's language system isn't triggered at the right time, it may never work. When is the right time? According to Chomsky, the language "iron" is hottest some time before puberty, during the first decade of life. If we don't strike when the iron's hot, we miss our chance. Left alone and in silence during this critical period, odds are that a child would never learn to speak. If the essential neural pathways aren't established before age ten, it's unlikely that they ever will be. So language, the hallmark of the human species, becomes possible only with the help of another human being.

But how would a scientist go about proving such a proposition? We've come a long way from the days of Frederick II when tiny babies could be "drafted" for experiments that could leave them handicapped for life. These days, we have to wait for someone's personal tragedy to become a scientific windfall. And that's exactly what happened. In the 1970s, a thirteen-year-old girl in California named "Genie" was found locked in a room. She had been there since she was a baby. She had never been spoken to, never even heard language spoken. She was, according to Chomsky, "brought up literally without language as far as anyone knows." She showed other signs of intelligence, but her grammar was that of a two-year-old.

This girl's tragedy confirmed Chomsky's theory that language has to be triggered in order to be learned. It also confirmed his theory that the language organ is *independent* of other parts of the brain. After being rescued, Genie did manage to learn some language, but she could never master grammar. The differences between various pronouns and between passive and active verbs were locked away in her mind—apparently lost forever. As a result, she spoke in short, mangled sentences: "Father hit arm. Big wood. Genie cry." Such statements were an eloquent testament to the tragedy that had robbed her of the capacity for articulate communication.

We can begin to get some sense of how complicated the process of speech is when we look at how complicated the speech mechanism in the brain is. The job is such a big one that it's divided up into parts and subcontracted out to three areas of the brain. First, there's an area in the left frontal lobe that controls the actual forming of words. It was located more than a century ago by a French surgeon

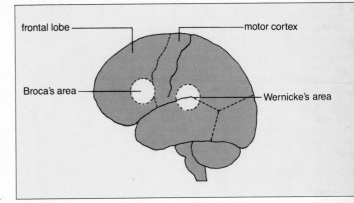

Incoming messages are deciphered in Wernicke's area, but responses are actually formulated in Broca's area. The exact location of these areas varies from person to person.

OVERLEAF: Human communication is an infinitely complicated process that spreads itself out all over the brain. Chinese characters, for example, are read in a different part of the brain than words written in English. Painting by Yang Wei-chen, 1360.

named Pierre-Paul Broca, who autopsied the brain of a man called "Tan-tan" because those were the only syllables he could say. The area was named, appropriately, Broca's area.

Soon afterward, the German neurologist Karl Wernicke discovered that Broca's area didn't do the whole job. The process of *understanding* language took place farther back, in the left temporal and parietal lobes. A person whose Broca's area was intact but who had suffered brain damage in Wernicke's area was still talking gibberish and unable to understand what other people said. For a while, it appeared that the speaking brain was a like a battery, with one input pole (Wernicke's area) and one output pole (Broca's area).

But subsequent research has shown that such a view was, like most early views of the brain, greatly oversimplified. For example, we now know that the exact location of these areas varies from person to person. By stimulating different spots in these areas, scientists have also discovered more subtle functions. For example, one part of Wernicke's area is responsible for naming things, another for repeating words. Damage to one area will leave you scratching your head at the sight of a "thin stick with a point at one end and an eraser at the other"; damage to the other will leave you speechless when the court clerk says, "Repeat after me." In addition to the spot in Wernicke's area that's responsible for naming things, there's another area below the visual cortex that's responsible for naming *colors*—just colors.

More evidence of how specific these functions are: If you're an attorney or a politician, you should avoid damage to the links between your main language areas. Because such damage interferes with the link between what you hear and what you say, it seriously affects your ability to "think on your feet"—to extemporize or respond to oral questions. If you speak English, damage to the back of Wernicke's area can be disastrous, but if you're Chinese, it's not so bad. Why? Because damage to this area isolates the rest of Wernicke's area from the visual input, seriously impairing your ability to read words—as in English—but not your ability to read pictures—as in Chinese characters; that skill is located elsewhere.

復既元師東

見皆与其

張能其編黑

雷見詩兒試一

梅畫後

余抚鶴
泊洞古舟傍波
主者為重
棕佛說茗
供⺘復連古清

Another indication of the complexity of the speech process is how much of it remains a mystery. To explain how you actually understand spoken words, we have only a theory that your brain repeats the words to itself, as if speaking, even though your mouth doesn't move. If true, this theory may explain why some children go through a stage when they drive their parents crazy by "echoing" everything they hear. It may also explain why some kids need to read aloud before they can read silently to themselves; and why some adults continue to move their lips when they read. Your brain may be doing the same thing every time somebody says something to you. When we say, "You put words in my mouth," we really mean that.

But the real core of our ability to speak, the infinitely subtle process of choosing the sounds that make up a word and arranging them in the right order, is still one of the many mysteries locked inside the human brain. How is an eighteen-month-old child able to get from input to output, from signal to meaning, from auditory or visual stimulus to *understanding?*

Here's what we do know.

Suppose someone says, "Do you know what time it is?" As every teacher and parent knows, the path from stimulus to response is hardly foolproof. Many things can happen along the way to upset the workings of this marvelous mechanism. For instance, when you hear that question, you have two options. If you're a woman in a singles bar, you may simply decide not to process the sounds at all—let the question go "in one ear and out the other." If you're in a meeting with your boss, you'll probably marshal your cognitive skills and process the information. The signals go from your ear to the hippocampus to the limbic lobe, where they're "scanned" as a whole to get a sense of what's being said. If you walk in the door at three in the morning and someone is waiting up for you with that question, it may sound angry, irritated, worried, or all three. It's here in the limbic system that you pick up on someone's tone of voice—as in "I don't like your tone of voice." You don't yet know what's been said, but you've got the "gist" of it. From here, the signals go on to Wernicke's area for a more detailed breakdown. Finally, you understand the question. Then it's on to Broca's area, where you formulate a strategy for responding. If you're home late, you may just say "No." If somebody has accosted you on the street, you look at your watch and say "I'm late." When a more complicated response is required, it's here at the last stage that you pick the grammar and syntax necessary to project meaning—as in "My watch must have stopped."

Speech, still largely a magical process, is a perfect example of how the human animal learns and, in learning, masters its environment. Not even sight, with its legions of dedicated neurons, involves the interaction between the neocortex and the outside world that speech does. Nowhere is there greater need for constant integration of signals, constant feedback, between the neocortex, the "thinking" brain, and the limbic system, the "feeling" brain. When we talk about talk being a uniquely human skill, we mean it in both these senses: it requires both more ad-

Nothing better shows how attentive children are than their remarkable ability to assimilate, just from ordinary conversation, the complexities of language.

vanced skills and better-integrated skills than any other animal can begin to muster.

So the next time you jot down a shopping list, prepare an interoffice memo, scribble a message to a child or spouse, take notes in class, write the great American novel, shoot the bull till the wee hours of the morning, or listen to a political speech, remember how much learning and how much biology are needed to make it possible. Not just possible, but relatively *easy*.

No exploration of language is complete without a look at the most enjoyable form of human communication: laughter. Although studies show that primates will "laugh" at slapstick gags, only the human animal has the capacity to appreciate humor in all its shadings. Far more complicated and challenging than everyday speech, humor involves integrating the higher cortex—the frontal lobes that can project what will happen—with the limbic system that generates the affective state of enjoyment. Curiously, no one knows exactly why we laugh—although almost everyone has a theory. Freud thought that laughter was a coping mechanism, a way of releasing repressed feelings. That's why so many of our jokes deal with sex, according to Freud. But, in fact, the reaction to humor—probably involving memory areas in the brain as well as the neocortex and the limbic system—varies so much from person to person that it's almost impossible to generalize about what makes us laugh.

Whatever laughter is—a crossed wire, a neural misfiring, a synaptic traffic jam

RIGHT AND OPPOSITE: No one knows exactly why we laugh. It probably involves memory areas in the brain as well as the neocortex and the limbic system. Whatever it is, laughter is one of the great joys of humanhood in all cultures, at all ages.

—it's a great feeling for the human animal, a feeling that no other animal enjoys. And best of all, it's something that we continue to enjoy throughout our lives. As Marian Diamond at the University of California has recently demonstrated, we never outgrow our childhood. We need never lose our ability to learn, our tendency to laugh, or our willingness to change. If we do lose them, it's because we choose to, not because biology takes them away like toys that we've outgrown. We hate to admit it, but most of us do have a tendency to fall back on old ways, established routes. To put it in neurological terms, we tend to use dendritic pathways that have already been forged, rather than forging new ones. It's certainly easier that way. Why bother to learn new vocabulary words when the old ones are sufficient? Why bother to write a letter when a phone call is enough? We're creatures of habit, after all.

It's in our nature to be nurtured. Ignorance and self-satisfaction seem to be the only natural enemies of the human animal. The great gift of language is wasted if we don't stay open to new possibilities, new ideas, and new solutions.

We bother to learn because there's no progress without learning. No new pathways means no new ideas, no new laughter, no new learning. Dr. Diamond has shown that brain development doesn't have to slow as we get older, that our capacity for learning remains intact even if we don't take advantage of that capacity. That doesn't mean it can't stop sooner. It's an enriched environment, a learning environment, she found, that keeps a brain active. Without it, even at a young age, a brain can go to seed like an untended lawn. What a terrible waste of a nonrenewable resource.

Of course, the same thing that happens to people in an unenriched environment can happen to a society. No new pathways, no new learning. This is the lesson of childhood development. It's in our nature to be nurtured. As children and as adults, we thrive on the constant interaction of stimulus and response. Ignorance and self-satisfaction seem to be the only natural enemies of the human animal. If we stay open to new possibilities, receptive to new ideas, and, most important, willing to change our minds as well as our patterns of behavior, new solutions and new insights will come just as naturally and inevitably as "Mama" and "Dada" follow "goo-goo" and "ga-ga."

LIFE & DEATH

16. Dreams that Come True

*Dreams are true,
while they last.
Can we say more of life?*

Havelock Ellis

"**W**hat animal walks on four legs in the morning, on two at noon, and on three in the evening?" If you were approached on some dark night by a man with a knife who posed that riddle and threatened to kill you if you couldn't solve it, what would you say? According to Greek mythology, that's exactly what happened to Oedipus as he approached the city of Thebes. The only difference was that the mugger in his case had the head of a woman, the wings of a bird, and the body of a lion. She was the dreaded Sphinx, and her unsolved riddle had been the death of so many travelers that the city of Thebes was perilously close to ruin.

What did Oedipus answer? "The human animal," he said. "It crawls on hands and knees in the morning of its life, walks erect in the midday of adulthood, and leans on a cane in the evening of old age." It was the right answer, and the Sphinx, in a fit of apoplexy, killed herself. As a reward for saving their city, the Thebans asked Oedipus to replace their king, Laius, who had recently been murdered by a stranger while traveling, and to marry Laius's widow, Jocasta. Oedipus happily accepted their offer and was crowned king of Thebes.

If this story had been a Walt Disney confection, everyone would have lived happily ever after. But it wasn't, and they didn't. Soon afterward, the all-knowing Oedipus discovered that the old man he had killed in an argument on his way to Thebes had in fact been the missing King Laius. As if that weren't bad enough, he also learned that Laius was his real father and that Jocasta, now his wife, was his real mother. The revelations would make even a soap-opera fan blush.

The ancient tragedy of Oedipus, a man who unknowingly murdered his father and married his mother, fascinated a Viennese doctor at the end of the nineteenth century who used it to help explain his new and controversial theory of human behavior. Previously, the human mind had always been the exclusive province of poets, philosophers, and mystics. But in the summer of 1895—about the same time that young Albert Einstein was riding a beam of light out to the edge of the universe

---

Oedipus and the Sphinx by Gustave Moreau, 1864.

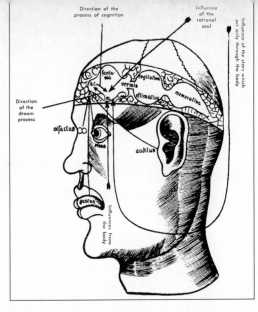

Direction of the process of cognition

Influence of the rational soul

Influence of the stars which act only through the body

Direction of the dream process

fantasia

a.c.

cogitativa

vermis

estimativa

memorativa

olfactus

nasus

auditus

gustus

Influences from the body

Scientists have been trying for centuries to pinpoint the different activities of the brain. Phrenology—the "science" of reading bumps on the head—was one such effort. A sixteenth-century attempt to diagram brain functions.

—this Viennese doctor turned the study of the mind into a science with a theory that disturbed and, in some cases, outraged his professional colleagues. If Charles Darwin was the reigning champion provocateur of public condemnation, this man must surely have been the runner-up.

The man was Dr. Sigmund Freud—the great "detective"—who, in starting the twentieth century off on its scientific quest for the mind, became the "third great revolutionist" in human self-awareness. The first two "revolutionists" were Copernicus, who declared that humans weren't the center of the universe, and Darwin, who declared that humans were also animals. Freud completed the trio by giving us the concept of an "unconscious": the idea that the mind's power was not limited by reality or perception; that its boundaries lay out there somewhere beyond the edge of Einstein's universe.

That milestone in the history of the human animal was reached in Dr. Freud's handsome house at 19 Bergasse in Vienna, Austria. It was appropriate that this new order would arise in a place like Vienna. Nowhere are the strict geometry and rational order of the Old World better preserved. The symmetry of the eighteenth-century Belvedere Palace and Gardens celebrated our earlier belief that the human

Sigmund Freud at thirty-five, just a few years before he began to shock the scientific community with his theories of the unconscious.

OPPOSITE: Symmetry, order, and rationality were dear to the nineteenth-century world. That was one reason Freud's theories were so revolutionary—and threatening. The Belvedere Palace and Gardens not far from Freud's office in Vienna.

condition was an orderly and rational one, that we were capable of complete mastery over the emotional, animal elements of our nature. Then Freud lowered the boom, and our confidence in the old conscious, rational mind would never be the same.

For the first three decades of this century, Freud applied his extraordinary intellect to the evidence provided by patients who came for treatment. Through the doors of Number 19, they brought their irrational impulses, strange mental associations, and tortured pasts. Looking deeply into these fragments of other lives, Freud caught obscure, tantalizing, often shocking glimmers of an unknown mental dimension beneath the surface of human consciousness. To enter Number 19 was to pass from the familiar, ordinary daylight world of the senses into the dark and unknown territory of the mind.

What was the key that unlocked this uncharted world?

Dreams. Freud called them "the royal road to the unconscious." Like all of us, he had been visited by the nightly floor show of bizarre images and disjointed experiences we call dreams. But unlike anybody before him, Freud wanted to understand these strange interludes between waking and sleeping. He felt that they had a language in common, a code of images, that could be deciphered to reveal the workings of the "other" mind, the unconscious mind. So he probed his patients' dreams—and his own—searching for the key that would unlock this secret language. He said, "We are lived by forces we know not of" and dreams are a vehicle by which we can catch glimpses of these forces.

It is only a little flip to say that Sigmund Freud was driving his fellow doctors crazy. He was actually saying, out loud, that dreams *meant* something. Before him, the only people who really believed that dreams could be "interpreted" were the same people who read palms and tea leaves. In the aggressively "scientific" world of the late nineteenth century, such things were considered nothing more than leftover superstition and paganism. So how did a rational, educated man come to such an "irrational" conclusion?

It happened on a hot day in July on a hillside overlooking the city of Vienna. Sigmund Freud was a thirty-nine-year-old M.D. escaping the heat of the city at a big guesthouse called Bellevue that has since been demolished. Bellevue had a breezy terrace restaurant with tables that provided a city view where Freud would quietly think about the dreams he'd had the night before.

On the night before this particular July day, Freud had retired for the evening, worrying about a patient who was not responding to his treatment, and smarting over the criticisms of a professional colleague. As he jotted down the details of the dream, Sigmund Freud believed he had found the evidence he was looking for. The dream featured a punishment of the disapproving colleague, and absolved Freud of failure in his patient's treatment. It was all very neat—much like a dream that anyone might have. If you or I woke up remembering such a dream, we might smile and say to ourselves, "Wishful thinking." That conclusion may seem obvious to us

The human animal's perception of itself was forever altered in Freud's office at 19 Bergasse in Vienna.

now, but, like all great ideas, it started off as one man's dazzling leap of imagination.

What was Freud's interpretation of the dream—his first "analysis"? Dreams are places where we act out wishes and desires we cannot admit while conscious. It was a moment of insight he would never forget. Five years later, on the same spot, he wrote to a friend: "Do you think that one day there will be a marble tablet saying: 'In this house on July 24, 1895, the Secret of Dreams was revealed to Dr. Sigmund Freud'?" Sure enough, although the Bellevue house is long gone, the plaque Sigmund Freud imagined is there.

Freud's insight at Bellevue shattered an old conception of the human animal and gave birth to a new one. Freud opened the door of this other human world, the unconscious, to science. Part of his achievement was to show that this is a world we all share, that it's not just the privileged sanctuary of a few artists, mystics, and geniuses. Every time you or I or any other human being falls asleep, we enter this separate reality.

What are these things called dreams? Shakespeare said, "We are such stuff as dreams are made on," but what do we know about them? We know that if you live a typical life span, you'll spend about twenty years of it asleep. We know that during that twenty years, you'll probably have somewhere around 300,000 dreams. That's almost one dream for every waking hour of your life. Given how much emotion, excitement, anxiety, or happiness can be packed into one dream, that means a lot of living takes place when your eyes are closed and your senses are turned off. One can't help wondering what's going on in there.

Despite the large role they play in our lives, we tend to see dreams as just an adjunct to "real" life—nothing for us to worry about. We may be rattled by a nightmare or thrilled by a dream that involves sex or flying or other supernatural feats, but we don't give it much thought during our waking day. In fact, we don't remember most of our 300,000 dreams at all. Only if we wake up in the middle are we likely to remember the details, and even then they quickly drift away.

Not everybody is so quick to dismiss dreams. More than 2,000 years ago, the Chinese philosopher Chuang-tzu dreamed he was a butterfly and, after he awoke, wondered if he was a human who had just dreamed of being a butterfly or if he was a butterfly who was now dreaming of being a human. Still, most of us are pretty confident about the difference between waking and dreaming. Although we can't tell we're dreaming when we're dreaming, we can tell if we're awake when we're awake. Can't we? People say, "Pinch me so I'll know I'm not dreaming," but is that an accurate test? Other societies, like the aborigines of Australia, believe that *this* world is a dream world and what we call the dream world is *real*. In other words, you're reading this book in a dream. Or else I'm writing it in a dream and dreaming that people will read it. The Senoi of Malaysia believe that dreams and "reality" are equally real. In the final analysis, how can we prove they're wrong?

There's even some scientific evidence that suggests they might be right. It turns out that the early hours of the morning, the time of most intense dreaming, are also the most dangerous. Dangerous sleep? Scientific studies confirm that most of the people who die in their sleep, usually from heart attacks, die during this relatively brief span—the bedtime equivalent of the Bermuda Triangle. Apparently, the dream state is so "real" that it can kill you. How much more real could it be?

There's also evidence that we have heightened powers of communication during sleep. No less an authority than Sigmund Freud suggested that "telepathic" dreaming might have been a form of human communication before language developed, and now there appears to be some proof. Montague Ullman of the Maimonides Medical Center in New York has conducted a controversial series of experiments aimed at verifying this phenomenon—with at least some arguable success. In his experiments, a "sender" mentally concentrated on a "target" image, often the image of a famous painting, and attempted to "transmit" it into the mind of a sleeping "receiver." The receiver was wired to a "sleep monitor," then awakened

OPPOSITE: The average person spends twenty years asleep and during those years dreams more than a quarter of a million dreams. In that world, we lead a separate and very private life. Self-portrait as a Dreaming Man, photograph by Doug Prince, 1980.

Controversial research indicates that the brain may have heightened powers of communication during sleep. In one recent experiment (right), "senders" concentrated on the George Bellows painting Both Members of This Club *(overleaf) and attempted to transmit the image to sleeping "receivers."*

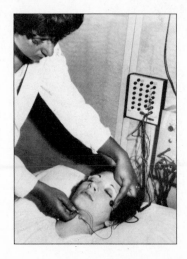

at the end of a sleep cycle and asked to recount the dream. In one experiment lasting eight nights, the image was successfully transmitted *every* night.

After being "sent" a painting of a boxing scene by George Bellows titled *Both Members of This Club,* a "receiver" described the painting with surprising accuracy: "There were a lot of people . . . There was a lot of activity going on. There were some strange characteristics about them in the way they were dressed." In response to the same painting, another receiver remembered a lot of "violence in the dream" and the violence "was exciting"—"I think I was betraying a great deal of violence, destructiveness, aggressiveness . . . you might say the raw aspects of nature more than the more refined aspects of a human being."

Ullman concluded that patients were most likely to be telepathic if the "target" material being communicated was material that evoked a sense of danger, either to the person sleeping or to someone close to him. Although many scientists consider the results of these tests highly questionable, they could conceivably explain why so many people have reported waking suddenly from a deep sleep, alarmed because they "feel" that something terrible has happened to a son or daughter or other loved one. It may mean that our telepathic communication line—if such a thing exists— works best when we're asleep and the line isn't clogged with competing messages, or when the telepathic message is urgent. Such research may be our first scientific inkling of the famous "sixth sense" that permits us to "feel" when someone is watching us. Whether or not these conclusion are waiting at the end of this exploration, the results of Ullman's experiments are an intriguing hint that the dream state may be a more important "reality" than we think.

But we don't have to speculate in order to find a basis for the special powers of the dream world. There are endless examples of our sleeping "consciousness" outperforming our waking consciousness. For example, after years of fruitless re-

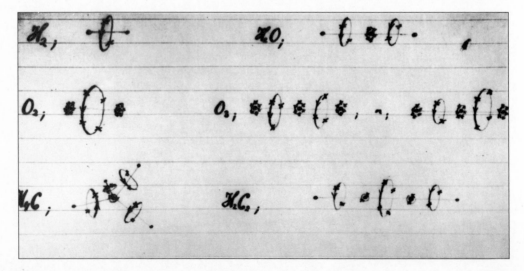

search on the structure of benzene, Friedrich Kekule dreamed of a snake that held its tail in its mouth. He snapped awake knowing that the elusive structure was a ring. Likewise, we owe our image of an atom as a nucleus with orbiting particles to Niels Bohr's dream world. Bohr dreamed that he stood on the sun, enveloped by burning gases, while planets attached to the sun by their filaments whizzed by him in eternal revolutions. The sun became the nucleus; the planets, electrons; and the connecting filaments the energy field of quantum mechanics.

On a more mundane level, inventor Elias Howe dreamed that savages captured him and told him that if within twenty-four hours he couldn't produce a machine that could sew, they would kill him. When his time was up—a mercifully short time in the dream world—he had nothing to show, so they hurled their spears at him. But just before the spears pierced his flesh he noticed that they had eye-shaped holes in their tips. He jolted awake with the realization that the sewing-machine needle he had been struggling to perfect should have its eye near the point, not near the middle or the top.

Once again, a rational person can't help wondering, What's going on here? What is this mysterious process that gives us "superhuman" powers? When you start to think about the dream world, it's like discovering that you're schizophrenic. There's another person inside you who leads a separate life, and the two of you know hardly anything about each other. Scientists have spent decades studying the mechanics of sight and hearing and the other senses, yet none of those rules apply when we're asleep. There's another world out there—or *in* there—where we spend twenty years of our lives. What do we know about it?

We know that the human animal, like all animals, needs sleep to stay healthy. A recent discovery indicates that when we're in deep sleep, our bodies produce a hormone that helps to build and rebuild the tissues of the body. But none of that

Frustrated in his attempt to diagram the atom, physicist Niels Bohr went to sleep one night and in a dream saw the relationship between the structure of the atom and the structure of the solar system. OPPOSITE: After he awoke, he made these drawings.

requires dreaming. What function do dreams perform? Do they serve some necessary biological purpose, or are they the neurological equivalent of the late movies—
just something to keep our overdeveloped brain entertained while our old animal
body gets a rest?

Scientists can't answer all of our questions about dreaming, but they can tell us
something about the mechanics. Although recent studies confirm what every
teacher knows—that you can dream when you're awake as well as when you're
asleep—most of our dream world exists in the darkness of sleep. The process begins
when some external cue—turning out the lights, for example—triggers our body's
built-in alarm clock, the pineal gland, located at the top of the brain stem. The
pineal releases the hormone melatonin, which in turn affects the level of serotonin
in an area of the reticular formation called the "raphe" nuclei. This sounds complicated, but it's really rather like a houseful of relatives tucking each other in, one by
one: first, the pineal, then the raphe nuclei, then the reticular formation.

But the last one, the reticular formation, never really goes to sleep. It is here,
after all, that scientists believe consciousness is located, so it can't conk out completely. It serves as the body's night watchman, monitoring the brain stem, which
in turn ensures that your heart continues to beat and your lungs continue to breathe.
If something should happen while the rest of your body is asleep—a burglar in the
house, a baby crying—the reticular formation will be able to sound the alarm.

Of course, it doesn't have to be dark for you to fall asleep. After a tense meeting
at the office or a hard game of baseball, some people can fall asleep in broad
daylight. Recently, scientists have discovered in the brains of animals a chemical
they call "Factor S." When they remove this chemical from the brain of one animal
and inject it into the brain of another, the second animal tends to get sleepy. Their
hypothesis is that we accumulate this Factor S throughout the day, and that when it
reaches a certain concentration, we feel "tired." This discovery may explain why
some people—those with an excess of Factor S—can fall asleep anytime, anywhere,
under any conditions, while others need to be in bed, in the dark—and even then
may have problems.

Once you're asleep, brain activity falls off as higher brain functions close down
for the night. Most of the millions of sensory messages are stopped and electrical
activity dies down. But there's a light on in the attic—the neocortex. Not everybody
in the house is asleep. This is the first stage of sleep; you drift in and out of
consciousness. In the next twenty minutes, your brain will pass through three more
stages of activity before reaching the dream world. At stage two, your eyes begin to
move slowly from side to side. You're still close enough to consciousness that a
noise or a touch can rouse you. In stage three, only a loud noise or a good shake will
do the trick. By the twenty-minute mark, you're in our deepest sleep of the night,
just one step away from coma and two steps away from death.

But you haven't yet arrived at the dream world. Many people mistakenly believe that if they're awakened in the middle of a dream, they've been dragged out of a deep sleep. In fact, there are no dreams during the deepest sleep stage, and a dreaming sleep is not too far from full consciousness.

From deep sleep, stage four, you move back through stages three and two. But instead of continuing into stage one, you take a sudden turn and pass over the threshold of the dream world into rapid-eye-movement, or "REM," sleep. Researchers believe this turn is triggered by the secretions of a small patch of dark cells at the top of the brain stem called the locus coeruleus. Whatever the cause, the effects are dramatic. Immediately, the cerebral cortex lights up. Noradrenaline, a chemical messenger produced in the pons and other parts of the brain stem, rushes through the brain, waking the whole house. It's as if the reticular formation decides to throw a late-night party and the entire cortex is invited.

Because we leave our physical bodies behind when we enter the dream world, we're not confined by the physical laws that burden us during the day. That's why so many dreams involve wish fulfillment, like winning the big game, and supernatural powers, like flying.

In fact, according to one theory, everybody is invited except the *body*. While all the parts of the brain that interpret sensory data (sight, sound, touch, taste, smell) are activated—along with memory—none of the corresponding parts of the body are involved. The reticular formation "paralyzes" the body so it can't react physically to the experience of dreaming—though occasionally signals do leak through, and cause the body to move as if the dreamed events were taking place in the waking world. In the dream world, you hear without using your ears, see without using your eyes, feel without touching. Normally the body's only movement is the rapid shifting of the eyes back and forth under the eyelids—the movement from which this stage of sleep gets its name—as they scan images that aren't there. In the dream world, the cortex is on its own.

"In most of the sleep states," says Dr. Arnold Scheibel, professor of neurobiology at U.C.L.A., "the relationship between the cerebral hemispheres, the cortex, and the brain stem changes very markedly. And in a sense, the cortex, the great think-

ing, analyzing part of the brain, is functionally cut off from the ongoing sensory input. As a result, the cortex becomes in a sense freewheeling. It's as if you step on the clutch in an old-type car. The cortex is free to follow its own operational moods, without being brought up to date on a moment-to-moment basis by sensory input and even without the organizing, pacemaking activities of the upper brain stem, which we know are absolutely necessary to valid conscious cortical operations."

Because we leave our bodies behind when we enter the dream world, we're not confined by the physical laws that burden us during waking hours. Time, distance, gravity are all suspended. But the mental activities remain the same. If the dream is exciting, our arousal mechanism will be triggered. If it's terrifying, we're terrified. In the dream world, brain activity corresponds exactly to what brain activity would be if the same events happened in the "real world." Not even an expert can tell the difference between recordings of brain activity made during the dream state and those made during the waking state.

If the dreams are pleasant, the period of REM sleep will last only minutes; then you'll drift back down into stages two, three, and four. The entire cycle, from stage one to stage four and back to REM sleep, takes about ninety minutes; most of us go through three or four of these cycles every night. If the dream turns into a nightmare, you may do a quick "reality check" of input from the outside world and jump into consciousness.

But where have you been? You've been on a journey through a strange land, but what does it all mean? Science can tell us what happens in the brain when we dream, but it can't yet tell us why. If the brain doesn't create these dreams in

OPPOSITE: The dream world is a world of its own. Science can tell us what happens in the brain when we dream, but it can't begin to explain the strange landscapes—sometimes enchanting, sometimes terrifying— that rush by us in dreams. Detail, *Hell* by Hieronymus Bosch.

Sigmund Freud was the first to study the relationship between the dream world and the waking world. Among his most radical ideas was that the unconscious mind could overthrow the conscious mind and direct a person's behavior.

accordance with the laws that govern waking life, what rules do apply? Why do things happen as they do? Or are they, as some have suggested, just the brain's daily "housecleaning"? Are you just throwing out the residue of the billions of bits of information—memories, thoughts, images—that pass through your cortex every day? Everyone has had the experience of thinking, for no reason, of an old friend during the day, then dreaming about her at night. Is that an example of the brain, not knowing what to do with an odd bit of information, throwing it into the "midnight stew" with similar scraps?

The incredibly intense "reality" of dreams suggests that perhaps the opposite is true. Perhaps what happens to us during the day is really just scraps left over from the more intense reality of our dream world. Perhaps the outside reality is secondary to the reality our brain creates inside. It seems to be our mental reality, our unconscious, more than what is solid, objective, and "out there," that constitutes our world. That, at least, was what Sigmund Freud thought.

By taking the often painful, sometimes frightening journey into his patients' dreams, and his *own*, Freud began telling the outraged scientific community that the irrational, unconscious mind—the dream world—had the power to overthrow reason and control a person's actions in the waking world. We are essentially slaves of passion, said Freud, but a passion so repressed that we're often not even aware of it in our waking lives. Only in our dreams, where "anything goes," are we free to express it. Dreams aren't just another world: they're the *real* world. What happens there helps us understand—may even determine—what happens here.

To test his theory, Freud needed a guinea pig. Since no one rushed to volunteer, he decided to use his own dreams—to put himself on the couch. He started with a particularly intense dream that had haunted him since childhood. "It was a very vivid" dream, Freud later wrote in *The Interpretation of Dreams*, "and in it I saw my beloved mother, with a peculiarly peaceful, sleeping expression on her features, being carried into the room by two (or three) people with birds' beaks and laid upon the bed. I awoke in tears and screaming, and interrupted my parents' sleep."

Thirty years later, Freud unraveled his own nightmare. It wasn't an easy job. Today, there are hundreds of pop-psych, self-help books that purport to teach us

The bird-headed creatures in Freud's dream turned out to be figures from the illustrations in a Bible that he had seen as a boy. Illustration from the Philippson Bible.

OPPOSITE: Freud was his own first patient. He began by analyzing a boyhood dream of his mother being carried by two bird-headed creatures.

the rudiments of dream imagery, but Freud had little if anything to guide him. He knew, as we all know from our own experience, that dreams are slippery subjects. In the dream world, unlike the real world, one event leads into another and one person is transformed into another in a way that eludes description even if we happen to remember that we *had* a dream. In the real world, there's a concrete wall between what really happens and what we want to happen. But in dreams, that wall disappears and what happens, what we want to happen, and what we fear will happen are constantly shifting and mingling.

Despite the problems, Freud set out to uncover the meaning of his dream. He managed to trace the bizarre birdlike creatures who had carried his mother in the dream to illustrations in a Bible that his father had given him when he was a child. "The strangely draped and unnaturally tall figures with birds' beaks," he wrote, "were derived from the illustrations to Philippson's Bible. I fancy they must have been gods with falcon's heads from an ancient Egyptian funerary relief." Freud also recalled that these same Egyptian motifs had been used to illustrate the biblical prohibition against incest.

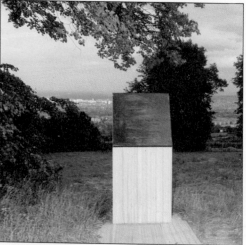

From a guesthouse on a hillside overlooking the city of Vienna, Sigmund Freud wrote to a friend: "Do you think that one day there will be a marble tablet saying: 'In this house on July 24, the Secret of Dreams was revealed to Dr. Sigmund Freud?' " Today the guesthouse is gone, but a tablet does mark the spot.

Of special interest to Freud was the fact that a woodcut of two similar figures carrying a funeral bed was used to illustrate the Old Testament story of King David and Joab, a story that involves death and the taking of a forbidden woman. Further detective work in his own past led Freud from the Philippson Bible to a childhood playmate named Philipp who had taught him a vulgar term for sexual intercourse, *vögeln*—a word derived from the word for "bird," *Vogel.*

What was Freud to make of this strange combination of sexual images, death images, and images of his mother? Today, most of us who were raised on soap-opera clichés and Hollywood psychoanalysis could guess the answer right off, but Freud had to carve his own path in the wilderness of the unconscious. It's a mark of his genius that he didn't hesitate to see the unpleasant truth. He saw, for example, that the dream reflected his troubled relationship with his father and his sexual attraction to his mother. He remembered when, as a child, he had seen his mother naked and been aroused. He remembered how much he had hated his younger brother, Julius, for stealing his mother's attention, and then, when Julius died, how he had felt responsible for his death.

All of these unexpressed feelings surfaced in Freud's dream. His fear that his mother was dying masked his anxiety over his own "obscure and evidently sexual craving" for her. After all, his experience with Julius had taught him that unnatural feelings could be dangerous. He was afraid that his mother would die because he wanted her sexually, just as he was afraid that his brother had died because he wanted him dead. And he was afraid that he would pay the price for thwarting his father's will (in craving for his mother)—castration.

Freud called this sexual attraction between a son and his mother the Oedipus complex after the legendary Greek hero who, unknowingly, killed his father and married his mother. Although very few males ever act out the Oedipal myth, said Freud, they do feel guilt over wanting—in their unconscious—to get rid of their fathers and have sex with their mothers. As adults, they're usually not consciously aware of these feelings, but that's only because they repress them. The feelings are still there, and they continue to feel guilty about them unless they can face them and somehow resolve them.

If taking dreams seriously was a crazy idea, then this one was a lulu. The suggestion that we harbor from childhood deeply repressed sexual wishes toward our parents and that those wishes can wreak havoc with our adult lives did not sit well in the upright and uptight Victorian parlors of the day. This was not a pretty world Dr. Freud was exploring, this world of dreams, this "unconscious."

As Freud realized, the myth of Oedipus is a perfect example of how complex and convoluted the human unconscious is. Why should we expect anything less from our amazing cortex? Since Freud's discovery, the science of psychoanalysis has mined this myth and found additional clues about the workings of the unconscious very much the way anthropologists analyze the skeletons of our ancestors to learn about the history of our conscious minds. Dr. David Peretz of Columbia University is one of those explorers who continue to find new insights in a very old story. He's especially interested in the first part of the legend in which Oedipus' real parents, Laius and Jocasta, warned by a prophecy that their son is destined to murder his father, order that the infant Oedipus be left on a hillside to die. Later, when Oedipus

The myth of Oedipus is a perfect example of how complex and convoluted the human unconscious is. Oedipus and the Sphinx, *kylix (drinking cup) with red-figure painting.*

is a young man, he flees the household of the couple who rescued and raised him in a state of doubt and confusion. It's Oedipus' flight from his adoptive parents that sets in motion the fateful chain of events leading to the murder of his real father and his marriage to his mother.

"Isn't this man's fate?" says Peretz. "We leave our childhood home—in this instance the home of Oedipus' adoptive parents—and yet because we're vulnerable and confused, we want the comfort and protection that we had as children. So we unconsciously seek out and marry our 'mothers.' And in so doing, we plant the seeds of later marital conflicts and problems, because a wife can never fully *be* his mother for a husband. So, if he hasn't outgrown that part of his quest, he's bound to suffer disappointment and frustration. I think it's there to some extent in every man: looking for his mother in a wife, looking for the ideal mother—the mother he was attracted to as a child—the one who loved, caressed, supported, comforted, and fondled him." The problem with "marrying Mother" is that if we do, we're destined to be put off sexually by the implicit "incest" of our acts.

Although Freud looked at the Oedipus myth only from the perspective of a son, Peretz thinks it can tell us just as much about what is happening in the unconscious of parents. "In the myth," Peretz points out, "Oedipus' real father, Laius, is warned that his son will bring about his death. In fact, this is what all sons represent to their fathers. Having a son moves a man into the position of his own father, and that much closer to his own mortality. In that sense, as much as fathers may love their children, they are threatened by them. If every boy, somewhere inside him, feels competitive with his father, and at some point wishes to replace his father, then every father remembers being a child himself and having those same feelings."

And what was happening in the mother's unconscious? Why was she willing to deny her maternal love and agree to have her infant son left to die on a mountainside? And why, in a plot turn worthy of any soap opera, did she marry a man young enough to be her son so soon after her husband's death? According to Dr. Peretz, she might have imagined that by marrying him she could "undo in some way the

Dr. David Peretz, psychoanalyst on the faculty of Columbia University: "Isn't this man's fate? We leave our childhood home . . . and yet because we're vulnerable and confused, we want the comfort and protection that we had as children. So we unconsciously seek out and marry our 'mothers.' "

OPPOSITE: The Oedipus myth suggests not only that sons may have sexual urges for their mothers, but also that mothers may have sexual urges for their sons. Mother and Boy by Mary Cassatt.

original crime that she committed. Also, she could have been trying to cope with aging and bereavement by marrying a younger man." Like her husband and her son —and all of us—she was a prisoner of her own childhood. "As little girls, women have often felt inferior," says Peretz. "They may have felt adored, but they may also have felt rejected in favor of a son. For such a woman, a boy child may become in a sense someone to identify with. He is what she wishes she could have been when she was younger."

Dr. Peretz also suggests that just as a son may have sexual urges for his mother, the mother may have sexual urges for him. "The Oedipus story suggests what, in my experience, is often true, that mothers often feel a strong underlying attraction toward their boys who are growing into manhood. I've had a number of women talk to me about how difficult it is having these highly sexual, strong young men parading around the house in their Jockey shorts. Jocasta, Oedipus' mother, had the oppor-

Recent research using PET (positron-emission tomography) scans has discovered observable differences between a normal brain (left) and the brain of a schizophrenic patient (right). Even though the patient's eyes are closed, there is considerable activity (seen as red) in the visual cortex at the bottom of the picture. The schizophrenic is "seeing" a world that isn't there. More than one third of schizophrenic patients show similarly abnormal patterns of brain activity.

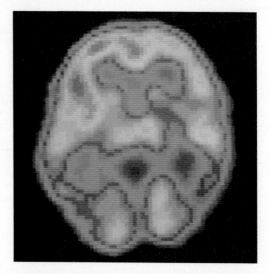

tunity to have just that: a man young enough to be her son but who didn't consciously remind her of her maternity."

There's no doubt that in revealing the hidden activities of the mind, Freud showed us aspects of ourselves that we probably would have preferred to keep hidden. Millions of people who have never read one of Freud's books but have heard his statements about our sexual feelings toward our parents will never forgive him. After Freud, we could no longer ignore that we are subject to many contradictory, often destructive impulses. Today, most of us recognize that our decisions aren't the models of rationality that we once thought they were. We understand that our lives are governed not so much by the careful weighing of options in the waking world as by a fierce struggle between the stated arguments of our conscious minds and the unstated impulses of our unconscious mind.

Most of us live successfully with this struggle. We become reasonably adept at keeping the two worlds separate. During waking hours, we submit to the "reality" created by our senses. At night, our minds create a reality that's independent of the environment, which is why psychologists say that the normal nightly experience of dreaming is very close to psychosis. But what happens when this compromise, this balance of conscious and unconscious, breaks down? The dream world is a testament to the power of the human mind to disregard the physical world outside itself; but what if this power gets out of hand?

By looking at a malfunctioning brain, a brain in which the balance between reality and the unconscious has been disturbed, scientists are getting their first glimpses of the actual structure of an aspect of the brain that wasn't even recognized a century ago, a look into the biology of the unconscious.

Dr. Arnold Scheibel has been studying schizophrenia for six years. His research

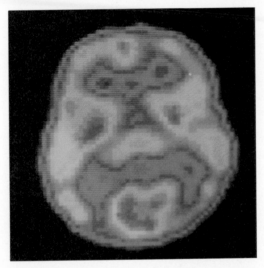

has uncovered observable differences between normal brains and the brains of schizophrenic patients. Although his work has not yet been replicated in other laboratories, it "suggests strongly that in schizophrenics, the pyramidal cells in the hippocampus—an important part of the limbic system—instead of being lined up like slats in a picket fence, are pointed every which way," according to Dr. Scheibel. "That means that their processes are pointed every which way too."

Dr. Scheibel has isolated a number of likely causes of schizophrenia, including faults in the embryological development of the brain, the "stickiness" of certain molecules on the surface of the pyramidal cells, virus infections, and the brain disease encephalitis. "As far as we know," says Scheibel, "it's very possible that schizophrenia is a disease package. Like pulmonary disease. We can think of fifty or a hundred causes for lung disease. It may be that the symptoms in schizophrenia

also reflect a number of different causes. We are at the beginning of our research, but we are finding some changes in the cerebellum too. So there obviously are many organic brain changes that go along with the schizophrenic process."

The research of Dr. Scheibel and other scientists indicates that the link between our physical bodies and our mental lives may be more direct than we ever thought. Dr. E. Fuller Torrey, a clinical and research psychiatrist in Washington, D.C., sees schizophrenia as a brain disease or diseases, organic in nature, and having nothing to do with childhood experiences or Oedipus metaphors. Dr. Torrey points out that Freud, many years ago, had the vision to understand that the remedy for schizophrenia would not be found in psychoanalysis.

No one ever said the brain was simple, and certainly the solutions to these puzzles, when they're discovered, won't be simple either. Other scientists have uncovered other tantalizing hints about the nature of the unconscious, including components of hallucinogens like LSD naturally present in the brain. Will these and similar discoveries lead us someday to a "formula" for consciousness, or even a formula for dreams? Will we be able to plumb the chemical workings of the unconscious the same way we can now plumb the workings of awareness—sight, sound, touch, taste, smell? Will Freud's unexplored world someday be so thoroughly researched and charted that you can walk into a drugstore and buy a pill that will induce a certain kind of dream—a pill for flying, a pill for having sex with your favorite movie star, a pill for getting even with your boss?

Possibilities like these raise the question of just how far brain research can go. Is there anything that happens in the brain that *can't* be explained in terms of chemical interaction? If all human mental activity exists along a continuum between the poles of normality and madness, then eventually all of those activities will yield to scientific scrutiny. That includes art and music, Einstein's insights and Shakespeare's poetry. Dr. Scheibel even has some evidence—*extremely* tentative, he emphasizes—that our religious concepts originate in the temporal lobe of the brain. And other scientists believe that a yet-undiscovered neurotransmitter like endorphin will prove to be the basis of the feeling we still quaintly call "hope."

Is this what lies at the end of the path that Freud opened up: God in the temporal lobe? Hope in a test tube? Or is there something more to human life, something intangible, something that will forever elude the poking and prodding of scientists? In the final analysis, will the human animal prove to be nothing more than the sum of its biological parts? Or is there an extra, secret ingredient—call it mind, soul, spirit, imagination—that makes us different from other animals? Is it just the conceit of our overdeveloped brain, or are we truly touched with immortality?

Are religious visions a product of the unconscious—another example of the mind's amazing capacity to create its own reality? Some scientists take the argument even further by suggesting that a yet-undiscovered neurotransmitter like endorphin will prove to be the basis of the feeling we call "hope." Detail from Mary, Queen of Heaven by the Master of the Saint Lucy Legend, c. 1485.

17. Stairway to Heaven

The most beautiful and most profound emotion we can experience is the sensation of the mystical. It is the sower of all true science. He to whom this emotion is a stranger, who can no longer stand rapt in awe, is as good as dead. That deeply emotional conviction of the presence of a superior reasoning power, which is revealed in the incomprehensible universe, forms my idea of God.

Albert Einstein

When we confront ourselves in a mirror, we see something no other animal sees. With our profound self-awareness and wide-ranging imagination, we see things that used to be, things that will be, and even things that can never be. We see ourselves as we once were, as infants and children, and as we will be in a few years. We have the dubious distinction of being the only animal that can see its own death coming. We see ourselves as we *want* to be, as we *fear* we are, and even, occasionally, as we really are.

Perhaps it's our godlike perspective on our own lives that makes us think we have a piece of something godlike inside. What do we know about this morsel of immortality? Is it the source of our hope, or our despair, or both? Is it, like the rest of our raw material, a product of the nature–nurture interaction of brain and environment, or is it "supernatural"—a tiny beacon from a different world altogether?

In 1967, a sixteen-year-old girl in California named Reinee Pasarow was pronounced dead. Here is her version of how she died and what happened afterward.

"I had gone to the doctor that morning with hives and gotten some shots. I hadn't finished dinner when my throat started swelling and I couldn't get any air. By the

time my mother and a friend got me out to the curb to race me to the hospital, I was unconscious and no longer breathing.

"A crowd of people gradually gathered around me on the sidewalk. I could not breathe, and I faded in and out of consciousness. I was aware of a crowd yelling, 'Come on, Reinee!' 'Breathe, Reinee!' I was aware of oxygen being forced down my throat. I was aware that I was going to die. I really fought to hang on to consciousness, but I reached a point where the struggle couldn't have been any better than death, so I gave up. I was very conscious of the blood stopping in my veins.

"The next thing I knew, I was outside of my body—about two feet from my body and about three feet in the air. It was as if I was an eyeball, because I had three-hundred-and-sixty-degree vision. I realized that the body on the sidewalk was my body. I remember the firemen screaming, 'Oh, my God, we've lost her!'

"I could hear them say how long it had been since I had a pulse, but I myself didn't have any sense of time during this. I said a small prayer, something like 'Oh, God, help me,' and then I cut my ties and started to soar.

"I started to move up as if I were a satellite, and I could see greater and greater distances of the landscape. I went all the way up, until I could see the entire earth as a whole unit. I turned away from the earth and headed toward a light coming out of a tunnel. I went through that tunnel into a place that seemed very confused, and dark, and full of other beings.

"At that point I was wondering if I was going to have to be alone, and the next thing I knew I encountered a deceased uncle of mine, my only deceased relative that I had known in life. It was as if I knew him very intimately, even though I didn't in life. He was welcoming but confused that I would be there.

"I remember light, movement, rhythm, and music in this area. I moved through it, totally enraptured by the beauty of it. Yes, I saw my life pass before me. I saw every significant incident, and I saw the effects of my actions on others as if through their eyes and also through my eyes.

"At that point, I was sort of ejected from this place to a place where everything

was constructed of light. People were there, and they beckoned me to join them, and I was running toward them very happy and exuberant, absolutely free. But before I could cross over to them, a voice said, 'It is not time.' With that, I was catapulted back down a descending rainbow of light toward earth. It was a tunnel now. I definitely sensed the tunnel.

"The next thing I knew, I heard a horrendous clang, and I saw my body again being lifted up off the sidewalk and being placed up on a stretcher and wheeled to an ambulance. It was very strange to me to all of a sudden see this. It was like looking through a microscope after looking through a telescope. Everything was so tight and tiny. I was heartbroken. I saw them placing the body in the ambulance, and at that point I realized I didn't have any choice but try to live."

When did you realize you were alive?

"I was *not* alive at that point," says Pasarow. "I was clinically dead. I was clinically dead when they put me in the ambulance and drove to the hospital. I was watching all this like an observer. There were two ambulance attendants, and they told the first doctor I was 'D.O.A.' And he said, 'How long has it been?' and they said, 'Well, it's been pretty long. I don't think you're going to bring her back.' Then I was lying on the table covered up with a sheet over my face while the doctor went to wash his hands. He had given up.

"My own personal physician came storming into the hospital and said, 'Where is she?' That's exactly what he said. And the other doctor said, 'There. She's D.O.A.' And my doctor said, 'The hell she is.' That's a quote. I'll never forget that. And he proceeded to order up six more injections of adrenaline. Finally, I think after the third or fourth shot of adrenaline, he managed to bring me back."

Are such experiences evidence of immortality? There's nothing in brain chemistry that can explain floating eyeballs and quick trips to cities of light to meet long-gone Uncle Fred. If we're ever going to leave the realm of science and enter the realm of religion, this must be the place. After all, life after death—immortality—

Reinee Pasarow's story of what happened to her after she died intrigues some scientists because it bears such a striking resemblance to thousands of accounts of similar brushes with death.

OPPOSITE: Life after death has long been the promise of religion. Now scientists are beginning to explore the world of "other worlds" and their discoveries often have surprising implications. The Archangel Gabriel by Masolino de Panicale, fifteenth century.

has always been the promise of religion. All science can hope to offer is a cure for cancer and an extra decade or two tacked onto the average life span.

But despite the incongruity of it, scientists are beginning to think that Reinee Pasarow's experience and others like it are worth looking into and trying to understand by some means other than faith. What first attracted their attention was that Reinee's miraculous experience as a teenager in 1967 and thousands of similar brushes with death resembled each other so closely. In fact, there have been so many of these experiences, and they look so much alike, that scientists have begun to refer to them by the shorthand phrase "N.D.E.," for near-death experience.

How common are N.D.E.'s? Dr. Michael Sabom, a professor at Emory University, interviewed 116 people who had suffered medical crises so severe that doctors expected them "to result in irreversible biological death in the majority of instances." Sabom found that 40 percent of these people had had near-death experiences.

How consistent are these experiences? Remarkably. According to Dr. Raymond A. Moody, author of a book on near-death experiences, most N.D.E.'s share these common elements: the subjects had difficulty in describing the experience in words; they heard the doctors and others *announce* them dead; they felt a great sense of peace and quiet; they heard loud noises, like ringing or buzzing; they felt as if they were moving through a long tunnel; they moved out of their own bodies; they met other spirits, primarily dead friends and relatives; they saw glowing lights in the shape of humans; they reexperienced, at great speed, the events of their own lives; they arrived at a boundary line beyond which there seemed to be no return; they enjoyed great knowledge; they often saw cities of light as well; they were "rescued" by another spirit and returned to life a changed person.

"Later [the subject] tries to tell others, but has trouble doing so," says Moody. "In the first place, he can find no human words adequate to describe these unearthly episodes. He also finds that others scoff, so he stops telling other people. Still, the experience affects his life profoundly, especially his views about death and its relationship to life."

According to Sabom and others, the *consistency* of these experiences means they couldn't possibly be hallucinations. Even under similar stressful circumstances—like dying—different people would have markedly different, idiosyncratic hallucinations. "I think it's scientifically verifiable," says Sabom, "since what they're seeing and later recalling is something that actually did occur. When they said they floated up out of their body, it seems they actually did—it's not a dream or a hallucination—because of the consistency of the reports."

Despite the evidence, the traditional scientific view has been that consciousness exists only in the human body, and when that goes, everything goes with it. Dr. Roland Puccetti of Dalhousie University in Nova Scotia, for example, scoffs at the notion that near-death experiences are trips back from the dead because, by definition, a dead person is someone who can't be revived. "Complete bodily death," he says, "the point beyond which there is no further life in the body, is when all the cells have died." In other words, dead is dead is dead, and if people like Reinee came back from the dead, then they weren't dead at all.

But not all scientists are so skeptical about the possibility of near-death or life-after-death experiences. No less an authority than Sigmund Freud wrote that "our own death is . . . unimaginable, and whenever we make the attempt to imagine it we can perceive that we really survive as spectators" in the next world. Charles Darwin seriously considered the possibility that spirits and ghosts are visions of the dead. And many of the experts who study N.D.E.'s today are reputable, well-credentialed members of the scientific community, hardly the crackpots and publicity hounds we tend to associate with U.F.O.'s, Bigfoot, and miracle cures.

Does this mean that we've finally found a phenomenon that science can't explain? Not exactly. As it turns out, the near-death experiences summarized by Dr. Moody are almost identical with the pattern of a typical hallucination, especially one brought on by drugs, anesthetics, accidents, debilitating diseases, fevers, and some of the physical processes that lead to death. Like the people who have experienced "death," those who have suffered through these hallucinations remember traveling through tunnels, seeing cities of light, floating out of their bodies, meeting spirits of dead relatives, and reviewing quick summaries of their lives.

In fact, scientists have *two* explanations for these experiences, one for the conscious mind, another for the unconscious mind. The first is a calm, rational, biological explanation. According to the latest research, when the central nervous system is stimulated in a particular way, neurons in the eye or groups of cells in the visual cortex are electrically stimulated to produce the same effect as light falling on the retina. There can also be, under certain conditions, a lowering of the threshold for the perception of electrical activity in the visual system, with the predictable result that the brain will "see" lights even in a dark room. The other, unconscious explanation for both near-death experiences and hallucinations, according to psychiatrist Adriaan Verwoerdt of Duke University, is that fantasies in which you leave your body may well be a mechanism for diverting the individual's attention from pain.

What about imagination? What about our unique ability to "see" things that we've never seen, to "go" places we've never gone, to imagine a reality that never existed? When we fantasize about being a famous rock star or having an affair with our favorite movie star, can these things too be reduced to a biological formula? To answer that question, we need to understand better just what the human imagination is capable of.

The death camps of Nazi Germany were perhaps the most successful attempt ever by human beings to create a hell on earth. That anyone could conceive such a massive crime is, I suppose, a kind of black testament to the powers of our imagination. But second to the question why it happened is the question how anybody could have survived such a system, a system designed solely for the purpose of extermination. The people imprisoned in such camps were powerless—almost. You may be able to lock up a body, but you can't lock up a mind.

Imagine what it must have been like to be confined to a so-called "standing cell" at the death camp. Your cell is divided into cubicles only three feet by three feet— barely big enough for you to stand in. If you're small, you might be able to sit, but forget lying down. You have to crawl in through a tiny opening near the floor, like a dog into a kennel. There are three other prisoners in your cell, night after night. You're forced to work all day. The life is designed to kill you, and you know it.

There was a Polish man, a painter named Josef Szajna, who was confined in one of these cells. Szajna knew that his keepers were trying to kill him, but he managed to survive. He lived because he focused his mind on the one thing he could see: a tiny blue patch of sky showing through a little window above his head. He used that square of light as a canvas upon which he painted dozens of pictures *in his mind* while he was imprisoned. When his *body* was finally liberated from the death camp by the Allied armies, he went home to his studio and painted every one of the images he had painted in his imagination, back in his little cell with the little blue patch of sky. All of his paintings were on small canvases, with a background of blue. Josef Szajna used the power of imagination to create the reality he needed to continue living, when all that the "real" world could offer him was the certainty of death. His mind's ability to go beyond the limitations of his physical body enabled him to adapt even to the environment of a death camp, and survive in it.

In the final analysis, how different is his situation from our own? We all live confined in this rather tight-fitting cell of a body, facing every day the certainty of death. But like Szajna, we rely on the power of our imagination to make it not just bearable, but sometimes downright pleasurable. Whether we use our imagination to conjure up great art, a life in the next world, memories of better times, or just what a swell time we're going to have this weekend, it is certainly our most uniquely *human* faculty.

Surely here is something that the scientists can't touch, a secret ingredient of humanhood, evidence of a divine spark inside each of us that can't be traced to neural discharges.

According to Dr. Arnold Scheibel of U.C.L.A., research on the brains of creative people indicates that there probably is a more down-to-earth explanation for people like the "death-camp" painter. In a visit to the laboratory of pioneering German anatomist Oscar Vogt and his wife, Scheibel examined the brain of a famous musician who was born with perfect pitch. "To be born with perfect pitch is an unusual thing," says Scheibel, "the kind of thing maybe Mozart had, maybe Beethoven. In this fellow's auditory cortex, the part of the brain that receives the auditory input, a specific layer in that cortex was at least twice as thick, twice as wide, as the cortex in a number of ungifted control people."

Dr. Arnold Scheibel, professor of neurobiology at the University of California at Los Angeles: "There is evidence of an organic difference in the brains of people with very specific talents."

A virtuoso on the piano at four, Wolfgang Amadeus Mozart toured Europe giving performances. At eight, on a visit to London with his father and sister, he wrote the piece below, his first choral composition and the only one he ever composed to English words. Scientists now think that Mozart probably had an unusually thick auditory cortex.

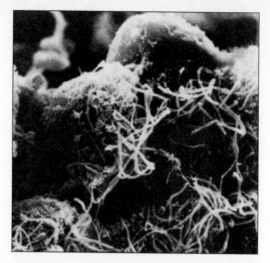

A cluster of neurons in the human brain stem, magnified 15,000 times in a scanning electron micrograph. In such clusters, the brain processes and stores information. These are the building blocks of human consciousness.

OVERLEAF: For thousands of years, Jerusalem has been considered the first step on the stairway to heaven.

Does this mean that our old-fashioned notion of "talent" is really just a question of the thickness of the cortex in a particular region? Scheibel is reluctant to make such sweeping statements, but he cites another example: the brain of a painter who, like the death-camp artist, had "eidetic imagery."

"You take a child with eidetic memory into a room that he's never been in before," says Scheibel, "and you point him at one wall where there are pictures and books on the shelf. You let him look for just two or three seconds. Then you whirl him around and have him face a blank wall. Then you say, 'Now tell me what you saw.' And a youngster with eidetic imagery can literally project an image of everything he's seen. When we say someone has a photographic memory we usually mean he has some form of eidetic imagery. In this artist who had intense eidetic imagery all his life, we saw in his primary visual cortex the same increased thickness, compared to nongifted control brains. There is evidence of an organic difference in the brains of people with very specific talents."

But most of these talented people spent a whole lifetime developing their talents. A man who loads trucks for a living develops big arms. In the same way, couldn't that feverish activity—playing an instrument, painting—account for the increased size of the corresponding areas of the brain? Was Mozart a great composer because he had a thick auditory cortex, or did he have a thick auditory cortex because he started using his ear from a very early age?

"It's the old nature-versus-nurture struggle. But someone like Mozart was already composing, he was already a virtuoso at four years of age. So that has to be nature. Of course nurture helps out a great deal too. They're obviously both important. But I very strongly feel that people like Mozart and Einstein and Newton are really the products of unusual brain structure and synaptic function. And we're just beginning to understand it all."

Does that mean genius and creativity are also on their way down the scientific tube? Can the magic of Mozart or Agnes De Mille or Michael Jackson be explained in terms of the effectiveness of their auditory cortex?

Dr. Marian Diamond, a professor of neurobiology, has found further neurological evidence that genius is in the brain, not in the stars. She has looked deeply into the gray matter of one of the greatest geniuses of our century, Albert Einstein. Her research indicates that Einstein's brain was no great shakes—little different from yours or mine—*except* in one area, the so-called "Area 39," a part of the brain located just above the ear, exactly where you tap your head with your finger when you have a bright idea or you want to indicate that somebody really "has brains."

Area 39 is perhaps the most complex area in the entire brain. It's the junction of the sensorimotor, visual, and auditory lobes, the hub, the hot spot, the HQ where the brain literally "puts it all together"—or at least much of it. Out of this spot, no larger than a 22-cent postage stamp, have probably come the wheel, Euclidean geometry, law, the steam engine, Newtonian physics, Mother Goose, and, if Dr. Diamond's conclusions are right, the theory of relativity. It appears that in Area 39 of Einstein's brain there was a significantly greater number of glial cells (support cells) per neuron. Clearly, if the imagination can be pinpointed in the brain, it's somewhere in the area of the inferior parietal lobe.

But if Area 39 is, in fact, the home of visionary concepts that transcend the normal functions of the brain—functions that can be expressed only in such things as higher mathematics—then it could also be the home of other visionary concepts, like fantasy and faith, that can't be expressed in words. In fact, this is the area where Dr. Scheibel has speculated that some kinds of religious experience may be located. Of course, it does make sense that leaps of imagination and leaps of faith would take place in the same area of the brain; but if God, heaven, Christianity, Islam, Buddhism, and all the rest came out of this same Area 39, along with the reciprocating engine and the laws of physics, what place in our lives does that leave for faith?

No examination of the human animal is complete without considering that one unique and universal preoccupation of the human mind, religion. We have variously worshiped the sun, the moon, the land, images, ideas, and even other people. Nowhere has this feature of the human experience played a more important role in shaping the history of a place than in Jerusalem.

If such things can be measured, Jerusalem is probably the most profoundly religious city in the world. It is the Holy City in the Holy Land. Here is the place where ideas have taken shape and events occurred that have shaped the behavior of half the human race. So much is sacred here that even the most cynical doubting Thomas might find himself walking more slowly, more reverently. Certainly no other city has had the access to God's ear that this city has. For several religions and millions of people, Jerusalem has been the first step on the stairway to heaven.

At the Western Wall, Kotel ha-Maaravi, Jews pray at the remains of the temple first built in the tenth century B.C. by Solomon. This is the "wailing wall," the

OPPOSITE: At the Western Wall, Jews pray at the remains of Solomon's temple built in the tenth century B.C.

The Church of the Holy Sepulchre marks the site in Jerusalem where Christians believe Christ ascended into heaven.

central shrine of one of the world's oldest faiths. It was here, at the Temple Mount, that Jews believe Abraham offered his sacrifice, that David spoke with God, and that the Jews were punished by God. The history of their triumphs and their suffering in and around this city leads Jews to proclaim: "This is my city."

Two miles away, at the Church of the Holy Sepulchre, built on a hill called Calvary, is Christianity's most sacred ground. This is the neighborhood of the earthly ministry of Jesus Christ. He walked the streets of this city, died at its edge, and ascended into heaven from a cave nearby. Three hundred years later, the first Christian emperor of Rome, Constantine the Great, would declare on behalf of Christians everywhere: "This is my city."

Four hundred years after Constantine, the Moslems ruled the city. The Dome of the Rock and other mosques, built beside Jewish temples and Christian churches, extended this city's ancient commitment to the oneness of God. Again, the door to heaven was open here in Jerusalem. Here, according to Moslem tradition, Mohammed ascended into heaven, not far from where Christians believe Jesus did the same thing. Next to Mecca and Medina, this is the Arab world's most sacred shrine and the basis for the Moslem's claim: "This is my city."

Not far from the Western Wall and the Holy Sepulchre stands the Dome of the Rock, a mosque built on the site where Moslems believe Mohammed ascended into heaven.

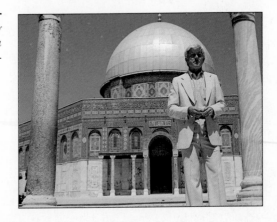

We shouldn't be surprised that all of these religions, *because* they felt Jerusalem was the gateway to heaven, fought each other for the job of gatekeeper. This city has probably been captured and recaptured more often by more groups of people than any other piece of real estate on earth. Ironically, a just God would long ago have abandoned any house where so much bloodshed, meanness, and pointless slaughter of innocents took place on the doorstep. The streets of Jerusalem, like the pages of its history, have been strewn with bodies.

Whether we look at Western faith or Eastern faith, ideologies of creation and creativity or of nationalism and war, the religious experience both exalts us and embarrasses us. It has produced great art, great music, great works of charity, selflessness, and forgiveness; but it's also produced the Crusades, the Inquisition, the Salem witch trials, Jim Jones, and the Ayatollah Khomeini. What does it all mean? What does it say about the human animal that we persist in the contradictions of religion, that we preach love and justice but practice intolerance and superstition, that priests bless the bombers on both sides of the fighting line? Is religion an inherent and inevitable part of the human condition?

Sigmund Freud was certainly familiar with the beauty of religion. At the incredibly ornate Karlskirche in Vienna, it's hard to think a bad thought about it. But Freud was practiced at looking past appearances, whether they were the stiff propriety of his Viennese clients or the gilded splendor of Viennese churches. In fact, at the end of his life he applied his theory of psychoanalysis to religious behavior and concluded, in effect, that religion was a very widespread form of mental illness. He wrote a book about religion which he called *The Future of an Illusion* in which he said that religion was "a system of wishful illusions together with a disavowal of

The absolutes of religious fundamentalism take the questions out of life, but often lead to atrocities. Past horrors that were religiously inspired include the Salem witch trials and the Jim Jones massacre. The Ayatollah Khomeini prepares to address a crowd in the holy city of Qum, 1979.

OPPOSITE: The religious experience has produced both great art and great agony. This illustration from Shah Tahmasp's Shah Nameh *is both one of the finest examples of Islamic art and a depiction of the wars that have plagued the Near East for thousands of years.* "Faridun Crosses the River Dijla," attributed to Sultan Muhammad, c. 1525–1530.

Sigmund Freud was unimpressed by the baroque splendor of churches like the Karlskirche in Vienna. Religion, he said, was "a system of wishful illusions."

OPPOSITE: Despite Freud's predictions, religion seems to be thriving as never before, even in an age of startling scientific and technological advancements. Television evangelist Robert Schuller's Crystal Cathedral in Anaheim, California.

reality, such as we find . . . nowhere else . . . but in a state of blissful hallucinatory confusion."

A strong prescription from Dr. Freud, essentially chiding us for our childish ways. "Grow up," he seemed to be saying, as if giving a child a spoonful of castor oil. Forget those silly old tales. There's no heaven, no hell, no angels, or devils or Gods or Saviors. Be brave and accept the natural world of science. Religion's eleventh commandment is "Thou shalt not question," and Freud saw in that prohibition a bar to scientific inquiry, which begins with questions. Science, he wrote, "is the only road that can lead us to a knowledge of reality outside ourselves." With that, Freud hoped he had closed the book on what he viewed as the neurotic human behavior called religion. He was certain that the exploding world of scientific discovery of the twentieth century would bring about its demise.

If he were alive today, Freud would have to admit that his conclusion was a bit hasty. To paraphrase Mark Twain: Reports of its death have been greatly exaggerated. For as this most scientific and secular of centuries nears its end, the human animal everywhere continues to devote huge amounts of time and energy to that most ancient and powerful dimension of the mind, religion.

In fact, science may have come a long way, but as far as religion is concerned, we are first cousins to the !Kung tribesmen of the Kalahari Desert. Except for the garments, their deep, religious trances might just as well be happening at a revival meeting or in the congregation of a fundamentalist TV preacher.

Contrary to Freud's prediction, religion has not only *not* gone away, it appears to be thriving as never before. Not that religious feeling in this country hasn't had its ups and down. In 1952, 75 percent of all Americans claimed that religion was "very important" in their lives. By 1978, the number had dropped to 52 percent. It may have been Vietnam or Watergate or both or neither, but that, apparently, was low tide. Within two years the number had risen to 56 percent, and it's been rising ever since—particularly among young people. In 1978, only 27 percent of all teenagers reported an interest in studying the Bible. By 1981, the number had jumped to 41 percent. These are the children of *Star Trek*, *Star Wars*, Pac-Man, and MTV. The Bible's continuing popularity amid a modern fun house of escapism is indeed impressive.

A massive survey of American attitudes toward religion recently found that 46 million Americans are "intensely religious." The survey predicted that morality and religion would play an increasing role in the American political process. The survey also found that religious commitment was a more accurate indicator of a person's values than economic level, age, gender, race, or political alignment. "The influence of religious belief," concludes the study, "pervades our activities in the home, the

community and the workplace, as well as our attitudes on social and political issues."

Some social scientists think that the resurgence of political activism on social-justice issues, like the nuclear freeze and equal rights for women, is powered by the same wave of "religious" sentiment in the country. Such causes appeal to "secular" people who are uncomfortable with traditional religious dogma but still have the very human need for a moral center, something beyond themselves, to face life. "The religious isn't just a Methodist church, or a Jewish synagogue, or an Islamic mosque," says Langdon Gilkey, professor of religion at the University of Chicago. "The religious is also an attempt to understand what it's all about—not only who we are, but where we're going, what we hope for." Apparently this wave of sort-of-religion is sweeping across class and economic lines, even in the secular hotbeds of higher learning. "There's no doubt about it," says Professor Harvey R. Cox of Harvard University. "There's a tremendous resurgence of religious interest here."

What do the scientists have to say about this phenomenon? What can we learn about religious feelings—whether they're directed toward a nuclear freeze or a Sunday Mass—from looking at the chemistry of the brain? Dr. Arnold Scheibel's research into the workings of the human brain has barely touched on the question of religion, but it may eventually shed some light on this most inaccessible corner of human consciousness. "There is still no evidence [for speculating about the origin of religion in brain chemistry]," says Scheibel. "This is the most tenuous and speculative part of the whole field. We do know that electrical storms (epilepsies) of the temporal lobe may start with an aura or hallucination. We also know that stimulation of the human temporal lobe during surgery may produce an intense dreamlike experience, often based on the patient's recent life. In addition, damage to one of

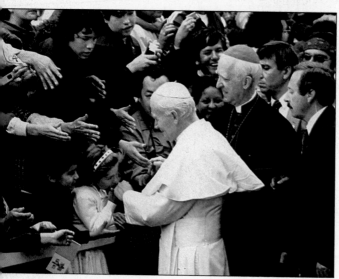

Despite the promises of technology and affluence, the power of religion endures. We hunger to be moved, to be freed from the limitations of our bodies and our world, to make contact with a higher power. LEFT: Crowd with hands outstretched to touch Pope John Paul II on his arrival in Quebec for a twelve-day visit to Canada. One girl kisses the pontiff's ring. OPPOSITE: The Pope at the Jasna Gora monastery in Częstochowa, Poland, home of the famous painting of "Our Lady of Częstochowa." Also known as "The Black Madonna," it is credited with having saved Poland from foreign invaders in the seventeenth and eighteenth centuries.

the temporal lobes produces a whole group of changes in mood, character, and ways of coping with the world. Thus it is conceivable that some intense religious experiences and 'mystic revelations' may be the result of unusual temporal-lobe activity.''

What if brain research does lead to the conclusion that Moses, Jesus, Mohammed, and a variety of lesser lights who thought they were chitchatting with God were actually suffering from hallucinations caused by a loose connection somewhere between their temporal lobe and a small mass of cells called the amygdala? What would be the implications for religion?

"I certainly am not the one to judge," says Scheibel. "I am very sympathetic toward all religions. But in trying to understand certain religious experiences organically and neurologically, I think it not unlikely that these phenomena may arise as intense neural experiences in the temporal lobes and then sometimes be interpreted as a great happening, as a miracle, or as a message that the individual has been chosen to carry a word or something. The emotional charge that goes with these experiences can last for long periods of time."

Science is a long, *long* way from proving that the world's great religions are based on a series of brain malfunctions mistaken for divine intervention; but speculations like those of Dr. Scheibel may help explain one of the fundamental contradictions in religious behavior: religious zeal. In our saner moments, we've always wondered how the Crusaders could slaughter women and children in the name of Jesus, apparently a gentle man who abhorred violence. Today, we ask the same questions about Shiite Moslem fanatics who, at the beginning of every chapter of the Koran, read "To God, the merciful and compassionate," then proceed to go out and paint whole countries red with blood. Or the I.R.A. terrorists in Belfast.

Religion and hypocrisy have always gone hand in hand into battle, and Scheibel's theory may explain why. Real zealots don't really fight for a belief: they fight in something like a neurological trance, like a drug-induced "high." They may have reached that high in a religious frenzy, but religion has nothing to do with the result. "We know that small amounts of some of the hallucinogenic drugs—like the ones used by the Southwest Indians in developing their religion and their culture—produce very powerful experiences, and these probably work at least in part in the temporal-lobe area," says Scheibel; "but we're just at the beginning of things now."

Dr. Marian Diamond has recently discovered additional evidence that may lead to a neurological explanation for another religious phenomenon: religious healing. "The brain's control over the immune system is what we might call a frontier in the neural sciences," says Dr. Diamond. "The thymus is a gland that regulates T-cells —a kind of white blood cell that is involved with your immune processes. We wanted to see if animals that have no thymus are deficient in cerebral cortex, and we find that, just as we predicted, the left cerebral hemisphere is deficient in an animal that has no thymus gland. This evidence supports other recent findings that these outer layers of the brain, which are under voluntary control, are related to the immune system."

In light of research like this, what are the prospects for religion in the twenty-first century? If visitations from God can be explained in chemical terms—and perhaps

OPPOSITE: Some social scientists believe that political activism may be a secular expression of what is fundamentally a religious sentiment—the affirmation of a moral imperative. Antinuclear rally in Central Park, New York City, June 12, 1982.

How can people die and even kill in the name of religious faith? Recent brain research may give us some insight into the paradox—some would say hypocrisy—of religious fanaticism. Funeral procession in Northern Ireland.

Dr. Marian C. Diamond, professor of neurobiology at the University of California at Berkeley, whose research may lead to new insights into subjects as diverse as faith healing and hypochondria: "The brain's control over the immune system is what we might call a frontier in the neural sciences."

even replicated in the laboratory; if the "miracle" of faith healing can be bought over the counter, will people still *need* religion? The answer appears to be a resounding yes.

In fact, as we move further from the life of ignorance and superstition in which religion has its roots, we seem to need it more and more. Even Dr. Scheibel, who understands as much as anyone the power of the human brain, doesn't see neuroscience replacing the worship service. "I must admit," says Scheibel, "that during my training in psychiatry I certainly came to agree with the classical Freudian position that religion represents, in a sense, the adolescence of mankind. But I think I've also come to respect the role that it plays as we try to become increasingly autonomous. In a sense, we are going farther and farther out, away from home, at least symbolically, and at the other end of the line we're feeling more and more vulnerable, more and more exposed. From that point of view, as long as we are sentient, as long as we are aware of the feelings we have, as long as we can say, 'I feel lonely' or 'I feel helpless,' then we will see the need for it. With the development of man's awareness of self and therefore of his condition, something like religion

Langdon Gilkey, professor of religion at the University of Chicago: "The function of the religious traditions in every culture has been to achieve some kind of basic, fundamental, and valid understanding of the human. Who am I? What am I here for? What should I do?"

becomes if not a requirement, then something darn near it."

These are scientists talking, men and women who are standing at the edge of our knowledge and looking off into the future. "There is abundant proof," says Stephen Gould, the chief scientific spokesman for evolution, "that the human body and brain got here via a process of evolutionary change. But that says nothing about religion, which is about ethics and values. It says nothing about whether there is a God who did or did not set up the laws according to which evolution occurred." No less a scientist than Albert Einstein went even further. Science and religion are not merely compatible, he said, they are *complementary*. The closer we come to a scientific understanding of the universe, the closer we come to an awareness of God.

Underlying the comments of these and other scientists is a recognition that however spectacular the discoveries of tomorrow may be, they can never explain everything about being human. No human system can do that. The human experience of the sacred remains—and probably will remain—an enigma beyond the brain, beyond what science can discover. "The problem with the idea that everything is ultimately explainable in biological terms," says Langdon Gilkey, "is that it's too easy to use it as a justification for denying personal responsibility—a scientifically modern form of the old excuse 'The devil made me do it.' That is the ultimate biological cop-out."

That idea of personal responsibility, of morality, of the human animal as something more than a slave of biology, is what religion provides. "The function of the religious traditions in every culture," according to Gilkey, "has been to achieve some kind of basic, fundamental, and valid understanding of the human. Who am I? What am I here for? What should I do? What fulfills me? Scientists who think science has answered these questions are mistaken. One of the reasons that people are going back to religion is that they don't know anymore who they are. That's one of the roles of religion—to supply a definition of the human. A picture of the human, an image of the human, a model of the human."

Why has religion become a force just when we'd have thought it would be losing ground to secularism? Part of the answer is a feeling that the power of reason just hasn't been the productive force it was supposed to be. "At the end of the eighteenth and to the middle of the nineteenth century," says Daniel Bell, a professor of social sciences at Harvard, "almost every enlightened thinker expected religion to disappear in the twentieth century. The belief was based on the power of reason." Of course, almost every enlightened thinker expected war and social injustice to disappear as well. In fact, the wars haven't disappeared; they've simply gotten bigger. "We've gained enormous power over nature via technology," adds Bell. "And yet the twentieth century is probably the most dreadful period in human history."

So we've been down this road before. As recently as the nineteenth century we looked to something outside ourselves—call it reason, enlightenment, technology—to solve our problems, and we came away disappointed. Today, it's all too easy to look to the scientists who are exploring our brain and our behavior and ask them to "make us right." Someday, they may be able to tell us why we act as we do, but they won't be able to make us change. And we wouldn't want them to if they could. Down that road lies mind control, Big Brother—Nineteen Eighty-Four.

Even if, in a hundred years, we're able to explain ourselves, will we really *know* ourselves? "Scientists talk about 'understanding ourselves,' " says Langdon Gilkey, "but when the Greeks said, 'Know thyself,' they didn't mean *scientific* knowledge. What they meant was knowledge of limits. That is to say, the kind of knowledge that leads to self-control. That's a very different kind of knowledge from knowing something biologically, pathologically, anatomically, or chemically. Self-understanding has been the real role of religion."

Science, if all works well, provides the knowledge, and religion provides the perspective; science the information and the means to control, religion the will to control. To go forward without either one is to deny the complexity and the subtlety of the human animal. Yet in the continuing debate over evolution and creationism, we continue to pit one against the other and, like a crowd at a cockfight, hope that one side walks away a winner. In our weapons and our eagerness to wage war, we've seen the perils and the limits of pure technology. In our troubled children, we've seen the effects of moral tyranny and intolerance. We know that certainty in science is good—although impossible—but certainty in religion is bad—although common. Yet we continue to believe that both are possible and desirable.

Self-awareness is the gift; self-understanding is the struggle. The best place to begin that struggle is with the information that science has gathered over the last several millenia on the subject of the human animal. We know, for example, that our biological evolution is pretty much over, that "what we see is what we got." The human body, from brain chemistry to foot size, isn't likely to change, so we might as well make the most of it. In human *culture*, however, what we see is what we *decided* to have. No other life form on earth has that option. The squirrel is dropped on this planet hardwired to do certain things with acorns for a snowy day. The human animal, on the other hand, can build greenhouses.

That is the good news. The bad news is that we have this remarkable ability to choose the shape of our culture at a time when the wrong choice can have catastrophic consequences. Our priorities and our prejudices are products of culture. So are our heroes and heroines, from the men and women we encourage our children to emulate, to the men and women we choose to marry. Culture determines not only what we expect from, but the very nature of, the State, the Corporation, and the Family. In short, culture determines values—no small thing on a planet covered with imaginary boundary lines and nuclear-tipped missiles. Now, more than ever, we need to be informed and to participate in making the decisions that will shape the world our children will inherit, for we can no longer afford the terrible consequences of behaving badly.

In the process of understanding ourselves better, we will find much to celebrate. The human brain is quite obviously nature's "crowning achievement," hundreds of millions of years in the making, an organ of exquisite perceptivity, infinite curiosity, and unlimited potential. It allows us to experience lives that are, by animal standards, incalculably rich and deep and varied. Amidst the doom and gloom of the nuclear age and the frustrations of daily routine, it would be a shame to lose sight of the things that make the human animal—even in a universe as big as this one— very special indeed: the capacity for love, a sense of wonder, and faith in the future. Whatever problems lie ahead, we are well equipped to handle them.

Cheers to us. Cheers to our future, to greater tolerance and freer inquiry, to more accommodation and fewer showdowns, to more caring and happier children, to sounder sleep and better dreams.

We are and always will be children. That is our great strength. We can always grow and learn and try, and try again. Nothing is permanently beyond our reach.

OVERLEAF: Dust to dust? Whatever we learn about ourselves from science, we will never stop believing that there's more to the human animal than mortal clay.

Credits

Special thanks to Cameron Beck, Jessie Cohen, Mark E. Gibson, Suzanne Szasz and to AP/Wide World Photos, Archive Pictures, and UPI/Bettmann Archive

Title page: © Cameron Beck; *9:* courtesy Phil Donahue; *13:* © Jeff Jacobson/Archive Pictures; *14:* © Suzanne Szasz; *16 (top):* courtesy the Circus Wald Museum, Baraboo, Wisconsin, and the New York Public Library; *16 (bottom):* courtesy NASA; *17:* Maisons des Clercs, Chartres Cathedral; *18:* © Marilyn Silverstone/Magnum Photos; *19:* National Gallery of Art, Washington, D.C., Chester Dale Collection; *20:* Vezio Melegan/ © Rizzoli Editori, Milano; *21:* © Mary Ellen Mark/Archive Pictures; *23:* courtesy HA! © Henson Associates, Inc. 1985. Reprinted by permission; *24:* © Mark E. Gibson; *25, 26:* UPI/Bettmann Archive; *27:* © Edward S. Ross; *28 (tamarin, orangutan, diana monkey, marmoset, mangaby, gorilla):* Jessie Cohen, courtesy National Zoological Park, Smithsonian Institution, Washington, D.C.; *(uakari, saki, proboscis monkey, mandrill, golden monkey, baboon):* Zoological Society of San Diego; *29:* courtesy Jutta Buck Antiquarian Book and Print Seller, New York; *30:* UPI/Bettmann Archive; *31:* courtesy Jeremy D. Pickett-Heaps, University of Colorado; *33:* Jessie Cohen, courtesy National Zoological Park, Smithsonian Institution, Washington, D.C.; *34:* © Lee Boltin/American Museum of Natural History; *35:* © Steve Ward/Anthro-Photo; *36:* © Lawrence Liphe, courtesy Stephen Jay Gould; *37:* from the collection of Mr. and Mrs. Paul Mellon, Upperville, Virginia; *38:* courtesy Thomas Road Baptist Church; *39:* courtesy the *Arkansas Democrat;* *40:* © Lois Lord; *42:* © Laura Van Dorn Schneider, model by John Allison; *44:* courtesy Michael Sacher, Mt. Sinai Medical Center, New York; *45 (top):* courtesy Paul MacLean, National Institute of Mental Health; *45 (bottom):* © Cameron Beck; *46:* Jessie Cohen, courtesy National Zoological Park, Smithsonian Institution, Washington, D.C.; *47, 48, 49 (bottom):* David Macaulay, from *The Amazing Brain* by Robert Ornstein, Richard Thompson and David Macaulay. Illustrations copyright © 1984 by David A. Macaulay. Reprinted by permission of Houghton Mifflin Company; *49 (top):* Jessie Cohen, courtesy National Zoological Park, Smithsonian Institution, Washington, D.C.; *50:* AP/Wide World Photos; *53:* © Charles Harbutt/Archive

Pictures; *54:* © Mark E. Gibson; *56 (left):* © Marjorie Shostak, courtesy Anthro-Photo; *56 (right):* National Gallery of Art, Washington, D.C., Chester Dale Collection; *57:* © Flo Fox; *58:* © Polly Brown/Archive Pictures; *59:* courtesy Atlantic Television; *61:* © Mark E. Gibson; *62, 63:* © Elizabeth Wilcox; *64:* courtesy, O.K. Harris Works of Art, New York; *66:* National Gallery of Art, Washington, D.C., Samuel H. Kress Collection; *67:* © Kevin V. Duffy; *69:* © Burt Glinn/Magnum Photos; *70:* UPI/ Bettmann Archive; *72, 73 (top):* courtesy Bethlehem Steel; *73 (bottom):* Walker Evans/ Library of Congress; *74:* courtesy Robert Reich; *76–77:* © Brian Brake/Photo Researchers; *78:* © Lois Lord; *79:* © Lawrence L. Smith/Photo Researchers; *80:* © Mark E. Gibson; *82–83:* courtesy International Business Machines Corporation; *84, 86:* © jun. and sen. Lautenschlager/ Eastern Switzerland Tourist Association; *87:* Niels Bohr Library, American Institute of Physics; *89:* courtesy New York Public Library; *90:* © John Deeks/Photo Researchers; *91:* © H. Peter Curran, courtesy the *Forbes* Magazine Collection, New York; *92:* AP/Wide World Photos; *93 (left):* courtesy New York Public Library; *93 (right):* courtesy Granada Television; *94:* UPI/Bettmann Archive; *95:* © Jamie Stobie; *96–97:* DoD Photo; *99, 101, 102:* courtesy Plasma Physics Laboratory, Princeton University; *105:* © Gregory White Smith, courtesy Gary and Amy Fitts; *106:* from the MGM release *Gone with the Wind* ©1939 MGM; *108:* courtesy Phil Donahue; *109:* Mrs. James Thurber; *110:* courtesy Fred Gilbert, Division of Pediatric Gastroenterology, Mount Sinai Medical Center, New York; *111:* courtesy National Cancer Institute; *112:* © Martha Swope; *113:* Claudio Bravo, courtesy private collection, London; *114 (left):* © Cameron Beck; *114 (right):* © Lois Lord/Bank Street School; *116 (left):* reproduced by special permission of *Playboy* magazine: copyright © 1982 by *Playboy;* *116 (right):* reprinted by permission of Jove Publications, Inc., copyright 1983 by Rosemary Hawley Harman, cover art by Heide Oberheide; *117:* © Laura Van Dorn Schneider, model by John

Allison; *118, 119:* © Suzanne Szasz; *120:* David Macaulay, from *The Amazing Brain* by Robert Ornstein, Richard Thompson and David Macaulay. Illustrations copyright © 1984 by David A. Macaulay, reprinted by permission of Houghton Mifflin Company; *121:* copyright 1983 by Bill Ravanesi; *122:* © Abigail Heyman/Archive Pictures; *124:* © Will McIntyre/Photo Researchers; *125:* UPI/ Bettmann Archive; *126:* © Laura Van Dorn Schneider/model by John Allison; *127:* © John Webb/Tate Gallery, London; *128:* courtesy Godiva chocolatier; *130:* © D. Heunemann, courtesy Irenaus Eibl-Eibesfeldt; *131:* © Irenaus Eibl-Eibesfeldt; *132:* Mrs. James Thurber; *133:* UPI/Bettmann Archive; *134, 135:* © Mark E. Gibson; *136:* © Nora Gruner, courtesy John Money; *137:* Zoological Society of San Diego; *138:* Cleveland Museum of Art, Hinman B. Hurlbut Collection; *139:* courtesy Kennedy Galleries; *141:* © Richard C. Wandel; *142–143:* © Michael O'Brien/Archive Pictures; *145:* © Abigail Heyman/Archive Pictures; *146:* from the United Artists release *Annie Hall* © 1977 United Artists Corporation/reprinted by permission of Woody Allen and Rollins Joffe Morra & Brezner; *147:* © Cameron Beck; *148:* © Mary Ellen Mark/Archive Pictures; *149:* © Leslie Wong/Archive Pictures; *150:* UPI/Bettmann Archive; *151:* courtesy Chippendales, Los Angeles and New York; *154:* © Suzanne Szasz; *156:* courtesy MTV; *157:* © Phil Ramey/AP/Wide World Photos; *158:* © A. Bernhaut/Photo Researchers; *159:* © Arthur Tress/Photo Researchers; *161:* © Cameron Beck; *162–163:* © Abigail Heyman/ Archive Pictures; *164:*© Mary Ellen Mark/ Archive Pictures; *167:* Jessie Cohen, courtesy National Zoological Park, Smithsonian Institution, Washington, D.C.; *169:* © Mark E. Gibson; *170 (top):* courtesy *Newsweek* magazine; *170 (bottom):* Supreme Court Historical Society; *172:* © Kevin V. Duffy; *173:* © Cameron Beck; *176:* courtesy Consulate General of Israel, New York; *177:* Metropolitan Museum of Art, New York, gift of Harris D. Colt and H. Dunscombe Colt, 1934; *179:* Vatican Museums; *180 (left):* © Abigail Heyman/ Archive Pictures; *180 (right):* © Suzanne Szasz; *181 (left):* © Cameron Beck; *181 (right):* courtesy Michael Lewis; *183:* courtesy David Nelson; *184, 185:* courtesy

Lajos Koranyi, Postgraduate Medical School, Budapest; *187:* courtesy NASA; *189:* © William T. Clark, courtesy National Park Service, U.S. Department of the Interior; *190:* courtesy Lucasfilm Ltd. © Lucasfilm Ltd. (LFL) 1980. All rights reserved; *191:* AP/ Wide World Photos; *192:* New Line Cinema; *194–195:* © Till Schwalm/Merkur Film Agency GmbH; *195 (right):* courtesy Simon Wiesenthal Center; *197:* DoD Photo; *200:* © Cameron Beck; *201:* Zoological Society of San Diego; *203:* © Napoleon A. Chagnon/ Anthro-Photo; *204:* courtesy Roderic E. Gorney; *205:* courtesy the *New York Post* and the *New York Daily News;* *207:* Mimi Cotter/ *People Weekly* © Time Inc.; *209:* © Michael C. Brien; *210:* © Elizabeth Wilcox; *213:* © Suzanne Szasz; *214:* © Bill Owens: from *Suburbia*/Archive Pictures; *216:* © Irven DeVore/Anthro-Photo; *217:* AP/Wide World Photos; *218:* © Bruce Bennett; *219:* © Richard Frieman/Photo Researchers; *221:* courtesy New York Public Library; *222:* Janus Films; *223:* AP/Wide World Photos; *225 (middle):* courtesy Consulate General of India, New York; *225 (left):* courtesy Consulate General of Israel, New York; *225 (right):* courtesy Central Office of Information, London; *226:* © Bill Owens: from *Suburbia*/ Archive Pictures; *227:* AP/Wide World Photos; *228:* © Suzanne Szasz; *229:* UPI/ Bettmann Archive; *231:* © Robert Goldstein/ Photo Researchers; *232:* © Irven DeVore/ Anthro-Photo; *233:* DoD Photo; *234:* © William T. Clark/Courtesy National Park Service, U.S. Department of the Interior; *235:* The British Museum; *236:* AP/Wide World Photos; *237:* Zoological Society of San Diego; *239:* © Hillel Berger/Anthro-Photo; *240 (upper left and upper middle two):* courtesy New York Public Library; *240 (upper right):* courtesy Simon Wiesenthal Center, from the film *Genocide;* *240 (bottom):* AP/Wide World Photos; *242, 243, 244–245, 246, 247:* DoD Photo; *249:* © Huynh Cong "Nick" Ut/AP/Wide World Photos; *250–251:* © John Webb/Tate Gallery, London; *252:* AP/Wide World Photos; *253:* UPI/Bettmann Archive; *255:* © Hans Namuth/Photo Researchers; *256:* © Jeff Jacobson/Archive Pictures; *258, 259:* © Harvey Stein 1978, from *Parallels: a Look at Twins* by Harvey Stein, published by E. P. Dutton, 1978; *260:* © Suzanne Szasz; *261:* National Gallery of

Art, Washington, D.C., Chester Dale Collection;   *262:* © Jamie Stobie;   *263:* UPI/Bettmann Archive;   *264:* © Lord Snowdon/AP/Wide World Photos;   *266, 267 (upper left and lower left):* © Ashley Montagu   *267 (upper right):* courtesy Phil Donahue;   *267 (lower right):* courtesy Phil Donahue;   *270:* © Jessie Cohen, courtesy National Zoological Park, Smithsonian Institution, Washington, D.C.;   *271:* © Charles Harbutt/Archive Pictures;   *272:* Courtesy Marian C. Diamond, Department of Physiology-Anatomy, University of California at Berkeley;   *274–275:* © Ed Lettau/Photo Researchers;   *276:* © Charles Harbutt/Archive Pictures;   *278, 279, 280:* © Suzanne Szasz;   *281:* David Macaulay, from *The Amazing Brain* by Robert Ornstein, Richard Thompson and David Macaulay. Illustrations copyright © 1984 by David A. Macaulay. Reprinted by permission of Houghton Mifflin Company;   *282, 285, 286, 287, 288, 291, 292, 293:* © Suzanne Szasz;   *294:* © Susan McCartney/Photo Researchers;   *295: Baby and Child Care* by Dr. Benjamin Spock. © 1945, 1946 © 1957, 1968, 1976 by Benjamin Spock, M.D. Reprinted by permission of Pocket Books, a division of Simon & Schuster, Inc.;   *296:* © Marjorie Shostak/Anthro-Photo;   *297:* © Elizabeth Wilcox;   *299:* National Gallery of Art, Washington, D.C., Chester Dale Collection;   *300:* © Cameron Beck;   *301:* courtesy Harlow Primate Laboratory, University of Wisconsin;   *302:* © Elizabeth Wilcox;   *303:* © Suzanne Szasz;   *304:* © Jessie Cohen, courtesy National Zoological Park, Smithsonian Institution, Washington, D.C.;   *305:* courtesy Hirshhorn Museum and Sculpture Garden, Smithsonian Institution, Washington, D.C.;   *306, 308 (top):* AP/Wide World Photos;   *308 (bottom):* © Harvey Stein 1984;   *309:* reprinted from *The Saturday Evening Post* © 1943 the Curtis Publishing Company;   *310:* © Alen MacWeeney/Archive Pictures; *313:* © Dick Swartz, courtesy National Institutes of Health;   *314, 315:* © Judith Grunberg;   *316:* © Jose Barrero, courtesy New York University Library;   *317:* The British Museum;   *318:* © Victor Engelbert/Photo Researchers;   *320 (top):* courtesy Noam Chomsky;   *320 (bottom):* courtesy New York Public Library;   *321:* UPI/Bettmann Archive;   *322:* © Lois Lord;   *323:* © Suzanne Szasz;   *324:* © Mark E. Gibson;   *325:* John James Audubon/New-York Historical Society;   *327:* © Joel Avirom;   *329:* © Suzanne Szasz;   *330:* © Susan McElhinney/Archive Pictures;   *331:* © **Suzanne Szasz;** *332–333:* Freer Gallery of Art, Smithsonian Institution, Washington, D.C.;   *334:* © Tim Davis/Photo Researchers;   *335:* AP/Wide World Photos;   *337:* © Johannes Wagner;   *338:* Metropolitan Museum of Art, New York, Bequest of William H. Herriman, 1921;   *340 (top):* courtesy New York Public Library;   *340 (bottom):* UPI/Bettmann Archive;   *341, 343:* © Johannes Wagner;   *344:* © Doug Prince;   *345:* courtesy Montague Ullman;   *346–347:* National Gallery of Art, Washington, D.C., Chester Dale Collection;   *348:* Niels Bohr Library, American Institute of Physics;   *349:* courtesy NASA;   *351:* © Cameron Beck;   *352:* Prado Museum, Madrid;   *353:* UPI/Bettmann Archive;   *354:* © Johannes Wagner;   *355:* © Laura Van Dorn Schneider;   *356 (left):* © Cameron Beck;   *356 (right):* © Johannes Wagner;   *357:* Vatican Museums;   *358:* © Sissie Weider, courtesy David Peretz;   *359:* Metropolitan Museum of Art, New York, Bequest of Mrs. H. O. Havemeyer, 1929. The H. O. Havemeyer Collection;   *360, 361:* courtesy Martin Buchsbaum, University of California at Irvine;   *362:* National Gallery of Art, Washington, D.C., Samuel H. Kress Collection;   *364:* courtesy NASA;   *366:* courtesy Reinee Pasarow;   *367:* © Jerry N. Uelsmann;   *368:* courtesy Reinee Pasarow;   *369:* National Gallery of Art, Washington, D.C., Samuel H. Kress Collection;   *372:* © Craig R. Dietz / courtesy Arnold Scheibel;   *373:* UPI/Bettmann Archive;   *374:* © Peter Duong, from studies by Fried, Paul, and Scheibel; courtesy Arnold Scheibel, Brain Research Institute, University of California at Los Angeles;   *376–377:* courtesy Consulate General of Israel, New York;   *378:* © Cameron Beck;   *379:* © Cameron Beck;   *380:* AP/Wide World Photos;   *381:* courtesy private collection, Cambridge, Massachusetts;   *382:* © Johannes Wagner;   *383:* © Julius Shulman, courtesy Robert Schuller Ministries;   *384, 385, 386, 387:* AP/WideWorld Photos;   *388 (top):* courtesy Marian C. Diamond, Department of Physiology-Anatomy, University of California at Berkeley;   *388 (bottom):* courtesy Langdon Gilkey;   *391:* © Suzanne Szasz;   *392–393:* © Cameron Beck.

Index

(Page numbers in italics denote illustrations.)